Praise for Sta

"Donna King-Nykolaycuyk's tribute t a Man *is truly amazing. This book was superbly written. Schools should include this book as reading assignments so our young folks do not forget the history of that era. I would really like to see the book made into a movie one day."*

—Jean Miller, Director of Development, Retired, Howe Military Academy

"Donna King-Nykolaycuyk profoundly captures Duke as a young man with a fighting spirit who became the battlefield warrior that made the Marine Corps legendary. Duke fought on beaches, jungles and hilltops against a ferocious enemy that neither gave nor took quarter. I am thankful to Donna for her devotion to Duke and for elegantly preserving the heroics of Duke "The Indian" Abdalla. I am honored to call Duke my friend."

—Richard C. Daniels, Attorney

"Donna King-Nykolaycuyk's writing about this WWII Hero is phenomenal. Duke's Battle experiences are described First Hand but what touched me most was the battle he fought when he came home with the memories of war and his price was the loss of everything, including his family. Duke's self-discipline to overcome in the years when PTSD was only talked about in whispers and his ability to overcome and do the right thing is inspiring!"

—Mick Grady, Founder- V-SPANN
Veterans Special Programs American National Network

"Donna King-Nykolaycuyk has written an articulate and brave message about an incredibly amazing Marine and a proud American Indian who honorably served our Country and went way beyond the call of duty to make sure America remained the Land of the Free. I am proud and blessed to know Duke, his grandson Doug and his grandson's wife."

—Robert Renteria
International Latino Author/U.S. Army Disabled Veteran

Stand Like a Man

The Story of Duke "The Indian"

DONNA KING-NYKOLAYCUYK

[signature]

Chesty Puller's
Marine Raider
Loren Duke Abdalla

King's Daughter Publishing

Algonquin, Illinois

by Jeanette Saubert.

Harriet Abdalla by red car, smiling © 1967, permission granted by Loren Duke Abdalla.

Duke standing with John Brady (fence behind them) © 1976, permission granted by Loren Duke Abdalla.

Loren Duke Abdalla at age eighty (80) in red cap © 2005, CPI Corp has granted permission for its customers to take their images, in whatever medium they are available, and have them printed or copied by a third party.

Illinois Marine Corps League Vice President, Gunnery Seargent Mike Ruffner (uniformed) © 2008, Permission by Gunnery Sergeant Mike Ruffner PDC.

Grandpa Duke, Doug Nykolaycuyk and Captain Rick Daniels © 2012, permission granted by Donna King-Nykolaycuyk.

Doug & his grandpa in front of restored 1963 Cruiser's Inc. wooden boat (Top Hat & Cane) © 2009, permission granted by Donna King-Nykolaycuyk.

House in Fox Lake that Duke built © 2012, permission granted by Donna King-Nykolaycuyk.

Flags flying at Duke's house © 2012, permission granted by Donna King-Nykolaycuyk.

Duke's eyes over fist wearing Indian Buffalo ring © 2012, provided by Donna King-Nykolaycuyk.

Cpl. Roland James drawing #1 Pavuvu © 1944, provided by Raymond J. Hill Sergeant, U.S. Marine Corps. NCO in Charge, 11 August, 1945 United States Marine Corps Central Procurement Division.

Cpl. Roland James drawing #2 Pavuvu © 1945, provided by Raymond J. Hill Sergeant, U.S. Marine Corps. NCO in Charge, 11 August, 1945 United States Marine Corps Central Procurement Division.

Earlier Marine photo of Duke © 1943, provided by Loren Duke Abdalla.

Youngest photo of Duke © 1930, provided by Loren Duke Abdalla.

George Abdalla wearing Running Bull's clothes/headdress © 1930, provided by Loren Duke Abdalla.

Engagement picture of Duke and Jeanette in teal-colored dress © 1948, Edward Fox Photography Edwardfox.com.

Warriors Watch Riders motorcade escort Duke - Welcome Home © 2012, provided by Donna King-Nykolaycuyk.

Warriors Watch Riders and Guests Group Photograph © 2012, provided by Michael and Susan Siciliano.

Al Costella kneeling in front of tents on Pavuvu © 1945, provided by Mrs. Vera Costella.

Al Costella standing in Marine Corps League uniform © 2009, provided by Mrs. Vera Costella.

Greenwood, South Dakota 1913-1930 Black & White photo of the town © 1925 by Loren Duke Abdalla.

Illinios State Capitol, Statue of President Lincoln - Loren Duke Abdalla standing below © 2014, permission granted by Douglas Nykolaycuyk.

Editor: Brittiany Koren/Written Dreams
Cover Design and Layout: Ed Vincent/ENC Graphic Services
Cover photographs Shutterstock

ISBN-13 978-0-9909627-0-0

Category: World War II Military Memoir

Printed in the United States of America

1 2 3 4 5 6 7 8 9 0

This book is dedicated to all of the men and women who have served, fought or died to protect the freedoms of The Greatest Country Ever— The United States of America!

Acknowledgements

I would like to thank first, my husband Douglas Nykolaycuyk, for his love and support during the arduous process of writing, preparing, and offering this book. I would like to thank my parents, Robert and Marian King, for their never-ending love and support of any endeavor I've made in my life. I am forever grateful to all of the men and women of America who fought and died to protect my freedom, and the freedoms of my family. And lastly, but certainly not least, I would like to thank Grandpa Duke for both his service—and this wonderful human story that he lived and shared with us. Thank you for your service, Corporal Loren Duke Abdalla.

Additional Acknowledgements

Captain Rick Daniels for hearing Loren Duke Abdalla's story and beginning the quest to have him receive the recognition he's earned and deserved, Gunnery Sergeant Mike Ruffner for all of his groundwork in obtaining witness letters and presenting Loren D. Abdalla's story to the Department of Defense, and Douglas Nykolaycuyk for his efforts to have his grandfather's story heard by the President of The United States of America.

Captain Michael Saubert, who so eloquently spoke on behalf of Grandpa Duke during the Warriors' Watch Riders Welcome Home, Phillip Grandinetti, who also spoke on behalf of Grandpa Duke and coordinated the event with the help of his brother, Brady Abdalla.

To All of the Warriors' Watch Riders for their participation in welcoming home all of our Veterans of War.

A.G. Liggett LCDR USN Director, White House Liaison Office in addressing a letter which so poignantly stated: *Please know that the value of your actions is not defined by awards received, but by the contributions you made to our Nation's defense during the Battles of Peleliu and Okinawa. You and your fellow Marines experienced untold hardship and demonstrated extraordinary courage. Your family, community, and Nation are forever indebted.*

Timothy K. Nenninger, Chief, Archives II Reference Section (RD-DC) for providing the military records requested by Congressman Joe Walsh on behalf of Corporal Loren Duke Abdalla.

Warrior Running Bull at the signing of The Treaty with The Yankton Sioux, 1858 – original resides in The Smithsonian Gallery.

Chief Running Bull at Fort Randall with a horsecart in the background.

Greenwood, SD 1913-1930 - Town where Duke was born, 1925. George Abdalla's Butcher Shop is fourth from the right.

Preface

Each of our lives has a beginning and a heritage that we seek to belong to. For those of us who embrace our heritage, it affects how we see ourselves, the choices we make in our lives, and the strongholds that we cling to when facing our greatest challenges. Whether it is with conscious thought or inherent subconsciously, it forms our nature and ultimately helps to distinguish who we become. From the late 1800s to the early 1900s, new rules of living were being established for Native American Indians by a painfully young United States government. Duke was only six years old when he became aware of his own ancestral ties to his great grandfather Chief Running Bull, and from that time became determined to achieve notability for himself. He, like his ancestors, experienced a time in history that will remain poignantly in the memories of those who lived through it—and in the hearts of those who have come to know its impact on our Country.

Beginning in 1803, President Thomas Jefferson commissioned the Lewis and Clark Expedition to explore the territories north and west of the Mississippi River in order to determine what natural resources were available there. He also wanted to determine whether or not there was a commercial advantage to the very recent Louisiana Purchase by mapping any viable waterways that reached or neared the Columbia River which then flowed to the Pacific Ocean.

In 1804, the explorers Meriwether Lewis and William Clark, while carrying out this objective, encountered a village of Yankton Sioux Indians camped near Calumet Bluff on the Missouri River, in what we now know as South Dakota.

At one of the tribal gatherings, the explorers were told that a male child had been born to one of the headmen of the tribe. Lewis asked to see the child, and when he was brought to him, Lewis wrapped the child in an American flag. It was prophesied that the child would become a loyal friend of the white man and a leader of his people. The child was called Struck by the Ree, and would grow up to become a Yankton Sioux Chief and the first Sioux citizen of the United States. He would proudly fly that same American flag outside his home the remainder of his life.

II

From 1803 to 1853, the United States' population expanded, due to the influx of immigrants to the country. Westward movement became inevitable for those who were searching for land to build homes and create a new life for their families. In order to create and maintain peace during the transition, The Yankton Sioux Tribe sent delegates to Washington D.C. to sign The Treaty of 1837, which ceded all of their lands east of the Mississippi to The United States of America. One of those delegates was a headman of the tribe named Zuyesa, which means "Warrior" in the Dakota language.

Born in 1826 to Headman Zuyesa, was Running Bull, who later would become one of the chief headmen when he came of age. Undoubtedly, he was influenced by his predecessor to seek peace with the white man, yet was still compelled to preserve his Yankton Sioux heritage.

In 1858, Running Bull and several other delegates accompanied Chief Struck by the Ree and traveled by horseback three hundred miles to Council Bluffs, Iowa. From there, they traveled by stagecoach to St. Louis, Missouri, and from St. Louis to Washington, D.C. by train. Once there, The Yankton Dakota Sioux Treaty was signed. It was meant to establish peace with The United States of America, define the boundary lines and institute The Yankton Sioux Reservation, and to procure safe passage for citizens traveling through the Dakota lands. The delegates' round trip took thirty days and their photo was taken at some point during the signing. Running Bull's picture resides in the Smithsonian Gallery in Washington, D.C., along with a picture of Chief Struck by the Ree and the other delegates who signed the treaty. Struck by the Ree passed away in 1889, and Running Bull succeeded him as chief.

Chief Running Bull married a woman named Pejutawastewin-Medicine Woman. She was known simply by her Christian name, Barbara. She gave birth to a daughter in 1880, Princess Minnie Running Bull (the title inherited due to her father being a chief of his tribe). Princess Minnie would marry George Abdalla, a man who was born in Beirut in 1860. Beirut was then a part of the Ottoman Empire.

At the age of twenty, George witnessed the murder of his father by a Turkish officer of the Ottoman Empire. He, in turn, killed the officer, avenging his father's death, then stowed away on a ship bound for America, along with his two brothers and nephew. When they arrived in the new land, George became a peddler, carrying and selling the wares atop his pack horses, as he worked his way west.

In the Dakota land, George traded with the Indians and settlers. He slept in snow banks and fought off wolves that tried to attack his horses. He was searching for a place to settle down on tillable land where he could make a home of his own. George eventually saved enough money to purchase a small butcher shop in Greenwood, South Dakota, which is where he would meet his future wife. Shortly after George and Minnie met in 1904, they married and moved onto the farm left to Minnie by her father. Chief Running Bull had passed away on July 22, 1900.

III

Together, George and Minnie had eight children: Carrie, Flora, Harriet, Jay, Marie, Ike, Thelma, and Bud. While the family lived on the farm, their daughter, Harriet Abdalla, met Loren Todd. Loren was a cowboy of Scottish descent who worked on the ranch next door, and he and Harriet became romantically involved.

Harriet became pregnant, and Loren Todd, not willing to make a commitment to marriage, abandoned both her and the baby. Harriet's son, Loren Duke Abdalla, was born on June 18, 1925. He was delivered by his Grandpa George, as no doctor was available. Shortly afterward, they lost the farm, and the family moved into the nearby town of Wagner, South Dakota.

Harriet, Minnie, and George remained housed together, the elder children having moved on to homes and lives of their own—though they visited regularly. Together, they taught Duke the importance of hard work, honesty, and honor. Raised during the hardships of The Great Depression, with no electricity or running water in the three-room shelter he called home, Duke learned to work hard for what he needed. The blood of his forefathers flowed strongly through his veins, and he meant to make them proud.

Known as "Duke, The Indian," he fought for the United States of America with the Marine Corps during World War II. He performed heroic deeds in the Battles of Peleliu and Okinawa, in the Pacific Ocean Theater. For these actions, Corporal Loren Duke Abdalla has been honored with a review for the Congressional Medal of Honor. He is a Marine to the core, an Indian warrior at heart, and a natural born fighter.

This is a portrayal of the life of Loren Duke Abdalla, that shows the development of his character in a time when hard work was expected. There were no handouts for this young man. He earned the respect of the people around him by doing what needed to be done, in the most expedient of manners. Courageous, practical, and determined are words often used to describe Duke. His matter-of-fact approach to life is inherent. This is his story.

Youngest photo of Duke, age 5.

Enthusiastic American citizen George Abdalla,
wearing a borrowed WWI uniform.

George Abdalla wearing Running Bull's clothing/headdress.

Chapter 1

Duke squeezed his eyes tightly closed, shutting out the faint light of the dawn that had invaded through the small crack in the bedroom door. He pulled the heavy quilt up to his chin to seal out the cold, then opened his eyes to watch his breath leave a faint mist as he exhaled slowly.

He slept on the floor on a goat-skin rug at the foot of his grandfather's brass twin bed. A quilt had been set beneath him, and two more lay atop him to ward off the cold. It wasn't even winter, but the pot-bellied stove had gone out during the night, letting the cold creep into the house.

He waited until the room had warmed up some before he jumped out from under the covers to dress. It was autumn where he lived in Wagner, South Dakota, and Duke was ten years old. School had started the day after Labor Day, and today was a school day, which meant he had to get up soon.

Knowing his mother would be in shortly to check on him if he didn't get out of bed, Duke got up. He splashed some water from a bowl on the dresser onto his face and the back of his neck. As he looked into the mirror, he could see his hair was long, black, and full of snarls. He didn't care to brush it much, that was for girls. He ran a comb through it quickly, then pulled on his pants and buttoned his shirt as the smell of flapjacks filled the air. His stomach grumbled as he thought about breakfast.

He lifted the lid of a cigar box that he kept his most precious possessions in on the top of the dresser. Inside was a newspaper clipping he had saved, with the librarian's permission, from the day before. Dated September 24th, 1935, it read **Joe Louis Takes Out Max Baer In Four Rounds!**

Duke eyed himself in the mirror and bellowed as if he were a ringside announcer, "Joe Louis knocks a man out with a six-inch punch from either hand!" With his fists raised in the air like a boxer, Duke punched hard one way, *Bam!* and then the other, *Bam!*, keeping his feet flat on the ground like his hero, The Brown Bomber. He took another look in the mirror and smiled with confidence before he turned to enter the kitchen.

Grandma Minnie stood at the stove in the kitchen, making cornmeal flapjacks. In the pot next to the skillet was a mixture of sugar and water that she stirred constantly. They didn't have syrup this week, so the heated sugar-water would be used to sweeten the flapjacks. They weren't so bad, with the sweetness added. Sometimes they had cornmeal porridge, too. Other mornings it was cornbread.

Duke had eaten cornmeal just about any way he could imagine it. It filled his stomach and that was all he cared about.

He watched as Grandma continued to stir the pot, slowly moving the spoon in a figure eight. "Come in and sit down, Duke. Breakfast will be ready soon."

He sat and as he did so, he admired his grandmother. She had smooth, tanned skin and dark black hair that she wore in two long plaits on either side of her face. She had braided them the night before as part of her nightly routine. Every night Duke watched as she brushed out her long, coarse hair; then neatly wove it into two tight braids.

He loved his grandma, and he knew she loved him, too. He was one of eighteen grandchildren, but he thought how lucky he was to be able to live with his grandma.

Just then his mother appeared from the smaller of two bedrooms, pulling a wrap closely about her shoulders as she entered the kitchen. She immediately got to work helping her mother prepare breakfast.

Duke watched the two women while he sat near the window, as they worked side-by-side. It was as if they moved to music, their movements nearly choreographed as they prepared the morning breakfast.

His mother was a petite woman, with her dark hair neatly pinned up at the back of her head in a bun. She put plates and glasses on the table and as she did so, smiled at Duke. "Good morning," she said.

He nodded. Duke wasn't quite awake yet, leastways not for conversation.

Mom had been almost a baby herself when she gave birth to Duke, at only fifteen years of age. Duke watched his mother working with his grandmother and wondered what it would have been like to have his father around. She didn't speak about him, and he knew better than to ask. Though it didn't stop him from being curious as to what had happened between them.

Grandpa George Abdalla walked into the kitchen and stood behind Minnie, leaning over her shoulder to see what they were preparing. His grandpa had taught him many lessons, some more painful than others. But most importantly, he taught him how to "Stund up like a man!" Grandpa George was of Syrian descent and spoke with a heavy accent. He had learned to speak English, as well as the Dakota Sioux language. He was a strong man with a broad chest, stout legs, and tough, leathery skin. His eyes were narrow and dark, and he wore a moustache in the shape of a triangle. Duke laughed at that. He never understood how his grandfather could get his moustache shaped that way.

Grandpa George was a stern man. He had learned from his father many valuable life lessons and endeavored to share them with his children and grandchildren, including Duke. That didn't mean Duke didn't still push the limits now and then, though he did respect him greatly.

One summer day, his cousin Duvie came over for a visit. He was a spoiled little boy with a foul mouth and was allowed to do anything he wanted to, without repercussions. Duke remembered he had been about six years old, and Duvie and he were sitting on the front porch talking. His Grandpa George was sitting at the kitchen table, as usual, playing solitaire.

16

Duke listened as Duvie told stories, using the foulest language. Feeling brave and not wanting to seem like a baby, Duke decided to try and swear around his cousin, so he chimed in with a four-letter word.

He felt, more than heard, the vibrations of the kitchen chair as it scraped against the wooden floor. His grandfather was getting up from the table.

Duke got up and ran so fast, he never looked behind him! He raced around the side of the house, his bare feet hardly touching the ground as he ran through the garden.

"Clop, clop, clop, clop!" He could hear footsteps following close behind him as he dashed forward.

"Clop, clop, clop, clop!" They were closer now. If he could just make it to the cornfield...

"Aghhhhh!" Duke screamed as he was lifted off the ground by his long, tangled hair.

Swat! He felt a sting on his backside, followed by "No swear!" uttered sternly by his grandfather. Another swat landed firmly on his rear end, followed by "No swear!" in a tone that brooked no argument.

His rear felt as if he'd been stung by a giant bumblebee! His grandfather proceeded to give him the beating of a lifetime, but Duke remembered one thing: "No swear." Duvie hadn't gotten in trouble at all.

Grandpa George sat down at the table for breakfast first, followed by Duke, Minnie, and then Harriet. Duke shoveled spoonfuls of porridge into his mouth, as he glanced at the time on the table clock. It was nearly time to leave for school.

He finished the food on his plate, used the back of his hand to wipe his mouth, then jumped up from the table, carrying his plate to the sink. He grabbed his jacket and stuffed his arms into the sleeves before he opened the front door. The morning sun's rays silhouetting his frame in the doorway, Duke turned back and yelled into the room, "Come on, Ring!"

From the corner of the kitchen, a black and white Border collie mix roused himself mutinously and made his way to Duke's side. The dog had a distinctive white ring around his neck with a white chest. Black fur surrounded the ring of white all around and down to the dog's toes. After shaking his head and body vigorously, Ring looked up at Duke and barked a hello. He was ready to go.

Duke hopped off the front porch, ran across the dirt yard, and headed straight into the cornfields, Ring at his side. It was a shortcut to school he had figured out a few years ago.

He stopped a moment to retrieve two folded strips of flannel from his front shirt pocket. After wrapping each strip of cloth around his knuckles, he continued into the field. He jabbed at the cornstalks on either side of him. *Bam!* He threw a cross with one fist, then *Bam!* a sharp hook with the other.

As he progressed through the field toward school, he continued throwing jabs at the stalks, both strengthening and numbing his hands with each strike against the uncompromising stems. Duke kept a sharp eye out for snakes as he ran. A prairie rattlesnake was the only venomous snake in South Dakota he had to watch out for. He knew the snake had a triangular head that distinguished it from other, harmless snakes. Duke had seen them before, but always managed to steer clear of the nasty reptiles. His mother had told him that as long as he could leave them alone, they would leave him alone. Duke continued racing through the cornfield, stalks crashing as he pummeled them aside.

Ring followed happily, barking every now and then to let Duke know he was still accompanying him. The words of the news article he'd read that morning replayed in his mind as he ran. He imagined Joe Louis throwing punches at Max Baer in the ring. Baer was a formidable opponent—four inches taller and twenty pounds heavier than Louis. He'd killed two men with his right hand.

But the Brown Bomber was a better fighter! Joe Louis could throw a punch with all his power focused on the connection, with all his might being delivered at the point of contact. This was a technique Duke practiced daily. Louis took Baer in four rounds—knocked him out cold. *Bam! Bam!*

A few last punches at the cornstalks for good measure, then he stepped out onto the grass that surrounded the schoolyard. Duke was ready for anything now.

He hugged Ring around the neck, patted him on the head, and ran toward the three-story brick building before the bell rang. He knew Ring would be waiting for him when he got out of school.

It wasn't his favorite activity, but school passed the time. He had made some good friends and shared fun memories with a few of them in particular. As he gazed out the classroom window, he daydreamed of some of those moments.

Back in first grade, he remembered watching Bitz Handley slide his tin of Copenhagen from his pocket, squeeze a pinch of chew out, and push it between his cheek and gum on the inside of his mouth. Duke was sure the teacher was going to catch Bitz chewing in class, but if the teacher got too close, Bitz would simply swallow the chew whole. He never got sick from it, either, which amazed Duke.

Then, there was Buzz Bastemeyer and Dolphy Greggor—the three of them were always hanging around together. A favorite topic of conversation between Duke and his friends was boxing. It was one of the greatest forms of entertainment, as far as they were concerned. Duke studied the boxing moves of many boxers, including Joe Louis.

Heavyweight champ Joe Louis was one of the most powerful and fastest punchers of his time. He was known for his right cross, thrown short and straight. His punches were sheer dynamite. The articles Duke read and shared with his friends described Louis as an extremely accurate puncher who wasted no motion. His punches could paralyze a man. But Duke's favorite phrase stated that Louis could "knock a man out with a six-inch punch from either hand." That was really inspiring.

Another favorite pastime was when Duke and the boys headed up to the north side of town after school to see if there were apples on the trees in the orchards. He and Buzz would hike up a tree and start shaking the loaded branches.

Dolphy, a heavy, stout boy, would scan the ground and gather as many apples as he could. The boys all stuffed their shirts and pants pockets with as many apples as they could fit.

One time, they were stashing apples in their clothes and heard some commotion coming from the farmhouse nearby. The next thing they knew, there was a black Model A police car stirring up dust as it headed down the dirt road toward the orchard.

Duke and the boys jumped down from the tree, dropping apples all over the ground, then ran as fast as they could to get away from the police. They ran across a field, toward the railroad tracks, saw the Model A racing down the road, and they simultaneously rolled under the railroad cars and out the other side before they were spotted. They looked for a place to hide in a farmer's corn crib, where they noticed several fifty-five gallon drums standing near the silo. They each hopped into one of the barrels just in time and the police car raced passed them. They waited for what seemed like hours in the drums, until they were sure they were safe, then jumped out and each ran their own way home before dark. Later, when they met during lunch time at school, they decided that one of them needed to stand sentry during apple pickings.

That made Duke think of his own lunch for today. He listened to the teacher for a little while then drifted back to his daydreams, remembering the good times with his friends.

While the weather was warm, Duke and his friends all liked to assemble at a place they called 'The Bottom,' where they liked to swim. The property was near Duke's Uncle Bruce and Aunt Maggie Pigsley's farm in Wagner, on land near the Missouri River. Sometimes, all the kids were called upon to help weed the Pigsley's garden, or do another chore on the farm. The kids' families always helped each other out in Wagner, cooperating in hard times.

One day during the summer Duke was nine-years-old, while pulling weeds on the Pigsley farm with friends, he took a hoe and cut into the dirt, lifting the weeds and soil as he went. Another boy grabbed and shook the dirt from the weeds, then tossed them into a large woven basket held by a young girl. The contents of the basket would then be piled up behind the barn, to be burned at a later time. Down a row they went, paying close attention to their job, when the girl gave out a scream.

Duke looked up from his task and jumped in front of the girl, who was pointing her finger at a prairie rattlesnake. Holding the hoe in front of him, conjuring up enough bravado for the young girl to see, Duke made a pass at the snake with the hoe. The snake made a short strike toward him. Duke swung the hoe in a half circle behind his shoulder, then *Wham!* down to the dirt and into the snake with such swiftness several of the kids jumped.

Rapidly repeating the stroke as he advanced toward the snake, he chopped it into small, harmless pieces. Then he looked up at the girl with his chest puffed up and smiled. She smiled back, her eyes twinkling with delight that he had come to her rescue.

Duke and his friends shared other adventures as well. On the side of the school building was a huge fire escape. It was a large, round tube that extended down to the ground from the third floor of the building. When the school had fire drills, Duke and his friends would leave the door open at the bottom of the tube. Later, after school let out, they would soak down their clothes, so that they didn't stick to the slide, then climb up the fire escape, and slide down it for fun!

"That's all for today. Make sure you read the next chapter in your reader this weekend." Duke heard the last sentence that his teacher had spoken and his daydream disappeared. After a long school day, he was ready to go home.

As he ran down the school steps and onto the grass, he called for Ring. He knew the dog would be nearby; he always was.

Sure enough, Ring scampered out from under the bandstand in the schoolyard, tail wagging, smiling from ear to ear, or so it seemed.

Duke slapped his thigh and said, "Come on, Ring! Good dog." They had to get home so he could carry out his chores before dinner.

Every evening before dark, Duke would carry in kindling and logs, stacking it beside the stove. Some of the logs would need to be split. Duke would stand a log up on its end on top of a larger log and swing the ax down smoothly, straight through the center of the log to be split. He knew he had to bring in enough wood to keep the stove supplied. At ten years of age, Duke had developed some muscular arms.

Once the logs were brought in, he headed back out the door to fill a bucket full of coal. There was a large bin around the side of the house that it was stored in. The coal would be layered beneath the wood in the stove to keep it burning throughout the night.

As he was setting the coal bucket down near the stove that night, Duke recalled an important lesson he'd learned. One his mother had taught him when he was younger. They bought their coal and wood from a man in town. His mother gave him seven dollars to buy five dollars' worth of coal and two dollars' worth of wood.

One day Duke decided to buy four dollars and fifty cents worth of coal and two dollars' worth of wood. He took the extra fifty cents from what was supposed to go towards the coal and went down to the local drugstore. There, he bought a malted milk with his "extra money."

Duke remembered how happy he was as he took another sip from the straw, it tasted so good! He was sitting on a stool in the drugstore, sipping that cold, frothy, malted milk—savoring every sip—when in the door walked his mother!

He pushed the drink away. His mother strode over and sat down next to him. "Finish your malted milk, Duke," she said, sliding the glass back in front of him.

Duke finished it obediently, although it tasted more like sawdust in his mouth now with his mother standing next to him. He swallowed with great difficulty.

"Pick up your change," she said.

He picked up the change off the counter, knowing he was in for it. Without so much as a word, his mother took hold of his arm and guided him all the way home. She took him straight to the woodshed, and he knew not to struggle. There, just inside the door of the shed, hung a half-length of a broom handle. She used that broom handle to mete out justice, to teach him a lesson, one that he would never forget. Money should be earned honestly.

His mother had told him while he was getting his malted milk that the coal and wood man made his day's deliveries. When delivering to the Abdalla house, the coal man mentioned to her that her son had only ordered four dollars and fifty cents' worth of coal instead of the usual five dollars' worth.

The last thing Duke did before he went in for the night was to fill two buckets full of water—one for cooking and one for washing up. After carrying them in, he set the buckets on top of the stove in the kitchen, then got ready for supper. There usually wasn't much to look forward to as far as dinner went, but eating anything was better than going to bed on an empty stomach.

***

On Saturday morning, Grandma Minnie asked him to go out to the field in back of the house and dig up some turnips and wild onions. Duke didn't mind this chore; he was skilled in handling a knife. He measured the weight of it in his hand, felt the curve of the handle against his palm, and had learned to wield it in the shortest strokes possible to accomplish his task.

When he got into the field, he pulled out the pocket knife he always carried with him from his back pocket, and turned up a dozen or so turnips from the ground in an amazingly short period of time. He followed suit with the onions.

Next, Grandma Minnie asked him to dig up some dandelions so she could use the leaves for a supper dish. She would throw the leaves in a pot, add some fat for seasoning, and cook it until the leaves became soft, like spinach leaves. Only it didn't taste much like spinach. It didn't taste much like anything other than fat-cooked dandelion leaves, mostly bitter and tasting something akin to dirt.

But Duke knew better than to complain. It was what they had to eat, so he ate it.

Since Grandpa George and Grandma Minnie had retired and lost their farm, there wasn't much food to go around. The butcher shop that his Grandpa George had once owned in town had become a general store. No more fresh beef on Sunday night. No more pork chops on Wednesdays. They were fortunate to have meat whenever they could afford it. When they did have meat, it was stretched to last as many meals as possible. Cornmeal, grains, and potatoes were the staples for most meals. Any vegetable growing wild that was edible was fair game, too. Choke cherries and wild plums were other naturally growing food items that Duke was sent to gather which Grandma Minnie sometimes baked into a pie. And then, there were the occasional apples.

Duke didn't know much about the butcher shop. He'd heard stories, though.

Grandpa George had owned the store when he was young and met Grandma Minnie. Minnie had come into the store with her mother, Barbara Running Bull, who was there to buy beef. When Minnie entered the store, George had noticed her right away or so he told Duke years later. She had walked closely by her mother's side, but glanced up shyly at Grandpa George from underneath her long, lowered lashes. She had thick, dark hair that fell to her waist. George thought she was beautiful and watched her as she followed her mother through the shop.

As he rang up their purchases, George grinned at Minnie and handed her a neatly-wrapped package of beef. The paper was folded perfectly, with corners tucked in neatly. Minnie smiled back at him as she took the package from his hand, his work-worn fingertips grazing lightly against her own.

Any time thereafter, when Minnie and her mother entered the store, George took advantage of the moment and conversed with her. Grandma Minnie was well respected by the townspeople and store owners alike. They knew she was the daughter of Chief Running Bull, and in the Tribe she was also known as Kiktewin, meaning Kills-for-Herself.

When Minnie walked down Main Street, her black shawl was tied loosely across her shoulders, her three-legged dog trailing along beside her, her head held high—people nodded and waved in greeting. Minnie always smiled sweetly in return, nodding her head in acknowledgment. Not long after they'd met, George and Minnie were married in 1904 in Greenwood, South Dakota, at the Presbyterian Church. Grandpa George wasn't one to waste time.

***

Grandpa George was a man to be reckoned with. He was very protective of his family, especially his daughter, Harriet, now twenty-five years old. There was another man who lived in the town of Wagner where they lived that was after Duke's mother. Grandpa George had told the man several times to stay away from Harriet. But this man didn't seem to want to listen to him.

One Sunday night, after dark, the man was at the house, calling for Harriet to come outside. What the man didn't know was that George kept a double-barreled shotgun, loaded, all the time, behind the front door.

Grandpa George heard the man outside, calling to his daughter. He jumped up and grabbed the double-barreled shotgun. Duke jumped up right behind him.

Duke followed him outside and around the corner of the house. The man was running fast toward the fence, and as he took a running leap to clear the top of the fence, George let loose with both barrels and shot the man directly in the backside.

The man fell to the ground on the other side of the fence and gingerly made his way away from their house. No report was filed. After simple questioning, the police determined that the man had been trespassing and was therefore deserving of his injuries.

At school the next day when the kids asked Duke what had happened, he had one thing to say—it's what his grandfather had said: "He got what he deserved!" The rest of the kids agreed and laughed.

When Duke was ready to make his way home after school, Ring was there waiting for him. They made their way home together, back through the cornfields—Duke jabbing at the stalks as they went, pieces of flannel cloth wrapped around his fists, to spare his knuckles.

As he arrived at the house, he heard his grandfather's deep voice. "Duck! Duck, is that you?" With his heavy Syrian accent, his grandpa always mispronounced his name.

"I'm home, Grandpa," Duke replied.

"Mind the house, Duck—I'm going to visit Abdush in town," Grandpa George told him.

Abdouch was a fellow Syrian and friend, who owned the pool hall in Wagner and who had also traveled to America to seek a new life. Grandpa George spent a lot of time at Abdouch's establishment. Duke didn't mind, it gave him more time to read about Joe Louis and be alone.

His mother and Grandma Minnie had gone to town as well, only they went to the General Store to purchase some cornmeal and sugar, if it was available. Sugar was one of the things that was highly rationed during the Depression, and they were lucky to get it.

***

The days grew shorter and colder. The stalks in the cornfields had begun collapsing, as much for the season passing, as from Duke's powerful punches. The Clemmons' farm, which was next door to Duke's house, had a large barn with rafters in the ceiling. The rafters would be perfect to hang a punching bag from, Duke decided.

He needed a place indoors where he could hone his boxing skills, and this was it. So one afternoon after school he approached Mr. Clemmons and asked him if he could hang a hay-filled gunny sack from the rafters in his barn.

The farmer considered Duke to be a good kid and knew of his interest in boxing. He slapped him on the back with endorsement and said, "Sure Duke, you can hang your punching bag in my barn."

Though it was a painstaking task, Duke worked hard on making his punching bag. With each shovelful of hay, he would climb into the gunnysack and stomp down on the hay as he pulled up the sides of the bag. The process was repeated until the bag was full and tight. Then, Duke took a length of straw rope and tied off the top of the bag as securely as he could. Finally, he had his punching bag in place.

Every day after school, once his chores were finished, he'd skip over to the Clemmons' barn and spend time punching his hay sack. At first it hurt his knuckles, the hay was so hard inside. But after two weeks of punching, it started to soften a bit and Duke got a good workout with the sack.

Duke spent a lot of time at the library, reading articles about Joe Louis. The librarian would occasionally allow him to cut out an article and save the clippings. He read about how the key to Louis's powerful punch was to amass all of his strength, and concentrate all of his energy into a single point as he delivered the blow.

Duke practiced this method as often as he could in the barn, punching the gunny sack with his fists wrapped in flannel—he couldn't afford to buy boxing gloves. He kept his feet planted flat on the ground, like Louis did, as he shuffled around the sack, learning his balance.

***

Winter soon arrived, dropping several feet of snow across the southeast corner of South Dakota. The kids at school were excited, because they knew Christmas would not be far off. But in Duke's house, they didn't celebrate Christmas. They never had a Christmas tree or decorations, except for the one year that Duke glued paper rings together to make a garland to hang around the house to add some festivity.

There were few presents that Duke ever recollected receiving from his mother. One Christmas he got three little furry bear figurines, each about the size of a quarter. Another Christmas, a sled. And three Christmases ago, the gift he received from his mother was a small truck with a seat on top. He used to sit on top of the little truck and slide it down the angle of the cellar door. Not a fancy ride, but it amused him.

Harriet was a young mother for her age. She was a hard worker and loving. It helped her financially that they lived with her parents on the outskirts of town.

Duke remembered a time when he was sick with a cold; he must have been about six years old. His mother kept him home from school that day. She fussed over him like a good mother would—wiping his forehead, doting on him with lots of attention. Then she asked him in her sweet, indulgent voice, "Is there anything you would like, son?"

He looked up at her and said, "I would like a grape pop."

In the dead of winter, Harriet bundled up and headed into town to buy a grape soda pop for Duke. A pop cost a whole nickel per bottle then, which was about what it cost to buy five pounds of sugar. When she returned home, she set the soda pop down on the small wooden table next to Duke. Boy, did that make him feel special!

Smiling at him as she pushed the hair back from his forehead, she sat down on the edge of her bed, where he was resting. Duke wished he knew more about his Indian ancestors, but it was not a frequent topic of discussion, nor was it entertained much. Feeling the warmth of her gaze, Duke searched her dark, brown eyes and asked his mother about how his Great Grandpa Running Bull had become a chief.

She indulged him with the story. Harriet spoke low about how, for the Sioux, the title of chief was earned for outstanding performance during times of war or peace. To be chief was considered an honorary title, achieved by unanimous vote of the council of the headmen of the tribe.

"I never told you before, Duke, but Running Bull's father had been a headman. His name was Zuyesa, which means warrior. It was a great honor to have been given this name. 'Ta Tanka Inyanke' is the Sioux name for Running Bull, who earned the honor, and the vote of the headman to become chief," his mother said.

Duke was proud to be the great grandson of Ta Tanka Inyanke, The Head Chief of The Yankton Sioux Tribe.

His mother explained about the Medicine Wheel that day, too. For the Sioux Indians, it symbolizes every individual's path in life and foretells of the steps they must take to achieve that path. It is round, to symbolize the circle of life from birth to death. There are four sacred colors: red, white, yellow and black. Red is on top of the wheel and stands for the North. It symbolizes wisdom and the last phase of the cycle of life: the afterlife. White represents the South and stands for friendship and youth. Yellow symbolizes the East, and the things in nature that are there for man to use and share. Black represents the West, growing old and death. The four colors are significant in that they represent the four elements—air, water, fire and earth; the four directions; and the four seasons of life: birth, life, friendship and death. Duke's mother never knew his great grandfather Running Bull, and many of the Sioux traditions were being forgotten with the merge of Indian and White Man. Symbols like the Medicine Wheel remained significant to those of Yankton Sioux descent and were displayed in Duke's mother's room, in a framed beadwork.

The next day he felt better, but he promised himself he wouldn't forget the stories his mother shared. Or perhaps it was the circumstances that Duke was growing up in: times were hard and he was happy to be alive. He respected life of all kinds. He respected the wisdom of his mother and grandparents. And he hoped to achieve an honorable path in his life.

***

In January, the winter seemed the coldest. Temperatures were often below zero—with or without the wind chill factor. One particularly cold Saturday morning, Harriet gave Duke three cents to run to the farm two blocks away to fetch a quart of milk for breakfast. Several times on his way to the farm, Duke's feet slipped into the deep snow, soaking his shoes, socks and the bottoms of his pant legs.

When he arrived at the farm, the lady of the house asked if he would like to come in and warm up for a while. Duke knew he was expected home in as short a time as possible, so he politely refused and headed back into the cold and snow, carrying the cold milk jar in his bare hands. When he stepped inside the door at home, his fingers were frozen stiff.

Grandma Minnie gently released his fingers from the glass of the milk jar, drew her black shawl more closely about her shoulders, and directed Duke back out into the snow. She believed in the old Indian ways, and rather than warm his fingers, she stuck his frozen hands into a snow bank, telling him to hold them there for several minutes before returning with him back into the house. As the flow of blood returned to his fingertips in the relative warmth of the house, the nerve endings protested with severe messages of pain. Duke decided he'd never go out into the snow and cold again without wrapping his hands with flannel, no matter how quick the trip.

"Thank you for bringing the milk, Duke. Once you warm up, we'll eat," his grandma told him.

He stood near the stove for several minutes, removing his shoes, socks, and rolling up his pants so he could feel his feet again. Before long, he was warm and his belly was full.

***

Because winters were so cold in Wagner, it was Duke's job to make certain that the outside water pipe was wrapped with a thick burlap cloth. Grandpa George asked him to do this so that the pipe wouldn't freeze up when the temperatures dropped below freezing. Duke always filled two buckets every evening with water and set them on top of the stove in the kitchen. Some mornings, when the stove had gone out during the night, the water in the buckets would be frozen when they woke. The ice that would form on top of the bucket would be two or three inches deep. Grandpa George would have to break through the ice with a chisel and hammer in the morning to get to the water beneath. It was mornings like these that Duke wished for spring and warmer weather.

***

When spring finally arrived and the days were growing longer again, Duke enjoyed spending time outside with his dog. This winter had seemed to take a toll on Ring, though. Duke had always been escorted to and from school eagerly, but Ring seemed more tired than usual as of late.

One cool morning when Duke left the house, he searched the yard for the dog, calling for him. "Ring, come on boy! Ring, where are ya' boy?"

Out of the corner of his eye, Duke saw Ring turning away from him, heading behind a shed. His tail and back legs were dragging on the ground behind him.

Even though he was worried, Duke knew he didn't have time to go after him. He had to get to school. He thought about Ring during class that day and wondered why he was acting so strangely. True, Ring was getting on in years and he didn't seem to be as strong as he used to be. He slept more often and followed Duke more slowly than he used to. He didn't have as much of an appetite, either.

The hours dragged by, Duke checking the clock that hung above the chalkboard often. He knew his dog would be outside waiting for him, and he was anxious to check on him.

As soon as the bell rang, Duke and his friend, Buzz, raced outside to find Ring. But the dog wasn't there, he wasn't sitting outside on the grass waiting for him.

Duke scanned the schoolyard. He had to be there somewhere! Duke ran around the school, Buzz tagging closely behind, calling "Ring! Come on, Ring! Where are ya' boy? Don't play games now, Ring. Come on out!"

Something wasn't right. Duke had to find him. He looked at the bandstand that stood behind the school. It was raised about a foot or so off the ground. He hurried towards it, a feeling of dread solid in the pit of his stomach. Buzz was right behind him. Duke dropped to his knees and leaned forward to peer underneath. It was dark, but he thought he made out a shadow near the stairs.

Inching closer, feeling the ground as he went, he stretched out his hand, and his fingers connected with soft fur. Hesitantly, he rested his hand on the mound. The body was stiff and cold. He knew at once it was Ring. Duke stroked his fur gently, quietly taking short breaths. His canine friend had crawled under the bandstand, into a hole that he most likely, had previously dug for a resting spot, and died.

Tears stained Duke's cheeks, now dirty from the dust and dirt that covered his face from the search. Duke turned to his friend and said, "He's gone, Buzz. He's dead."

The boys worked silently to gather dirt from under the bandstand to cover the dog. Tears streamed down their faces as they worked in unison to give Ring a proper burial.

"I loved that dog," said Duke, wiping the back of a dirty hand across his eyes as a sob escaped from the back of his throat.

"I know ya' did," said Buzz, patting his friend gently on the shoulder.

Later, when Duke went home to tell his mother the news, she hugged him. He didn't cry in front of her, and he kept a stiff upper lip in front of his grandma and grandpa, too. But his heart ached at losing his long-time friend, and sleep eluded him that night as he curled up at the foot of his grandpa's bed, reminiscing about the adventures he'd had with Ring by his side.

Ten-year-old Duke, 'Billy' goat, and Grandma Minnie on their home porch.

Chapter 2

The Memorial Day parade and picnic was in just a few days. That meant the rodeo would be here soon. The town of Wagner had taken to setting up a boxing ring in the middle of Town Square on Main Street every year for the occasion. All of the boys age twelve or older by the end of the summer had a chance to box each other. Boys would be matched up by age and weight, with the youngest ones boxing first. It became such a popular event, that the process was repeated for Independence Day and Labor Day.

Duke enjoyed boxing so much, it gave him greater incentive to study the boxing techniques of his idol Joe Louis. He studied the information seriously; he wanted to be the best boxer in the ring. For the last two years, he had continued to read any articles he could find from the town library regarding Joe Louis and his boxing style. He returned to his routine of punching cornstalks and zigzagging his way to and from school through the field.

Then, every day, after he'd done his chores, he would pummel the burlap sack filled with hay that hung in the Clemmons' barn. Duke was grateful for his makeshift punching sack and took advantage of any spare time he had to devote to practicing his boxing techniques in the relative warmth of the barn.

It was Memorial Day, 1937. Duke was nearly twelve years old, so he qualified to participate. The boxing ring had been set up in the center of the square, downtown Wagner. People gathered all around the ring to watch.

The announcer called Duke's name, and Duke stepped into the ring. He puffed out his chest, proud to be a contender. He was matched up with another boy his age. The practice was, that they went three rounds per match.

Duke boxed all afternoon. He didn't count how many fights he fought, but he won them all. He handled himself well in the ring. So well, that the rodeo promoter who had been watching from the stands, approached Duke after his last match.

The rodeo promoter offered to pay Duke three dollars a fight in the upcoming rodeo on Independence Day, all he had to do was box any kid his age and weight that would challenge him. That was a lot of money to Duke, and he wanted to box! So he accepted.

He practiced all summer, never missing a day with his punching sack which was getting put to the test.

On June 22nd, the whole neighborhood gathered at his Aunt Flora's house to listen to the Joe Louis/James Braddock fight for the Heavyweight Championship Title. Aunt Flora's house was the only one on the south side of town that had a radio.

The match took place in Comiskey Park, Chicago, Illinois in 1937. The family listened intently as the boxing began. It sounded like it was anyone's fight in the beginning, Duke thought, but he knew his hero would come out on top.

In the first round, Braddock threw a right upper cut to Louis' chin, knocking him to the mat. Louis managed to get up in short time. Throughout the next five rounds, Louis took charge, and Braddock lost his composure. Braddock won the seventh round, putting up a good fight, pouring out a lot of energy, perhaps looking for an early end to the bout.

The final blow came in the eighth round, when The Brown Bomber threw a left hook, knocking Braddock's arm aside, then a right cross to the chin, knocking Braddock to the mat for good. The whole neighborhood cheered as the announcement was made. Joe Louis was the new Heavyweight Boxing Champion of the World! Duke couldn't have been happier.

Duke knew that his mother was proud of his boxing, she was happy that he dedicated himself to the sport, and that it gave him a sense of purpose. When the Fourth of July rolled around, Duke couldn't wait for the day to begin. He'd hardly slept the night before, knowing this time when he boxed at the rodeo, he was going to be paid for it. He dressed quickly and rushed through a breakfast of grits and cornbread. The first of the day's events was a parade that would be conducted through the center of town.

Duke had worked along with the other kids from school to build a float. It was created to look like a football field. The Hoefer twins were chosen to dress in cheerleading uniforms and ride on the float on either end near the goalposts. Doris and Dorothy Hoefer wore white sweaters with a large, red "W" emblazoned on the front, and red, pleated skirts. They rode on the float along with Duke's pet goat, Billy.

Since the loss of Ring, Duke had adopted a new pet. Billy had been a young goat when he lost his mother, a goat they had had in the family for several years. Duke fed the goat and gave him lots of affection. Billy became quite attached to Duke. Like his dog Ring had done before, Billy followed Duke to and from school.

When Duke left the schoolyard and headed through town, he'd call for his goat, "Come, Billy! Come here, Billy!" Billy would appear from around the corner, running sideways down the street toward Duke. It made Duke laugh every time.

All the school kids loved Billy and wanted him to ride on the float with the Hoefer twins. So Duke agreed to let him. The girls sat at either end of the field on the goalposts, their blonde curls bouncing atop their shoulders, and Billy stood between them on the miniature football field. The float passed through the center of town, people cheering and clapping as it went by. Billy became so excited, he began to urinate in the middle of the float. The Hoefer twins turned their heads, embarrassed, pretending not to see it. The crowd laughed heartily, but Duke knew he'd be cleaning up the mess when the float finished its course.

Still, he was excited about what was to come. The boxing tournaments were one of the events following the parade.

As Duke stood in the ring, the announcer spoke through a megaphone offering to any boy Duke's age and weight a challenge to a three-round boxing bout. Duke stood solidly in the center of the ring, wearing the boxing gloves that the rodeo promoter had provided for the contestants.

The first challenger entered the ring and Duke sized him up. The boy was knocked completely out of the ring in the first round. The kid didn't know what hit him! Duke had the flat-footed stance that Joe Louis used and delivered a punch that sent the boy literally flying out of the ring.

The announcer called in another boy, who warily stepped into the ring with Duke. It wasn't long before the second challenger succumbed to his adroit maneuvering and fierce punches. Duke became well-known for his boxing skills, and never lost a fight that day. He appreciated the opportunity to earn a decent amount of money doing something he enjoyed. Times were hard and any chance he had to earn an honest dollar, he jumped at it.

Grandpa George and his mother were very proud of him that day, and Grandma Minnie baked a homemade apple pie in his honor.

***

Duke worked hard at whatever job he took and always gave his best effort. He had several jobs in his youth, one of them working in town for Rife's Grocery Store. He was paid ten cents an hour to unload the delivery truck. All the goods had to be carried in from the truck and down into the basement. Then, once the truck was completely unloaded, Duke restocked all of the shelves in the store. After he had completed his tasks, the grocery store owner would lay him off work until he was needed again.

When he wasn't working at the grocery story, Duke was working at the granary for a man he called Zip, the elevator man. For ten cents an hour, he shoveled corn from the silo into the bins that were set out to be filled. The first time he'd eyed those bins, it brought back memories of apple-picking and how they'd saved his backside from a late night whipping!

One day Duke was working hard at the granary when it was nearing noon. Zip approached and asked him if he knew how to drive a car. Duke recalled how his Uncle Jay had shown him how to work the pedals and stick shift of a car once. Though he hadn't yet driven one, Duke nodded yes. Zip told him that he could drive his brand-new 1937 Model A Coupe home for lunch and handed him the keys. Duke jumped into the car. He didn't go back to his house, knowing there wasn't anything to eat there, anyway. He passed by instead and headed straight to the racetrack.

Duke drove around the dirt racetrack over and over, watching in his rear view mirror as the dust rose behind him as he circled the track. He opened up the Model A Coupe and drove the car with a big, fat smile on his face. He was driving all by himself—what a thrill!

When he arrived back at the granary, he simply drove up into the lot and parked the car. No mention was made of where he'd been and what he'd done. But at twelve years of age, for the first time in his life, Duke had driven a car!

***

Over the next few years, Duke continued to work and play hard. Perhaps it was part of the times that made him a serious-minded young man. He didn't just want to play a game, he wanted to compete and he wanted to win.

At the age of fifteen, Duke enjoyed playing baseball in the Junior League for the American Legion, in Wagner. In August, his team played in a tournament for the state championship in Pierre, South Dakota. Of the teams that participated, Wagner was the only team that was so poor they had to borrow a bus from Ravinia High School to attend the tournament.

On the bus ride there, the air was hot and muggy so they rode with the windows open. Swarms of grasshoppers covered the grill of the bus by the time they arrived in Pierre. After driving on gravel and dirt roads, the boys were covered in dust. Since there were no shower facilities available, they were forced to jump into the Missouri River with their clothes on to get their uniforms clean.

Duke played either shortstop or second base. Between his boxing workouts and the strenuous daily chores he performed, he had become very strong and quick. He was able to cover a lot of ground and handled either position equally well. His friend Bitz Handley was the catcher for the Wagner Juniors and the boys enjoyed hanging out together. Walt Pigsley, Duke's uncle, was proud of his small team and to be their manager.

The league in Pierre had won the State Championship the year before, in 1939. Wagner beat Pierre in this year's tournament and became runners-up to the Aberdeen Eaglets, who won the state championship. The Wagner Post reported that Aberdeen was able to select from eight Junior teams from a city of twenty thousand people—while Wagner had a rag-tag team chosen from a population of only twelve hundred.

The game against Pierre was broadcasted over the radio, with Harriet, Grandma Minnie, Grandpa George, and the rest of the townspeople listening intently. When the Wagner Juniors won the game and returned home, the whole town greeted them. It was as if they'd won the World Series!

Later, Duke read the article where the paper described Pierre as an ideal host, entertaining the boys at free swims and picture shows. He knew the reality was the boys slept in cabins near the river where they bathed. They were fed bologna sandwiches for meals.

In the years of participation in the championship tournament, the Wagner Juniors had achieved either championship status or runner-up status each time. Duke was proud to have been a part of this team. Baseball had taught him a lot about teamwork, honesty, integrity, courage, trust, a sense of fair play, and a love of the game. Between baseball and boxing, Duke stayed healthy and fit.

A few months later, Duke entered the Golden Gloves Boxing Tournament. The tournament was presented in Mitchell, South Dakota, sixty miles from Wagner. He rode on a bus with several other boys from town.

After he arrived and checked in, Duke fought one fight with a young, Scandinavian blond man who had a sturdy frame. They went three rounds, shuffling their feet, jabbing and throwing punches at each other with a fervor, until a ref called the fight and determined it a draw they were so well matched. It was a day Duke would never forget. It was the only fight he boxed in that day, but it was the most challenging of his experience. He was proud to say that he had qualified for, and fought in, a Golden Gloves Tournament.

***

In the spring of 1941, Grandpa George died of advancing age. He was eighty-one years old. Grandma Minnie passed away four months later, having suffered from tuberculosis. She was only sixty-one. It was a tough year, having to bury both his grandparents. Duke carried fond memories of them both. One phrase that his grandfather had spoken often Duke took to heart: "Stund up like a man!" The words made a significant mark on his life.

Without Grandpa George around, Harriet and Duke were forced to move into what amounted to a tool shed, in the heart of Wagner. There was a county yard near the railroad where the county trucks were parked. Duke and his mom were allowed to move into the small dwelling on the property without having to pay any rent. The shed had no windows, no electricity or running water, and they were forced to heat their meals over a small kerosene stove, which also served as a heater.

They continued to live sparsely throughout the next year, barely having enough money for food. Duke never complained about his circumstances, though he did dream of a better life for them both.

He and his mom had a close relationship, and he knew his mother was proud of him. She encouraged him often, remarking on his skills and abilities, expressing confidence in all of his accomplishments.

Chapter 3

On December 7th, 1941, the whole world was stunned when the sneak attack on Pearl Harbor by Japanese forces was announced. Never before had the United States been assaulted on their own shores. Duke and his mother were shocked and listened to the news about the war whenever they could. Not having electricity in their own home, they would visit his Aunt Flora's house as often as possible to hear the latest news from around the country.

There were several appeals made to young men in America to join in the fight. Many young men wanted to defend against and fight to remove the threat of the cruel German and Japanese forces. Young men that Duke knew lied about their ages to join the United States Army, Navy, Air Force or in rarer circumstances, the Marines. The Marines were known to be the toughest and fiercest in their fighting, and Duke knew when he turned eighteen he'd sign to be a Marine.

***

In the summer of 1942, Duke turned seventeen. He was a slender young man at six feet tall, with black, wavy hair and steel grey eyes.

One night he and his friend, Noel Troxell, attended a dance in town. Noel escorted Elsie, a girl that lived in Chicago, and Duke and two other friends from Wagner escorted three girls from the high school to the dance. Elsie and her girlfriends all worked at a place called Stewart Die Casting Company in Chicago. She wanted Noel to move to Chicago.

As much as Duke wanted to stay in Wagner with his mother and finish high school, he was eager to begin working and experiencing life outside of the small town. That night, Noel invited Duke to move with him to Illinois—in hopes of acquiring a job at the same company where the girls worked. Duke didn't have to think twice about the opportunity. As the big band played in the background, he thought about all the money he could make in the Windy City.

After the dance was over he asked Noel to drive him home. When they arrived, Duke turned to his friend and said, "I'll only be a minute."

Walking inside the tiny home they had made for themselves, Duke told his mother he was leaving for Chicago, packed everything he owned into a cardboard oatmeal container, kissed his mother good-bye, and headed out the door in a minute flat. His mother hadn't shed a tear. Instead, she believed her son would achieve great things and hoped for the best for him.

Early the next day, they set out in Noel's car. Duke and Noel got the jobs in Chicago, due to the association with the four girls Noel knew: Elsie, Kay, Eleanor, and another girl named Eleanor. The girls lived in an apartment together, and Noel and Duke got an apartment in the same building right down the hall. It wasn't a large apartment, but Duke enjoyed being self-sufficient. Though in time he knew he'd miss his mother's cooking.

The company Duke worked for was a defense plant that made mortar shells and other metals to support the war. His job was building frames for fighter airplanes. When he first began working, he made forty-four dollars a week. After a few weeks in Chicago, Duke decided to work Saturdays to make extra money. His weekly income went up to fifty-six dollars per week. He had never earned so much money in all his life!

Each week he sent money folded up into a letter home to his mother and told her how things were going for him and Noel. Chicago was quite a change from Wagner, he wrote, "Here in the city, people dress up when they go out. For any reason. If you are going out to dinner, you put on trousers and a shirt. If you are going to the movies, with or without a date, you put on a tie. People take pride in their appearance here." His mother replied that she'd like to see that and sent her love.

Chicago was a welcome change for Duke. This type of life he had never experienced before. He began to get a taste for his independence, and enjoyed it fully. Duke took a streetcar wherever he went in the city. He worked hard at the factory, but spent nearly every dollar he made, as fast as he made it. For the first time in his life, Duke felt like he was his own master. He could do anything he wanted, as long as he could pay for it himself.

The rest of the year went by quickly, but the one thing he knew for sure was that he still wanted to fight in the war and be a Marine. His eighteenth birthday was fast approaching, and he couldn't wait.

Duke returned home to Wagner when he turned eighteen to approach the draft board. He told them he wanted to enlist in the Marines. The men there directed Duke to go to Nebraska to enlist with the Marine Corps so he took the train alone to Omaha.

He had a lot of time to think while he was on the train. He thought about his Grandpa George and Grandma Minnie and how much he missed them. He thought about how tough things had been growing up and how hard it was on his mother. But the one thing that was always constant was his mother's love and support of him.

As Duke walked into the auditorium in Omaha where he was to enlist, the heels of his shoes clicked against the large, square floor tiles and echoed in the vastness of the high ceiling of the building. He noted a myriad of sounds in the auditorium as he took a seat.

Sitting on the fold-out wooden chair, he listened to the murmur of voices and scraping of chairs against the floor. He turned in his seat to view a hundred or so other men who were there with the same purpose as him—to enlist for military service. Men of all ages were there to join. There were a lot of young men, some too young to join—but so eager to fight for their country. There were older men, too. Much older than he was, anyway.

A director raised his voice over the murmur of voices and asked, "How many men are here to join the Army?" Tens of hands rose suddenly, and those men were directed to one corner of the room.

Then he asked, "How many men are here to join the Navy?" Tens of more hands were raised, and those men were directed to another corner of the room.

Duke looked around at those left in the room. Not too many men were left. Then the director asked, "How many men are here to join the Marines?" Duke and one other man named Don Vogel raised their hands. Don was from Duke's own home town of Wagner, South Dakota but he hadn't seen Don since before he left for Chicago.

Duke approached the recruiting officer where the director had told him and Don to go, handing the recruiting officer his identification card. "I want to be a Marine and I want to see action!"

The recruiting officer glanced at Duke's identification card. "Oh, you're gonna' see some action, all right. So you're eighteen?"

Duke said, "Yes, sir!"

"What is your heritage, Mr. Abdalla?" asked the officer.

"I'm Yankton Sioux, Syrian, and Scotch, sir."

The officer filled in the boxes next to Duke's name on the enlistment form. Race: Sioux Indian. Complexion: Ruddy. Height: 6 feet. Weight: 160 pounds. Hair Color: Black.

After transferring the information from Duke's identification card, the officer looked up at Duke and said, "We could use more Indians like you in this war; you're natural-born fighters."

After completing a few physical checks, the officer told him to sign the application and have a seat. When the officer had completed Don's application form, he rose and walked to where Duke was seated. Offering his hand to Duke, the officer shook it, saying, "Welcome to the United States Marine Corps young man, you are about to serve your country. You'll be reporting to Camp Elliot in San Diego, California. Get your gear together; you'll be taking the train to California—you might enjoy the ride." Then the officer went on to give Don his orders as well.

Duke hadn't known what the officer meant by enjoying the ride to California until he arrived at the train station. Standing at the gate he was told to report to, Duke couldn't take his eyes off the shiny metal of the Pullman car that mirrored his reflection. His gaze traveled up the reflection from his dark-brown shoes, to his lighter brown pleated-front trousers, to the dark-brown wool sports coat with his crisp white linen shirt unbuttoned at the neck. After adjusting his brown felt Fedora, Duke checked the gate number to make sure he was in the right place.

A recruiting officer approached him within a few minutes, asking for identification and paperwork. Duke pulled it out of his pocket and handed it to the man. After a quick review, the officer pointed Duke toward a train door and told him to climb aboard and stow his luggage in his assigned bunk.

As he entered the train car, Duke couldn't help but be awed at the luxurious interior of the car. He looked up at the mirrored ceiling above him and saw his own astounded face looking back at him. The mirrors were framed by finely-etched wood rails. Small paintings covered the panels that lay in rows beside the mirrors. He saw that the train seat backs were covered with a soft mauve, velvet cloth with a tapestry flowered pattern on the seat bottoms, accented by the rich, carved wood frames that supported them.

As he made his way to his sleeping area, he felt the plush, cushioned carpet give way to softness beneath his feet. He had never before experienced this kind of superfluity. He stowed his bags in the storage area and looked up to see what would be his bunk, the rounded bottom of it suspended from the ceiling of the rail car. The soft, velvet seats below adjusted to become another bunk beneath.

Recalling the goatskin rug on the cold, hard floor in Wagner, Duke reached up to feel the thick, soft mattress with the velvet bedcover above. "This is the life," he said to himself.

He hung up his jacket and left his bunk and headed to the dining car. As he stepped through the doors, a wondrous aroma assaulted his nostrils. Braised beef with succulent mushrooms, boiled potatoes and steamed carrots, freshly roasted coffee—the smells teased his appetite and made his stomach grumble.

The luxurious accommodations extended to the dining car. The seats were a deep brown leather upholstery, the dark walnut tabletops polished to a bright sheen, the lampshades made of the finest silk, and the carpets that lined the aisles were of the softest wool. He found the table with his bunk number on it and sat down.

On the table was a vase with a single fragrant, red rose and a menu. The seats were cushioned and extremely comfortable to sit on. A waiter approached wearing a white suit jacket, white trousers, and a white-collared shirt with a black bow tie, and asked what he would like to drink.

Duke thought for just a moment and asked, "Do you have a cold glass of milk?"

"Certainly, sir," the waiter replied. He left the table briefly, returning a few moments later with his tray.

After the waiter had set the glass on the table, he asked: "Have you decided on your order, sir?"

Duke looked the waiter straight in the eye and said, "I'll have the beef and potatoes."

"Certainly, sir," the waiter replied and left.

Duke looked down at the table and noted the crisp white linen tablecloth with sparkling sterling silverware laid atop neatly folded white linen napkins. He took a deep breath, wanting to remember this moment.

When the waiter returned, he placed a delicate china plate in front of Duke. It was loaded with a large serving of savory, braised beef with sautéed mushrooms in a delectable red wine sauce, tender golden buttered potatoes, sweet, juicy steamed carrots and tasty, flaked biscuits with a golden brown crust. Then the waiter placed smaller dishes laden with all the butter and jam he could want. Duke finished his meal with a mouth-watering peach cobbler topped with smooth vanilla ice cream. Duke thought a moment to himself. He hadn't eaten a meal like this since he had been living high on the hog in Chicago. He never knew that people traveled this way by train. This type of extravagance was something he could get used to. The meal was delicious and he took a few moments to relax at his table.

A lot had happened in the past two years. He had left South Dakota and his mother. He had faced a new world in Chicago, along with the freedom that money could afford. He always knew that he wanted to fight in the war. It was a spirit that sought to rise within him. He couldn't place the moment that he had decided to join the Marines; he only knew that once he had made the decision, it was the only path for him. To experience the honor of fighting for his country, to know he was contributing to freedom from oppression was extremely important to him.

He walked slowly back to his bunk, swaying with the movement of the railcar. He pushed back the curtains, entered the sleeping area and began to undress down to his boxers. He neatly folded his clothes as he set them on the bedside table. Then, he climbed up to his bunk and scrambled beneath the soft, warm covers and promptly fell asleep.

The next morning, Duke awoke to the aroma of freshly brewed coffee. He quickly dressed and hurried to the dining car. He couldn't wait until the waiter handed him the menu. Swiftly he scanned the contents until his eyes landed on an interesting item. The Pullman Special. It was a large platter that offered three eggs, cooked any way, a large ham steak with hash browned potatoes, and freshly baked biscuits—with or without gravy. He was offered a fresh-squeezed glass of orange juice and a bottomless cup of hot coffee with sweet cream. This was an entire day's fare back at home, minus the orange juice. Duke placed his order with the waiter and began to wish that this train ride would last forever.

He had one more day to enjoy the luxury, then he was off to boot camp. Tonight's dinner would be rich and filling and he would enjoy every bite. Later, a fellow passenger showed the dinner menu to him and Duke chose this night's meal: roast leg of lamb with mint sauce, browned potatoes, steamed asparagus, and a small, moist round cake with Neapolitan ice cream on top. He would savor every morsel.

When the train arrived in San Diego, Duke hopped off with other young men who were there to join the Marines. Several more men had boarded the train along the route to California, and there were buses waiting to take them to Camp Elliot.

When the men arrived at the base, they immediately disembarked from the bus and were directed to their tents by half a dozen drill instructors, where they plopped their gear on their cots. Duke chose his cot and hoisted his gear atop it, then turned to fall in where the drill instructors were waiting to direct them. The men proceeded to the supply building where they were issued their uniforms. They marched in single file as they passed through the building, stopping only for a moment at each station to announce their size for the boots, pants, shirts, cap, socks, belt, and skivvies as the clothing was piled on top of each other in the outstretched arms of each man. The men returned briefly to their barracks to stow the new gear.

Without a moment to dawdle, still marching in single file, they trod off to another building where they would receive the standard Marine haircut. Inside were eight barbers set up strategically in the building, ready to buzz each head that stopped, then passed beneath their clippers.

Duke walked into the building with a full head of dark hair and walked out along with his companions with a head as smooth as a baby's bottom. He reached up briefly and felt his divested head. It would take some getting used to after having such long hair all his life.

When they returned to the barracks, there were three drill instructors waiting for them. They were directed to the showers, where each man stopped for a few minutes to soap his nearly bald head and body with a bar of soap that was dark, brown, and rough like sandpaper—and Duke thought—could take the paint off a wall.

Duke made his way along the edge of the shower stalls and grabbed the towel from the stack at the end of the line. He quickly wrapped it around his waist and proceeded to his bunk to dress for dinner. First he put on his skivvies—they had drawstrings on either side—then he put on his white tee shirt. Next, he reached for his dungarees. The slacks were made of a forest green herringbone weave of jean-like material; the shirt was twill and a similar color of green with buttoned pleated pockets on both front sides. The shirt also had buttons on the sleeves that extended the length of each wrist, and the shirtfront was to be buttoned all the way to the top at the neckline. The belt was a two-inch wide woven cloth belt with a dark brass buckle. The socks were like white tube socks, thick and soft, and Duke liked the feel of them, especially after that rough soap. The boots were called boondockers and were made of a stiff, black leather, rough on the outside with a smooth inside, and soles that were like tire treads and heavy to walk in.

Again, he fell into line and marched single file with the rest of the men to the chow line, each grabbing one of the metal trays that were stacked in front of the tables. They continued moving forward, stopping just long enough to hear the splat of the slop that was dumped into one of the five compartments on their tray.

For a brief moment Duke allowed himself to remember the generous, tasty meals on the Pullman car. He shook himself back to reality and noticed his tray was full. He found a seat and ate without complaining. Then he returned with the rest of the men to their tents, where Duke laid down on his cot and fell asleep quickly.

The first day of training, Duke and the others were told to wear their boondocker boots with no socks. Duke wondered why, but he figured he'd learn the answer soon enough.

Then the drill instructor proceeded to run them through a river of water that soaked their boots thoroughly. Next was an obstacle course that included crawling under fences, climbing towers, racing through tire tubes, climbing up ropes and running endlessly until the boondockers had dried onto their feet. This way, the drill instructor said later, each man's boots were formed to fit his feet.

When the men returned to their tents that night, their feet were aching and blistered all over, including Duke's. But after taking his shower, he dressed and attended the mess hall with as much fervor as ever.

Over the next several weeks, Duke was introduced to an intensive training of mind, body and soul. It began in the morning with trumpets blaring "Reveille" before daylight and ended each night with "Taps" playing softly in the background as his weary body fell fast asleep.

During those first few days, Duke and the other men came to know each other well. Everyone had a story, and everyone knew each other's story. Duke had shared his stories of life in Wagner; boxing in rodeos and on holidays in town. And he had heard many interesting stories from others.

On Sunday, they were allowed to enjoy an exercise of their choice. The men were so tired from being run so hard, they didn't want to do anything except write letters home. A few of the drill instructors brought over a box that was made of plywood, three feet wide by three feet long. In it were various pieces of gym equipment. There were bats and baseballs, basketballs and other equipment. But what caught Duke's eye was the pair of boxing gloves that were draped along the side of the box.

Of the three drill instructors on the grounds, the youngest of them was named Sergeant Crick. Duke suspected the man wanted to get something going, as he walked to the midst of where the men were lying and sitting down and yelled, "Abdalla!"

Duke jumped up and snapped to attention saying, "Yes, sir!" All of the men were so tired, lying and sitting around the parade grounds. No one else made a move.

Sergeant Crick said, "I hear you've done some boxing."

"Yes, sir!" Duke replied.

The sergeant pointed to the boxing gloves hanging over the side of the box and said, "Put 'em on!"

Well, Duke thought, that was like throwing a grenade into the middle of all the men. They all jumped up, formed a circle, and were winking at each other, swaying back and forth on the sides of their feet on the dirt.

Duke reached down into the box and put the gloves on, then one of the guys laced them up for him. Duke looked back at the drill instructor and watched him dancing up and down. Duke looked at Crick, now facing him, and Crick looked back. After sizing each other up, they met in the center of the circle of men. Duke moved in and then he moved back, then he moved three inches to the right, feet sliding like his old hero, Joe Louis.

When Duke moved in again, Crick threw a pitty-pat jab, soft, like a pillow to his face. In response, Duke slid to the side another three inches and got a perfect shot. He moved in again and threw a right cross to Crick's chin. Crick dropped to the ground so hard his head bounced back up. He was out!

The other two drill instructors grabbed Crick by each of his arms, smirked at each other, and dragged the young drill instructor to his tent. Afterward, a little guy from Texas stuck his head above Duke's shoulder and squealed in a high-pitched voice in Duke's ear, "Did you hit him as hard as you could?"

Duke answered, "Yes, I did."

Every day thereafter, the diminutive Texan would say to Duke, "Crick better not mess with me, or I'll knock him right on his ass!"

Duke looked at his enthusiastic face, and laughed.

***

Three weeks into boot camp at dusk, they were ordered to fall into formation by Sergeant Hazzard. The men were told they were being called upon by the City of Los Angeles to control and disband a group of rioters known as *pachucos.*

Four platoons consisting of about fifty men apiece took buses to Los Angeles from Camp Elliot, and each Marine was issued a wooden nightstick. The men filed out of the buses and surrounded the area where the pachucos were rioting, nightsticks in hand.

At a time when national obedience was everything, the pachucos were singled out by servicemen for being poor citizens. Not only were the pachucos dodging the draft, but the zoot suits they wore violated fabric rationing regulations in the proportions of their cut. Pachuquismo was a complete contradiction of military discipline, order, effort and practice. The pachucos were seen as lazy. They showed their defiance through their clownish attire, openly inviting hostile attention from servicemen. These rioters created havoc in the city by breaking store front windows, turning cars on their hoods, setting fires throughout the city and threatening citizens and servicemen. There were too many of them to be controlled by the police department, so the Marines were called in.

When the Marines were sighted by the rioters, they quickly disbanded, scampering to the basements of the city and leaving the area in peace.

This was Duke's first duty outside of basic training, and he liked feeling the power of the Marines. This was part of why he had joined. His efforts showed a purpose.

***

41

Following his boxing bout with Crick the drill instructor, Duke earned the respect of the new recruits as a fighter. He worked hard, and set his sights on becoming a member of The Marine Raiders. The Raiders were an elite group of Marines, singled out for their outstanding abilities and fighting spirit. He'd been told he would have to be hand-picked for such an honor. Duke was scheduled to train immediately in machine gun school. So, for the remainder of boot camp, he spent several weeks training with both a machine gun and a rifle, and learning the tactics of amphibious warfare along with the standard Marine training. The basic strategy in the Pacific Theater incorporated island hopping, the military tactic used for weakening and flushing out enemy forces on islands that were swarming with Japs.

Duke learned this was a brand-new technique just introduced. It involved heavy bombing runs by jets and artillery fire from nearby battleships. This made it easier for infantry attacks. They would take one island, then continue to take the next, then the next and so on until they were able to obtain several islands. As they hopped from island to island, they were able to shorten the distance to Japan and establish forward land bases and air fields for supply purposes. With all the islands in their possession, it would be easier to launch a huge offensive on the homeland of Japan.

After the intensive training of boot camp and graduation day, Duke was promoted to Private First Class. The cadet graduates were given a two-week furlough to go home to visit their families, and every man packed his belongings and prepared to leave camp.

As Duke headed toward his tent he was halted by a sharp call from one of his drill sergeants.

"Abdalla!" Sergeant Hazzard called.

"Yes, Sir!" Duke stood at attention.

"Monday morning you're shipping out on the USS *President Polk* and heading to the island of New Caledonia. The Marine Raiders are still occupying the island." The sergeant smiled, patted him on the shoulder, then said, "Good luck, Marine!"

Duke had shown a natural adeptness in military skills during his weeks at Camp Elliot and had been chosen to be a Marine Raider. He had proven himself to be a good fighter.

Duke allowed himself a moment to consider his mother. She had always wanted the best for him, and he missed her. He wouldn't be able to go home, but he'd make sure to send her a letter sharing as much as he could. His sense of duty was strong, though, and he couldn't wait to embark upon the journey ahead of him.

Duke and his good buddy and fellow Marine, Don Youngbluth managed to enjoy what little time they had in San Diego before Duke was shipped off to New Caledonia. Don was of Bohemian heritage and the two of them shared an unspoken understanding concerning Duke's status in the Marines. He was valued for his fighting abilities, but escaped segregation due to the fact that Indians were well accepted in the front lines. Yet, they both knew he would not be given the same recognition that was standard for white soldiers.

The two friends went to Oceanside Park near the ocean that night. It was an amusement park where some of the cadets had gone on a Sunday afternoon, and Duke knew lots of young women would be there.

It was the perfect night to go, with the weather a balmy 85 degrees. Duke looked around. There was a roller coaster, a high-flying Ferris wheel, a merry-go-round, and a water-ride. They ate cotton candy and popcorn, corn dogs and caramel apples. Duke knew it would be the last time he would sample such fare in a long time.

On Monday morning, Duke grabbed his gear and hopped on a bus that took him to the USS *President Polk*. It was an uneventful ride. Once on the ship, Duke was assigned a partner for the duration of the trip. His name was William Louis Veeck.

Duke and Bill managed to grab a piece of the blistering hot steel deck to spread their blankets on. It was just underneath a hanging Higgins boat, a thirty-six foot long landing craft with a wide, ten-foot ramp at one end where the men could disembark in larger numbers as opposed to single file. Duke looked up at the boat above their heads and for the moment, appreciated the shade it offered.

He and Bill took turns going to the galley to grab bologna sandwiches, one man always standing guard at the blankets to ensure their spot on the deck. The first time Duke went to fetch the sandwiches, he watched as the cook took a large cleaver and whacked off the end of a tube of bologna, then whacked off the end of a loaf of bread. The two pieces of bread weren't the same thickness across, and it was a lop-sided sandwich that Duke handed off to Bill with a grin. Neither of them seemed to care, as they wolfed the food down.

During their journey, Duke learned through conversation that Bill's father had been President of the Chicago Cubs. Growing up in the business of baseball, Bill Veeck worked as a vendor, ticket seller and junior grounds keeper. When his father died in 1933, Bill left college and eventually became club treasurer for the Chicago Cubs. Duke learned that in 1937 Veeck planted the ivy that decorates the outfield wall at Wrigley Field.

The men were packed as tightly as sardines in a tin can on the top of that ship, and the course of travel was deliberately a zigzag pattern so as to avoid enemy detection. The journey to Noumea, New Caledonia took seventeen very long days and their final destination would be located well below the equator, not far from Australia. Bill Veeck was assigned elsewhere on the island, and Duke doubted they would cross paths again.

In the Pacific Theater of the war, operations were changing as the Marines approached the larger islands, which were more heavily guarded with greater numbers of Japanese forces. More troops were needed to combat the enemy. Duke learned the majority of Marine combat operations used the Raiders as regular infantry to fulfill those requirements.

Also, during this time, he noticed a building resentment within the Marine troops against the Marine Raiders. The titled "elite force" had been singled out, and the resentments resulted in a withdrawal of the trial force. Before Duke even reached the island the Marine Raiders were disbanded.

The majority of the troops were sent to the island of Guadalcanal, but many remained in New Caledonia. Some members of the Raiders Fourth Battalion stayed on the island, and they relayed some of their experiences in battle to Duke. He was impressed with the regaling of their stories, eager to hear of what he may be facing when fighting the Japanese enemy. As a member of the Corps Replacement Battalion, Duke's duties were relegated to guard duty.

Duke was stationed on New Caledonia for several months, awaiting orders regarding his transfer to a unit in the South Pacific. During that time he kept busy with general guard duties on the island. It afforded him time to relax, something he hadn't experienced in a while; the lack of excitement was a welcome change.

In June of 1944, nearly a year after enlisting, Duke received his orders. He was assigned to Pavuvu Island as a rifleman/machine gunner with the First Marine Division, First Regiment, First Battalion, A Company, First Platoon, under the command of Colonel Lewis B. "Chesty" Puller.

Duke in his Marine uniform.

Raider Patch that Duke hoped to join on New Caledonia.

Chapter 4

Duke felt the spray of the sea air in his face as they traveled toward Pavuvu Island, water splashing up the sides of the ship as they crashed through the waves. The sun, hot on his back, reminded him of how far he was from home and for a brief moment he thought of his mother all alone in South Dakota. His ship would be landing soon, and he didn't have time to reminisce. Memories could get him killed. He thought about the weather again to keep his mind on track. Even though he had been trained to fight in and endure the climate, he could not have imagined living in it.

Disembarking at the wharf after the ship had docked, Duke arrived on the island and purveyed his surroundings. Pavuvu was the largest of the Russell Islands, lying some sixty miles from Guadalcanal, ten miles wide at its widest, and fifteen hundred feet high at its tallest. The moderate climate in New Caledonia was pleasant in comparison to the sweltering heat here, just above the equator.

As in the other Solomon Islands, the natives had cultivated and harvested coconut trees in an expansive grove which covered almost all the level land on the island. Long left unattended due to the war, the grove was covered with a carpet of stinking, rotted coconuts. As he walked ashore, Duke's nostrils were assaulted by the odorous rotting smell. The sun was a searing flame on the skin of his neck. Coral and sand crunched under his feet as he walked onto the island. It was hotter than he ever remembered it being anywhere. "So this is Pavuvu," he said aloud to no one in particular.

He looked around, using his shirt sleeve to wipe the sweat from his forehead and wondered how in the heck they were gonna make this place livable.

He heard Captain Jennings, company commander of A Company, barking orders, then pointing Duke to where his company was to assemble. As Duke approached the area, his feet were sticking in the deep mud with each step he took.

Though the sun was blazing now, rain had saturated the grounds during the night and in the early morning hours. He saw Sergeant Aubertin, platoon sergeant of the first platoon, directing him and the other men as to where to drop their gear. The sergeant was a seasoned warrior, having fought in the Battle of Guadalcanal. Duke recognized the authority in the man's voice and stance, and immediately respected and responded to him.

The men were scrambling to find a spot to lay their gear, their feet slipping in mud that was nearly up to their knees this far from the beach due to the heavy rains that had pelted the island. Initially, there were no tents to be set up for their living quarters, let alone was there ground firm enough to accommodate them. Instead, each man strove to find a spot to lay his rubber poncho and claim it for his sleeping area.

Duke gathered as many leaves as he could find to solidify the mud, placed his poncho over the leaves, then laid his sleeping blanket atop it. There was no order to the arrangements; it was every man for himself that first night on the island. Any semi-solid piece of ground that could hold the weight of a man without giving way to sinking was claimed.

Sergeant Frank Aubertin informed the men that K-rations were to be used for meals as no supplies had arrived yet. The K-rations consisted of firm, crusty chunks of cheese, hard, thumb-sized chocolate bars, strips of beef jerky, and rock-hard biscuits. Although it wasn't tasty, it was still nourishment.

As Duke ate his rations, he dug in his pack for the chocolate bar. The chocolate was so hard, Duke couldn't bite through it. He had to place it inside his cheek and let it slowly melt over several hours' time. That night he didn't sleep well. Tiny black gnats tickled his face and crawled up his nose, and he spent hours swatting them away before exhaustion took over. He woke early the next morning, relieved that the heat of the day's sun kept the gnats in hiding. His stomach rumbled loudly, causing him to seek out morning chow.

The first eating quarters on the island was any dry or semi-dry piece of ground or stump a soldier could find. There were no mess halls or recreation buildings on Pavuvu, but at least some supplies had arrived during the night. A buddy of Duke's grabbed a wheelbarrow to sit in while he ate his rations, as Duke grabbed a nearby stump. Chow lines were outdoors and mess-men balanced large metal food pans on tree stumps as they dished out the morning meal rations.

Each man was issued a three-piece silverware kit consisting of a knife, fork, and spoon. Duke noticed most soldiers would carry their spoon with them at all times. Duke would stick the handle of the spoon into his boondockers on the outside of his foot at the base of his ankle—it was a perfect fit! He liked to keep the spoon handy in case he had need of it; he never knew when a stray can of peaches or fruit cocktail might make its way from a supply crate.

After chow, Duke rummaged around in his pack until he found the bottle of small yellow pills he was required to take once daily. He was told it was Atabrine, a drug issued to each soldier to ward off malaria that could be contracted from mosquito bites. The mosquitoes came out in droves after dark Duke had learned quickly that first night. Any exposed skin was subject to bites, so despite the heat, the men wore long-sleeved shirts and pants all day, and slept in them as well.

He noticed some of the men's skin turned yellow from taking the drug; Duke was lucky not to have that happen to him. His skin remained brown and tanned. He lived in mud with the other men and had no place to shower for days. No wells had yet been dug, so Duke and the other soldiers managed to capture rainwater by strategically gathering the drops as they fell onto their ponchos and funneling the water into their canteens. Water, especially clean water, was a scarce commodity on the island.

At night, Duke was sure to check his blanket before climbing under it to make certain that no snakes, rats, or land crabs had decided to make residence there. Land crabs especially liked boots. He and the other men came to an understanding regarding these pests. They outnumbered the men in masses and became, therefore, an accepted nuisance and part of the way of life on the island. During the night, Duke almost inevitably heard the patter of little rats' feet scurrying, or he occasionally witnessed one scrambling across another man's face so he slept lightly.

It was nearly the end of the first week on the island before the Seabees arrived to bulldoze the rotten coconuts into piles to be burned. The Seabees were Navy military engineers brought in to prepare the island for occupancy. A lot of work was needed on Pavuvu to make it inhabitable. Besides bulldozing to get rid of the putrid, rotting coconuts, there was a need to solidify the mud for roads traveled by jeeps and trucks.

A coral pit on the island was mined. After being excavated, the coral was crushed and truckloads were dumped strategically to form roads for each of the division's companies to set up camp.

In Duke's unit, the men marched in lines from the coral vein, carrying crushed coral in their helmets to pave the muddy roads and eventually, their tent decks.

Another man from his unit, John Brady from Rhode Island, remarked on the task one day. "I've never seen this much mud in all my life!"

"Me, neither," replied Duke, carrying a load of coral up the muddy path.

"This island isn't fit for pigs!" remarked Brady.

They both laughed, and continued on with their task.

Alfonzo Calliqurei from Ohio, walked the path ahead of Duke, shaking his head and muttering, "Pigs would know better than to live in this mess."

"You ain't kidding!" piped in Al Costella. Al was from Brooklyn, New York. Pavuvu to him was about as far as he could get from the paved streets of the big city.

The men worked all day until nearly ten thousand helmets-full were used to fill that slippery, muddy mess.

Tent gear was issued after supply ships finally arrived, and Duke would often return to his tent to eat, as it was usually raining on Pavuvu. Mosquito netting was arranged around his cot, and he carefully climbed under it. Plopping down on his cot, he balanced his tray on his stomach and against his knees to eat.

The Seabees dug wells on the island to obtain fresh water, although it was a few weeks after arriving that the wells were finally dug. Even then, since fresh water was nearly impossible to find on Pavuvu, the men were rationed to one helmet-full per day.

Often times a soldier who decided to use the island's many rains to shower in would find himself completely soaped-up when the precipitation ended, leaving him to towel off the lathered mess. Duke found himself in that predicament only once, but it was enough.

The Seabees built docks so supplies could be more easily unloaded. And they built the stage and theater for the entertainment area, as well as erecting other structures such as the mess tent and tables for food to be served or stored on. One evening after dinner, just before dark, Duke decided to take a stroll along one of the other company roads, for a change of pace. Pavuvu Island was home to the First Marine Division, following the hellacious battles at Guadalcanal, New Britain, and Cape Gloucester. The Fifth and Seventh Marine units were now on the island as well, preparing for war on the Japanese islands. It wasn't long after he'd been roaming that Duke ran into Colonel Chesty Puller. He knew the man before introductions were made. There was no denying the firm set of the jaw, eyes narrowly placed at the top of his nose, brows drawn together in concentration, or the stout, barreled chest that signified his name. All troops knew about and respected Chesty; his bravery and "give 'em hell" attitude made the colonel a Marines' Marine.

Duke saluted the colonel as Chesty approached. He smiled at Duke as he removed the pipe from his mouth and said, "At ease." Then the colonel asked, "Where are you from young man?"

"South Dakota," Duke said.

Their conversation led to Duke sharing memories of boxing, and he told the colonel how much he'd enjoyed it. Duke spoke of the hometown rodeos and how he had participated in boxing matches whenever they were in town.

Chesty had a few stories of his own about boxing, including his building a boxing ring at his home in Virginia. He built it in the stables of the barn, and many neighborhood boys gathered to box there.

Then the colonel spoke with an understanding of the hardships they all faced here on Pavuvu. The conditions were deplorable and it was an effort to keep their spirits up. He knew that although some of the men hadn't yet faced battle, they shared an inexorable determination to defeat the Japanese enemy and to stop their ruthlessness. Tipping his hat to Duke he said, "Good night, soldier."

Duke responded with admiration. "Good night, Sir!" He watched as the colonel walked away, a slight limp in his step. He knew from stories that had circulated about Chesty that shrapnel remained in his leg from an old battle wound he'd received on Guadalcanal. Duke was proud to be serving under him.

***

Duke was one of six men in his tent from the third squad, first platoon, A

Company. After the battle-worn Marines had joined the First Division on the island, he began to hear stories from the men who'd endured battles on Guadalcanal and/or in Cape Gloucester on the island of New Britain. As they told their stories, Duke felt as though he were experiencing the battles firsthand.

Heavily forested, Gloucester's terrain seemed as much of an enemy as the Japanese soldiers' fire. The land was laden with waist-high sink holes, and in late December, just a year before, coinciding with the onset of a monsoon, the First Marine Division began their attack.

Water backed up in the swamps on the island—just rear of the shore line, making it impossible for any wheeled or tracked vehicle to pass. During the entire operation the troops were soaked to the skin and their clothes never did dry out. The joke among Marines who survived the ordeal was that no watch was New Britain waterproof. Everything rotted in Cape Gloucester.

From the soldiers who had survived Guadalcanal, stories were told of one of the most critical campaigns there had been: the Battle of the Ridge, or Bloody Ridge, or Edson's Ridge as it was sometimes called. The names all referred to the Marines who successfully maintained their strategic position in a particularly grueling battle in Guadalcanal, as well as their killing more than six hundred Japanese soldiers.

They, too, had to survive terrain and conditions that challenged them almost as much as the battle itself. None of them chose to speak specifically about the battles. Instead it was of the countrymen they lost. The visions in their minds of men being blown apart by grenades, or their limbs being torn off with a samurai sword, or helplessly watching their comrades bleed to death before help could arrive in the form of a corpsman. Even when a corpsman was available, there were plenty of soldiers who couldn't be saved. The men the Marines ate, drank, slept, and fought with side by side, had died all around them. It wasn't part of a normal conversation, but somehow it hung in the air as Duke listened.

It strengthened their bonds, these men who shared stories. Stories of war, pain, and death mingled with stories of where the men had grown up, what sport they'd played, or how beautiful their girl at home was. They would talk about what their home town was like—the colors and smells and sounds of it. Those who spoke of it felt closer to home for having been there not long ago, and those who listened felt closer to home because their memories had been renewed by shared moments. As he listened, Duke imagined a strong wind blowing across his shoulders as he sauntered toward the house after a long days' work. For a brief second he could actually feel the coolness of the breeze, smell the aroma of a fresh-baked pie, and see the sweet smile of his mother as she welcomed him home.

Stories traveled, too, from tent to tent. And when Sergeant Aubertin heard about Duke's boxing skills, he sought him out to assign Duke the duty of designing and building a boxing ring with the Seabees. The sergeant considered him to be fully prepared for the Marines, as a machine gunner with specialized skills. And survival itself, on this island, was proof of a man's savvy. It was important to keep the men's morale up as well, and boxing seemed to keep their minds off of melancholy thoughts. It kept them active, too, in a climate that made you want to lie down and be still, so as not to increase body heat any more than was necessary. The constant heat and humidity was wearing on a man's body and mind.

Duke enjoyed keeping busy building the ring with the Seabees, and understood his role in providing entertainment for the troops. This was his ticket out of standard training on the island as well, and anything was better than that.

Duke took the job seriously and went to work building the platform that would house the boxing ring built next to the theater for the troops.

It was a few weeks since his arrival on the island when he and the Seabees finished building the ring. Boxing matches were set up at various times during the week for any man who was willing to fight. Duke fought every week, and often had two very special audience members as his biggest fans. Colonel Chesty Puller and Major Ray Davis, his battalion commander, would sit in the first row on the rolled logs that served as seating, giving a wave and a 'thumbs up' to Duke whenever he entered the ring. Every week, they were there to watch "Duke, The Indian" box. It was a nickname that Duke had picked up since he started boxing on the island. It never bothered him that they recognized his heritage or his skills as a fighter.

He stood six feet tall and weighed in at one hundred sixty pounds. He was a solid mass of muscle, and having studied the quick-sliding foot maneuvers of Joe Louis, was light on his feet. And Duke never failed to deliver a punch that was packed with power. Whoever was on the receiving end of that punch never forgot who had delivered it. Duke, The Indian soon became the A-1-1 Boxing Champion on Pavuvu.

Once his afternoon duties for the day had been accomplished and the area was policed, Duke and the other men were allowed to eat. Dinner was corned Willie cakes, or Vienna sausage, with dried vegetables and coffee. Most men ate in their tents to avoid flying pests looking to share their meager rations. The routine on the island was fatiguing, time passing slowly as the days dragged on.

Both to occupy his time and to keep his knife ready, Duke would remove his Ka-Bar knife from its leather sleeve and sharpen it on a stone, first spitting on it to lubricate the surface of the stone. Then, to test its razor sharpness, he would slide the blade along his forearm, slicing the hairs that stood up against it. *You could always tell which was a soldier's power hand, because the opposite forearm was generally hairless from having been tested with the blade of his knife.* Duke would sharpen the blade of his Ka-Bar frequently to keep it ready at all times.

One thing that struck Duke the most about Pavuvu was that it was so quiet at night. Once all the coconuts had been bull-dozed, all the roads had been built and all the tents erected, there was little or no noise on the island. The men became attuned to the quiet, and could practically hear a pin drop onto the soft, mossy, jungle floor. Sometimes he'd hear the rain pouring down on the tent top and sides, or the scurrying little feet of a rat that had fallen out of a palm tree.

Of the more frightening sounds on the island, one was that of a fellow soldier screaming in the night as the "Mad Ghoul" attacked yet another slumbering Marine. "Asiatic" was a term often used on Pavuvu to describe the man who had gone off the deep end or lost touch with reality.

The story that all the men on the island knew, was that an Asiatic soldier stalked the battalion by rising in the night with his machete and sneaking into an unsuspecting tent. Tent flaps were kept open due to the intense heat, and it was easy for the man to enter. He would then choose a man to stand over, his machete raised in the air above the soldier's chest. If the man so much as moved in his sleep, the machete would come down—severely injuring, or at the very least, slightly wounding the sleeper. Marines determined to capture this ghoul had filled as many cans as they could find with stones. Then they tied the cans together and placed them strategically around their cots as a sort of alarm system. During a night intended for terror, the Mad Ghoul sneaked into a tent, tripping over an assembled alarm. He ran from the tent and was chased by six men all the way to the ocean. The man had cracked up—he was loony—and had to be locked up. All the men slept better after the attacker had been shipped off to the hospital on Guadalcanal for observation and treatment. Although Duke never bothered with making an alarm for himself—he always slept lightly—he did sleep easier knowing that the crazed attacker had been caught and detained.

There were other sicknesses and wounds that were treated on the island. Things like jungle rot, a type of fungus that grew on the men's feet, armpits, buttocks, or any crevice on a man's body that remained moist. Each soldier had originally been issued two to three pairs of socks. They were quickly torn to shreds on the island, the terrain heavily laden with sharp coral. Most times the fungus caused severe itching, especially of the feet, due to daily trudging in wet mud. But the fungus became so bad for some men that they could not walk. It had become debilitating.

Then, there was malaria. The men who were bitten by infected mosquitoes came down with fever, chills, headache, sweats, fatigue, and sometimes nausea and/or vomiting.

Dysentery was another threat. It was a disorder of the digestive system that resulted in severe diarrhea containing mucous and blood. If left untreated, Duke knew dysentery could be fatal. It was important to keep the men hydrated with fluids during recuperation. Living on Pavuvu was an experience that Duke would not soon forget, and he believed no civilian back in the States would ever understand. It was a long way away from Chicago or a Pullman car.

There were many reasons why a soldier struggled to sleep on Pavuvu. One of the most disturbing sounds ever heard in the night was the sound of a single gunshot or the crack of a rifle reverberating in the dark, quiet hell that was Pavuvu. It signaled the self-surrender of yet another man's life on the tortuous island.

"Who was it this time?" was the general thought that passed through the tents of the survivors. "Was it a 'Dear John' letter? Or was it a family member passing away at home?"

Duke knew many men felt abandoned. Some were stressed about the thought of returning home with memories of war that haunted them daily. They wondered if they would ever be able to return to their old way of life, if it even existed the way they remembered it.

Others were so downtrodden with their current living conditions or illnesses that they struggled to survive each day. Then there were men, like him, that looked forward to battle. It held a fascination that only few could understand. It was an opportunity to prove their bravery and honorableness. Something to give credence to their involvement in the war.

***

After surviving another night on the island, Duke had breakfast to look forward to. The morning meal on Pavuvu varied in color and size, though taste was rather general. A mass-produced kind of French toast was a standard breakfast. It was soaked in a diluted syrup that helped to wash it down. Other mornings they had oatmeal, a cardboard-like substance soaked in water until it became a gray mush he shoveled into his mouth with a spoon.

This morning they had powdered eggs. Duke watched as the eggs sat on the mess tray for a few minutes, then a puddle of water formed around the ugly, pale yellow-green scrambled mass. Disgusted but hungry, he shoveled it down his throat, hoping it would land gently in an already ravaged belly. There were some soldiers who opted to have just coffee in the morning. At least that didn't come back up your throat to attack twenty minutes after ingestion.

The arrival of supply ships always caused a stir among the men. Men were asked to volunteer to unload food and supplies from the ship. Every man raised his hand, including Duke, though not every man was chosen.

Duke's tent had a team that would organize a rotating assembly line, with each man carrying several six-foot measured pieces of string in his pocket. The first member of the tent chosen to unload would board the ship, scanning the food offerings quickly and measuredly. At his first opportunity, he would find, say, a six-inch bologna tube. Using a piece of string from his pocket, he would tie one tube of bologna to one end of the string and either another tube of bologna or a block of cheese (or other fair game) to the other, draping the string around his neck, carefully concealing the food under his loosely worn buttoned shirt and pants. Next, he picked up a small load to carry to the food storage pile on shore.

Dutifully, he'd set down his load on the pile, then continue onto his tent, whispering clues over his shoulder as to where certain food items were located as another tent mate took his place in the assembly line. Each man was sure to keep his load small, wanting to extend their time to attain as much "treasure" as possible from the ship. Once he arrived at his tent, the man would find a spot to hang his loot from the ceiling of the tent. The tent mates would share their goods with each other, and occasionally, barter with another tent to swap for desired fare.

When Duke was chosen, he made his way quickly to the ship, feeling his shirt pocket to make sure he'd grabbed his measure of string. He found a large tube of bologna and a good-sized chunk of cheese to balance it as he arranged the items beneath his loosely worn shirt. This particular ship's bounty included two fresh eggs that Duke got his hands on. Later, when he had the chance to cook them, he never thought two fried eggs could taste so good!

Fresh food was scarce on the island and even certain canned items were considered to be a delicacy. One night, after a shipment of food had arrived from Australia, Duke made his way to the back of the mess tent, lifted the flap and got his hands on a can of pineapple he kept for his own. Opening the can with his Ka-Bar knife, he savored the flavor of the pineapple and ate the entire can right there at the back of the mess tent. It was only a few hours past evening, after having returned to his tent, when he regretted having consumed the entire contents of the can. He hadn't felt this sick to his stomach since he was a kid.

Lying on his cot with his stomach in painful knots, he remembered the time he had won a box of chocolate-covered cherries from a penny-punch card at the drug store back in Wagner. A whole pound of chocolate-covered cherries! His cousins were visiting that day, and they were at home, waiting for him to arrive. If he took that box of candy home, his cousins would surely eat the entire box.

Well, Duke wasn't going to let that happen. He found a secluded spot on the way home and ate the entire box of chocolates himself. It was a mouthful of heaven! And boy, did he ever regret eating the whole thing. Hours later his stomach was making noises he'd never heard before. And it hurt. It was a reminder to him he couldn't fill the emptiness too quickly. Being deprived of something for so long creates a hunger that seems to momentarily overtake a man. Satisfying a craving, even if it makes you sick, made him feel human again somehow.

There weren't many moments on Pavuvu that allowed that. Most of the food items hauled ashore were readily shared with their tent mates, feasting on the fare.

***

It wasn't unusual for Colonel Chesty Puller to have a surprise inspection of a tent at random. One day he walked into Duke's tent, Major Ray Davis and

Captain Jennings having preceded him, and the men in the tent quickly stood at attention where they were.

"How you doing, son?" Chesty said to Duke, smiling. "At Ease," he added, as Duke returned the smile and relaxed. Chesty strolled through the tent, inhaling the pungent aroma of what Duke was certain the colonel knew to be jungle juice fermenting in the back of the tent. Jungle juice was an alcoholic concoction formed from a cooperated effort of all six tent members, dropping whatever food items they could find that could ferment quickly and well, into a five-gallon drum.

The men relaxed and watched him proceed through the tent, noting the cleanliness and remarking on it. When the colonel reached the back of the tent, where the jungle juice was kept, he asked the Marine standing next to the drum, "How's the juice comin'?"

The thin young man answered in a drawling, Southern tone, "T'aint ready yet, sir!"

The colonel smiled broadly, and continued on with his inspection. It was well known throughout the regiment that he kept his own vat of juice on hand. One thing Chesty did not tolerate was any soldier or officer living above the means of the other men. He lived the way they lived. He ate what they ate. He slept the way they slept.

Duke remembered a time when the colonel caught a company commander with a cushioned pad on his cot. He threw his thumb over his shoulder at the door and said, "Get that outta here!"

Without waiting for the man to respond, Colonel Chesty grabbed the pad himself and threw it out the door.

So things like jungle juice helped them cope with the isolation and hardships of war while they prepared for battle. In Duke's tent, Chicken Boyd was in charge of the jungle juice. Boyd was a skinny young man from Virginia and weighed about ninety-eight pounds. He liked to share stories of his family while he chewed tobacco, and he sure knew how to make jungle juice. He had the men in the tent dropping pieces of pineapple or other fruit, bread, carrots, potatoes, powdered yeast (which was shared with other tents to help speed fermentation), and other items into the drum, then he'd cover it with a piece of cheesecloth.

After a few days of fermenting, Boyd would lift up the fly-ridden cheesecloth that covered the juice, then push back the cottage-cheese looking film that covered the top, dip his cup into it and taste it—shaking his head and remarking in his southern drawl, "T'aint ready, yet."

After a series of these revelations, and just when the cheesecloth seemed to be solid black with dead flies, Chicken Boyd would roll back the cloth releasing the tell-tale fragrance of the fermented liquid that permeated the tent, and announce, "It's ready!" Then the men would gather to partake of the jungle juice and share stories about home.

Horace T. Clark was renowned in A Company for brewing his own version of jungle juice. Many a night Duke could hear Clark, brought up in Georgia, singing at the top of his half-breed Indian lungs, drunk as a skunk from the poison he brewed in his tent. "I got the knot-hole blues, I got the knot-hole blues, I peek through the knothole in the shed, I peeked there 'til my face turned red. I got the knot-hole blues, I got the knot-hole blues!"

Some of the men got tired of hearing him drone on and began yelling, "Shut up, you drunken hillbilly!"

Having imbibed so much juice, Clark would run out of his tent with his fists held high in the air, challenging the man who had demanded his silence, "Come out ch'yah! You hear me, come out ch'yah!" *Come out here.*

Duke, or none of the other men ever took the challenge.

While making jungle juice one time, Duke recalled, Clark accidentally turned the lid on the container, screwing the lid entirely closed. The standard procedure was to at least leave the lid sitting loosely on top of the drum, so that gases could escape while the concoction fermented.

With temperatures on Pavuvu reaching into the one hundreds, the gases built up quite rapidly under the lid until it exploded violently, sending pieces of whatever had been dropped into the container flying across the tent. Duke thought it was a sight to see H. T. Clark jump up and try to gather as many drops of juice and fermented pieces of food as he could into his helmet, whilst attempting not to trip over the cots in the tent.

His tent-mates couldn't stop laughing. It hadn't been a good day for Clark. Waiting for jungle juice was like waiting for his next dose of sanity, and it would be weeks at best before he could partake again.

Another man that captured Duke's interest on Pavuvu was a character named Shade. Shade made his own jungle juice, too. Only, when the ordinary ingredients weren't available, he chose a different method to make his juice. He opened a can of "heat" used for heating food. He'd pour water over it bunched in his handkerchief, then strain it into a container—repeatedly. Duke thought it smelled just like kerosene. Shade drank that foul-smelling liquid until he passed out.

Duke remembered a night when Shade slept outside through the night in the pouring rain—passed out cold. When he touched Shade's arm, he was as stiff as a board. By mid-day the next day, Shade was back in motion.

Unique characters abounded on the island and an Indian friend of Duke's named Case was another. He was one hundred percent Cherokee Indian. One of the largest men on the island, he haled from Oklahoma and was in the third platoon of A Company. He was a good friend and trusted Marine. The other men nicknamed him Chief, with due respect. He never had a bad word to say about anyone and often gave sage advice regarding judgment of other men's souls.

Roland James was a skinny, dark-haired young man who served as a news correspondent for the war. He took an interest in Duke one day, as he listened to Duke's story. He wrote about the nostalgia that kept Duke motivated during the trials on the island and facing the furor of battle with a realizable death awaiting him. During the interview, Mr. James sketched a drawing of Duke, as he gazed down at a small, glowing kerosene lantern that dimly lit the tent.

Excited about the interview, Duke wrote a letter home to his mother telling her to watch for the story, including the picture that the news correspondent had given him.

Entertainer Bob Hope heard about the pathetic situation over at Pavuvu and redirected his troupe from Guadalcanal there to try to cheer the men in Pavuvu. When the Marines heard that Bob Hope was bringing his troupe to the island, most of them didn't believe it, including Duke.

It wasn't until they arrived on the island that they knew it to be true. Over sixty miles of open sea, the troupe came over two at a time and landed on a coral-paved road which served as the only airstrip on the island. All the men gathered to see the crew disembark from the two Piper Cub aircrafts.

As Duke watched on, he saw Bob Hope, a well-known actor and comedian; Frances Langford, a movie star; Martha Raye, a well-known actress/singer/ dancer; Patty Thomas, a young tap dancer who was only eighteen years old; and Jerry Colonna, another comedian.

Duke hadn't seen a woman in months. There were other Marines on the island who hadn't seen a woman in a year or two. A hearty Marine welcome was given to the entertainers.

While nearly every man attended the USO show, a few lucky men were asked to participate. A friend of Duke's got to dance with Patty Thomas. Patty wore a short black skirt with tights and Mary Jane pumps. She was light on her feet and wore a smile on her face. Martha Raye sang several tunes for the men, including some songs that brought tears to the eyes of soldiers who hadn't been home in a long while.

At another point in the show, Bob Hope told a comical story as Jerry Colonna grabbed a scoop shovel, sneaked up behind Hope, and shoveled air right behind his feet as the comedian spoke. Duke and the rest of the division hadn't laughed that heartily in ages! It was nearly the last moment on Pavuvu that they all got to experience some human, American moments.

***

A few days passed by as Duke and the other men began preparing for an imminent battle in a yet unknown location. Although rifles, Ka-Bars and other weapons were maintained, they were cleaned with a new respect in anticipation of their upcoming use. Fewer complaints were made concerning chow, the ungodly heat, and the unwelcome pests that took up residence in personal space. A sense of purpose returned to the men who had been forced to live idly. Fear and excitement mixed in Duke's gut as he considered facing and killing the enemy.

The night before they left Pavuvu, the men were called to assemble at the theater. Colonel Chesty Puller addressed the men after they gathered. Gruff as ever, Chesty emanated strength and resolve, evoking loyalty and determinedness from his soldiers. He sympathized with the men over their recent living conditions and rations. He drew from the fortress that had been built within the regiment; the stories that had been shared and appreciated, and the strength of loyalties made in a service of men of the highest bravery and brotherhood. These men were about to face one of the fiercest enemies they had ever encountered. They needed to be as prepared for hell as they could be.

The colonel bellowed over the men, "We're goin' in to kill! I don't want no prisoners! The truth is…some of you men won't be coming back. And remember, if you aren't coming back, you take as many of those bastards with you as you can! These Japs are ruthless. They will fight you to the death just as we will fight them to the death! Don't you forget that you're the finest regiment of the finest division that ever walked the earth!"

After a long sigh and a deep breath, he pointed a stout finger at the men and said, "I'm gonna tell you one last thing. You boys get in off that beach as quickly as you can!"

The next morning Duke boarded his assigned ship. The words Chesty spoke the evening before played over in his mind. The single thought that remained gave him the resolve he needed for his final preparation. He was a member of the First Marine Division, and he was going in to kill!

Duke with a Seabee –
"A Marine's best friend".

Duke cleaning supplies on Pavuvu.

Al Costella kneeling in front of tents.

Corporal Roland James' drawing of
Duke on Pavuvu.

Ringside theater seating where Bob Hope
and gang performed for the troops.

Row of tents on Pavuvu.

Time for chow.

Chapter 5

September 4th, 1944, the Marines shipped off from their station on Pavuvu. Colonel Puller's words whispered in Duke's ears as he stared at the bottom of the bunk above him. *"Japanese soldiers are ruthless. They'll fight you to the death! Get in off that beach as quickly as you can!"*

Several days passed as the ship traveled to an unknown destination. During this time, Duke was able to recall the stories he'd heard from soldiers who had already been in battle—frightening tales of men being torn apart in front of their eyes. He remembered, too, the fierceness in the eyes of the servicemen who had recalled killing a Japanese enemy, particularly after a comrade's life had been sacrificed.

He thought back to his youth, memories of himself sporting boxing gloves. He remembered the rhythm of shuffling his feet across the canvas, waiting for his opportunity to throw a right cross, decking his opponent. He liked to think that his quick reflexes would be of use in the battle. One thing he did know, he was determined to fight the way he always did—to win!

After several days of traveling in a zigzag pattern toward their destination, A Company was ordered to assemble on the ship's deck. Duke made his way along with the rest, as they gathered to hear their orders and their battle destination from Captain Jennings. He had a map pinned up on a board for all the men to see.

"Peleliu…a strip of island just two miles wide and five miles long. The island is surrounded by, and completely made up of, coral reefs, thick jungle vegetation and sink holes. The Navy is set to bomb the island continuously until the Marines are in place to arrive. The First Regiment is to land on the shores of the southwest side of the island, named 'White Beach.'" He pointed on the map.

The captain's voice was stern and full of purpose as he finished. "The regiment will then work their way to the left and north, headed for Bloody Nose Ridge, the highest point on the island. The Fifth and Seventh Regiments are to land on the south and southeast ends on 'Orange Beach.' The Fifth Regiment will cut straight across the island and the Seventh Regiment will head to the right of the island. The First Marine Division's objective is to capture the island in three days, cutting off access to the Japanese and securing the use of the air strip for the Americans."

The men took a collective deep breath. A few asked questions. Then there was silence as each man was left alone with his own thoughts. Duke couldn't fathom what lay ahead for him, he only hoped that he could make it out alive.

The ship arrived a few miles off the shores of Peleliu. Duke could hear the bombing runs being made by carrier-based aircraft. Naval ships launched rockets, whose explosions could also be heard from his vantage point on the ship. The bombardment seemed endless. It was a constant blasting and exploding, and it made Duke feel secure that they had the support of the Navy and their bombs. It lasted for three days.

On September 14th, Admiral Oldendorf of the U.S. Navy aborted the bombardment of Peleliu a day ahead of schedule. Duke learned he declared the Navy had run out of targets. The airstrip, aircraft and several buildings surrounding the airstrip had been destroyed.

D-Day, September 15th, 0333 hours, stillness was interrupted by "Reveille" blasting from the deck of the ship. Duke made his way to breakfast. Steak and eggs were on the menu this morning, traditional battle fare. Short, thick pieces of steak sat next to a large, fluffy, yellow pile of real scrambled eggs on his plate, and Duke ate heartily.

This near to Peleliu, the sounds of explosions from mine charges set by Navy frogmen to break up the dangerous underwater coral reefs could be heard from the ship. They were to prepare the way for amphibious vehicles, called amtracs, to get to the island and allow the Marines to land on the beach. Amtracs, also known as landing-vehicle-tracked or LVT's, were amphibious vehicles with a track-wheel system much like that of a tank. It allowed for travel on uneven, treacherous ground such as the sharp coral mounds that beleaguered the beaches of Peleliu.

After breakfast, Duke walked back to his bunk to ready and pack his gear and equipment. He counted the four smoke grenades, six explosive grenades, two medic packs, and checked to see that he had his Ka-Bar knife, machete, M1 rifle with a ten-inch bayonet, and a .45mm handgun. He also had two canteens filled with fresh water. After having lived on Pavuvu for so many months, he knew the value of uncontaminated water.

Next, Duke sat down and placed the small mirror issued for shaving atop his bed table. He pulled out a foil-wrapped pouch and proceeded to cut off the top of it with his Ka-Bar. Slowly, he squeezed out a small amount of black grease paint into the palm of his hand. Using the fingers of his other hand, he dipped them into the paint and applied it to his face, covering every visible sign of skin. It was part of the camouflage to be used in battle. Once completed, Duke stood up, grabbed the mirror from the table and took one last look at himself before he packed his final items.

The shirt he wore had four pockets sewn into the front. In the top two pockets, he placed the four smoke grenades, two and two. In the bottom pockets, he placed the six hand grenades, three and three. He was ready, knowing he hadn't forgotten a thing.

Duke stepped up the stairs to the deck, cool sweat dripping down the sides of his face. He stood poised near the edge of the ship where the rope ladders had been dropped, the weight of his pack loaded on his back, camouflage steel helmet in place.

No going back now. He heard the words resound in his head.

He watched from the ship as LCM rocket launchers fired onto the reef in front of them. Bill Costello, from Missouri, stood next to him watching the onslaught. He turned to Duke and said, "Duke, I got a feelin' I'm not coming out of this one."

Duke had no verbal response, he simply nodded.

They all knew that some of them wouldn't make it out of this war alive. In his mind, though, he was determined to survive.

Captain Jennings ordered the men over the sides of the ship and into the amtraks. Duke hiked over the side of the ship onto the rope ladder, hustled down, then off, and jumped into the floating craft.

Several Navy ships continued to launch shells and bombs at the island while the Japanese returned fire. The First Marine Division struggled to land on the beach. Duke's thoughts were jumbled. *How could there be this much resistance?* How could the Japanese have retained their numbers, shelling and bombing the beach continually, as the American troops floundered in their attempts to gain the shore. Mortar and artillery shells pelted the island as black smoke rose into the air above it. The noise was deafening!

They had been told these weren't just any Japanese soldiers; they were the never-defeated Manchurian Imperial Japanese Guards—an elite Japanese fighting force. They were fierce and single-minded in their focus, and they were focused on killing Americans.

Shots landed all around Duke as the amtrac made its way to shore at about five miles per hour. The Marines were packed tight into it like sardines in a can. A torrent of shells rang off the metal of the amtrac while still more shells expelled water from the surface of the sea, creating a symphony of gunfire and cacophony of destruction that exploded in Duke's ears.

On either side of him, and as far as he could see, several other amtracs were being blown out of the water. Big guns housed in caves on the island were pinpointing and annihilating the amtracs! These guns were nearly as large as cannons, and from their vantage point, several times more lethal. Machine gun nests filled with two to three Japanese soldiers each were raining bullets on the men as they made their way to shore. Snipers hidden in various yet undetermined positions were picking off the Marines as they landed on the beach.

As the amtrac moved toward the beach, it stopped at a wall of coral. Stationary in about a foot and a half of water, and about one hundred feet from the beach, the vehicle's ramp was lowered in the back, and Duke moved to the port and rear side of the amtrac. He made his way into the water as the sound of shots and explosions rang around him. A body floated into his path, and he couldn't help but look to identify the man. There was no mistaking the hulking form of Case, the big Cherokee Indian that Duke had grown so fond of. Chief's eyes stared emptily back at him.

Duke stepped over the body quickly, eyeing the beach for a place to take cover. He moved as fast as he could through the water, feeling the weight of his boots as he ran. As he reached the sand, the shock finally settled in and registered. His friend, Case, was dead.

No sooner had he found a shell hole, before another man jumped in beside him, barely escaping Japanese gunfire. It was Chicken Boyd. Boyd proceeded to remove his helmet and set it on the ground next to him on the edge of the shell hole. A mortar shell went off nearby, and a fragment of the mortar shell hit Boyd's helmet with a *ping* and the two of them watched as the helmet rolled several feet away.

The seventeen-year-old had a mouthful of chew, and he spit a stream of brown liquid into the sand, looking at Duke apathetically and remarking, "Mighty close, wadn't it?"

It was an odd moment, his apathy so out of place as they listened to another loud barrage of fire from the enemy.

Duke didn't have to ask Boyd why he had removed the helmet; the heat was a sweltering 117 degrees Fahrenheit on Peleliu. The grease paint Duke had applied before leaving the ship as part of his camouflage ran down his face and into his eyes. He had no time to worry about it now though as he kept low and moved to join his platoon, wiping the paint from his eyes.

Peering through the blackish-gray smoke that rose all around them from the ground, he looked over his shoulder at the amtrac that he'd just left. He watched in amazement as it took a direct hit from a mortar shell, permanently immobilizing and destroying the vehicle.

Marines poured onto the beach as LVTs landed on shore. Duke and Boyd watched in horror as men toppled, sprawling in gross formations on the ground. Body parts flew through the air as the Japanese hit their marks. He had never before witnessed the utter destruction of war. Destruction of men, of reason, of sanity. Soldiers all around him were wounded or dying. Men that they had lived with on Pavuvu were being killed and maimed. There was no time or possibility of tending to them as they fell.

Duke heard the boom of a big gun, and in half a second he witnessed four men being blown into the smoke-filled air, limbs flying. Their lifeless bodies joined those of the men who had fallen before them, creating a sheet of dead bodies that stretched across the blood-soaked beach.

More men fell at the hands of snipers. As they made an attempt to join their captain just off the beach, soldiers were being picked off by the Japanese.

Looking up into the palm trees that bordered the beach on the right, Duke yelled to Chicken Boyd, "Go, now!"

As Boyd threw on his helmet and ran up the beach toward Captain Jennings and A Company, Duke caught the flash of the sun on a rifle barrel aimed at his friend. Three quick pumps from his rifle, and the Jap fell from the tree, dead. Duke moved his eyes quickly from palm tree to palm tree, expeditiously marking and shooting at least half a dozen Japanese snipers who would otherwise have killed his comrades. Grateful for his marksmanship after having been pinned in their positions on the beach, several men from his company were able to move and unite at the forward location.

Duke's attention was drawn inland as his captain motioned for him to join what was left of his company. As the men were waved off the beach, they joined the other men at the top of a low-lying hill.

Captain Jennings was barking at the soldiers to jump across a small cart path so they could make their way north toward Bloody Nose Ridge. Duke watched as the men before him attempted the eight-foot jump. Several of the men were wounded as they were picked off by sniper fire as they attempted to cross the path.

Captain Jennings continued to wave the men across. Determined to clear the path and stay alive, Duke went into a dead run, his heart pumping, and with a running jump, he dove over the path, just clearing a log on the other side of it. He landed on another body, that of his gunnery sergeant. The sergeant was lying just on the other side of the log, wounded. Duke pulled him carefully to a safer position, knowing a corpsman would tend to him shortly.

The men in his platoon were told to move up to make room for the other soldiers coming from the beach. Duke moved up quickly, heading straight north, working his way in between the bamboo that grew about six to eight inches apart. He acknowledged he was in a swamp as the water became deeper with every step he took.

Glancing around, the thunderous sounds of gunfire and mortar shells spurring him on, he realized he had been separated from his company. The rest of A Company had swung to the left to move around the swamp behind him, while Duke had continued to move forward, directly into the swamp.

He was now alone in a small swamp surrounded on three sides by the enemy. He had nowhere to go. If he tried to move forward, the Japs would surely kill him. And if he tried to move back with his own troops, he would most likely be killed from not being recognized in the confusion of gunfire and smoke. The bamboo was so thick, that any Marine noticing movement among the stalks would consider him to be a Japanese soldier and fire.

So he waited, keeping his body lowered, keeping his chin at the top of the water level, to remain undetected.

Duke heard the loud roar of a Japanese tank as it crashed through the stalks of bamboo directly in front of him. He hunkered low into the swamp as the tank came to a halt not fifteen feet away. He watched closely for any signs of movement from the vehicle. Several moments passed.

Then, as he watched, a creaking, groaning noise accompanied the turning of the wheel atop the tank's hatch. He held his rifle in a ready-fire position as he stayed low in the swamp. His eyes never strayed from the top of the tank.

The wheels stopped rotating.

He waited.

Several moments passed as Duke trained both his eyes and the nose of his rifle on his target. Slowly pushing up the lid of the hatch, a Japanese soldier emerged from the tank. Cautiously, he placed his hands on either side of the tank opening and pushed himself up to sit on the edge of it. He peered all around him, glancing at the stalks that hid Duke.

Duke zeroed in on the man, and made three quick pulls on the trigger of his M1, killing him. He waited to see if any other soldiers would emerge from the battered tank. For a moment, he entertained the thought of dropping a grenade into the tank, but he considered that he might reveal his position. After a long wait, no other soldiers appeared.

Duke remained in his position in the swamp for the rest of the day, the voices of enemy soldiers and gunfire surrounding him. He was sure they would discover him.

The sun was scorching hot, and the air was dank and humid as he waited. He thought about having killed the Japanese soldier. As his enemy raised himself up on the edge of the tank opening, he'd looked like any other man Duke might encounter on the streets of Chicago. Only he wore a Japanese uniform, so that made him a target. Duke knew his duty, to kill as many enemy soldiers as he encountered. Take no prisoners was the order. It was different when the man was sitting fifteen feet away from him, but he'd seen the results of the vicious attacks from these men while crouching for cover on the beach.

Friends he'd suffered through Pavuvu with had fallen in the water and on the beaches in minutes upon entering the shore. The memory of their lifeless bodies and vacant stares made pulling the trigger easier, more satisfying somehow. It was more than revenge, it was justice.

When he'd finished drinking the water in his canteens, he was desperate for more water to sooth his parched mouth and throat. Every move he made, he made slowly, stealthily, so as not to draw attention to his position in the shallows of the swamp. Carefully, he unscrewed the cap from the first canteen and lowered it into the swamp water. He watched as the canteen filled, water infused with white larvae seeped into the container. He repeated the process with the second canteen.

Duke cared less what was in the water at the moment. Water was water. He had no food, and this bacteria-laden liquid was his only means of sustenance. He drank heartily, then crouched low in the water as the hours crept by. Every sound was measured. Every movement of the trees was noted and assessed. As quickly as the morning had passed, the day lingered. Sounds of the battle pursued his senses.

As nightfall arrived, Duke continued to stay alert. Mortar shells and gunfire continued to sound all around him. Flashes of light in the dark were his containment. He could hear the Japanese guns on three sides. He hunkered down lower in the swamp and waited.

He didn't sleep that night and felt the sun before it rose. The moisture in the air began to warm, brightened by the rays as they descended. When morning broke, Duke realized he would have to make a move.

He laid his body flat in the water and began to snake back in the direction he believed his company to be. About every three feet or so, he would raise his head above the swamp grass and yell in a whisper, "A Company!" then slink back into the murky swamp.

Continuing in this manner, Duke managed to gain some ground. Not certain if his voice would be heard but determined to rejoin his company, he'd let out another whispered shout, "A Company!"

After what seemed like ages, he finally heard what he believed to be an American voice in reply. "Over here!" the man responded in a whispered shout.

The soldier turned out to be with F Company and directed Duke back down below, near the beach area, where he could rejoin A Company.

The men of A Company were taking cover in a Japanese tank trap along the beach. The Japanese soldiers had dug a tank trap into the ground about twenty feet deep at its deepest, and eight feet wide. From the bottom of the trap, the sides sloped gently to the top, creating a means of escape. It was fortuitous for the men of A Company, as it was their only means of cover on the wide expanse of the beach. Duke hustled from the cover of some shrubbery, bullets flying over his head and pelting the ground around him, while sand flew into the air, and he hurriedly jumped into the trap.

As he joined the men, he listened as they revealed that Captain Jennings had been shot in the neck, their platoon leader had gone into shock on the beach, and Sergeant Aubertin was now in command of the company. Duke also learned that he, himself, had been reported as MIA—missing in action.

He glanced around the trap, noticing a log at the far end of the hole. On the other side of the log was a dead Japanese soldier. Sergeant Aubertin and the runner, Dempsey, laid down their rifles at the entrance of the tank trap and walked toward the log where the dead man lay. They were going to strip him down and search for souvenirs.

As they approached the log, the Jap jumped up and shoved his bayonet at Sergeant Aubertin's chest. Duke and fellow Marine, Stan Bitchell, watched as he attacked. Bitchell grabbed his Browning Automatic Rifle (BAR) and fired multiple shots into the chest of the soldier, cutting him in two as he collapsed to his death.

As the man fell, Sergeant Aubertin and Dempsey stripped the soldier of his belongings for souvenirs. While the men waited for their orders, they continued to hear the shots being fired over their heads, shells exploding on the beach that surrounded them.

After a short time, the bombing became too close for comfort, explosions spilling sand into the trap. The men looked at each other, the dawn of realization registering at the same moment. A single explosion inside the trap could kill all of them.

Sergeant Aubertin reviewed their maps. He explained to the men that the next order of business was to capture a blockhouse that housed Japanese machine guns, called Nambu's. They needed to make their way north, off the beach. Four Marines were chosen for the task.

As the four men—Duke, Bureau, Barnard and Bitchell—approached the blockhouse, BARs in hand, they were fired upon heavily. From the caves shielding the big guns and the men that operated them, shots were fired and shells were dropped, all around the blockhouse they were to secure.

Hell bent on securing the place, the Marines proceeded to follow the routine—smoke grenades were thrown, followed by either rifle fire or an active, explosive grenade being hoisted at the building, or at any movement detected in the landscape nearby.

Then the men charged the blockhouse!

Firing shots with their BARs and strategically throwing grenades into the blockhouse to smoke out and kill their enemies, they gained the advantage. Their determination won out as they captured it.

Duke noticed a Japanese soldier running from the end of the building, and watched as he dove behind a tree stump a few feet away. Duke aimed his BAR at the stump and bark flew as he hit his mark with a burst from his rifle.

He jumped up and ran toward the stump, rifle in hand. As he took his next step, the ground shook where his foot landed, earth exploding into the air and at his face. The soldier had unpinned a grenade and held it to his chest while blowing himself up, in hopes of taking his enemy with him.

Duke was fortunate to have been spared. He glanced down at the dead body and surmised that he was a boy who could not have been more than seventeen years of age. The kid's chest was blown wide open, his ribs were splayed apart with the tips reaching heavenward into the sky. Death was a horrible thing to witness, especially a gruesome, bloody one. And the death of one so young was difficult to register in his mind.

With a grim, determined expression on his face, Duke acknowledged that the blockhouse was secured, their objective complete.

Duke and his team moved up a few feet at a time. It was all the ground they could gain under such heavy gunfire and shelling pinning them down. They found a safe place behind coral, their positions in a jagged line of attack.

Night had fallen with the darkness. As they held the line, the men took turns on watch, sleeping lightly when they could—ever aware of the night sounds. Behind the coral wall that hid Duke lay a dead Japanese officer. Safe from rifle fire passing overhead, Duke decided to search the officer for souvenirs. He found a matching set of pearl-handled knife with pistol, a Japanese flag, a compass and a few other items, and stuffed them into his pack. All of the men gathered souvenirs when they could; it became a right of war. A Company spent the night there behind the jagged protective wall of coral.

LTV's making their way to the shore.

Deck of boat approaching beaches of Peleliu.

Marines Calliqurei and Aubertin reenacting Jap pointing gun while in tank trap on Peleliu.

Chapter 6

D-Day plus two. Duke's company, along with General Chesty Puller's First Regiment, continued on to their objective—to secure Bloody Nose Ridge. It was the area most heavily infested with Japanese soldiers.

Duke had a machine gun team assigned to him. He carried the tripod for the machine gun straddled over the back of his shoulders held in place with one hand, while he carried his M1 rifle in the other hand. Costello, the fellow Marine from Missouri, carried and operated the machine gun, and two ammo carriers carried the ammunition.

As they moved up the ridge a few feet at a time, the bombardment of gunfire and shelling continued, making their progress slow. Duke scanned the ridge until he located a target. Japanese fire was streaming from a ledge on the ridge.

He motioned for the machine gunner and the ammo carriers to set up on a plateau that faced the ridge and gave them the best shot at their target. The procedure became routine. They only had a matter of seconds to fulfill their task.

Duke yelled, "Go!" and the team ran to the assigned plateau. Duke spiked the tripod, Costello placed and aligned the machine gun, and the ammo was loaded by the carriers. The machine gun peeled off several rounds as Costello fired, successfully annihilating the enemies holed up on the ledge. Without taking time to celebrate, the team moved on to the next objective.

Duke listened to the difference in the sound of the Japanese nambu as opposed to the American machine gun. The quick-firing nambu made a distinct "Brrrrrt, brrrrrt!" noise that jarred his senses. After each round from the Japanese sub-machine gun, he watched as his comrades fell around him. It was a bloodbath, made bloodier by the mortar fire spewing from the big guns that rolled out of their hidden fortresses on tracks. Focusing on the next vantage point to spike the machine gun kept him steady.

Duke didn't count how many times they fired. It was all one exceedingly loud, visual terror—a blur. Several times over, he would determine a target, motion or yell for the team to go, tripod down, machine gun loaded, ammo loaded. Then he'd yell, "Fire!"

The advancement was gradual, but as the tip of the spear, they continued to move upward. Then their movement ended abruptly as they found themselves surrounded on three sides, in the heart of Bloody Nose Ridge. *Strange, how routine develops,* Duke thought. It was almost without thinking that Duke continued—dedicated to the task, blocking out fear, determined to win. He motioned to a spot, ran to it and spiked the tripod yet again, the machine gunner set up the gun, the ammo carriers began to load it, and Duke pointed at the target he had in mind. His finger froze in mid-air.

A big gun rolled out of the cave where Duke had been pointing. A flash of smoke rose up from the end of the gun. The explosion was palpable, the vibrations pulsing through his body. He was shoved backward and into a wall of coral, the ribs in his back breaking with the impact. Duke felt fire-hot metal slugs burrowing their way into both of his thighs. The pain was excruciating!

Blood poured out from the wounds in both of his legs. Momentarily stunned, he felt liquid dripping out of both his ears and somehow registered it was blood. Both of his ear drums had been blown out from the explosion.

He looked around him. Costello and the two ammo carriers had all been killed. He knew he had to move.

Using his elbows to pull himself along, he crawled into a crevice that kept him out of the range of fire. Duke knew he had to stop the bleeding to survive. Using his Ka-Bar he made two slits to elongate the holes already made by the mortar shells, one in the top of each pant leg. Then he opened the medic packs at his waist on his belt and pulled out two sulfanilamide packets. The sulfur mixture was used to stop wounds from bleeding. The hole in his left leg was about the size of a nickel. He opened the end of one packet and poured the entire contents into the hole in his leg. Then he took his finger and shoved the powder deep into the wound. Next, he opened the other packet and repeated the process to the other leg.

Shaking off the shock that penetrated his senses, he started back towards help in the form of medical attention. Again, using his elbows he made his way down the steep decline of coral, the weight of his body assisting him.

The coral cut through the sleeves of his shirt and into his skin. He was oblivious to the pain in his arms as his legs sent a message to his brain, throbbing in agony. Floating in and out of consciousness, Duke somehow found himself at the bottom of the ridge.

Al Costella, who hailed from Brooklyn, recognized the bloody form of his friend, Duke Abdalla. Calling for another soldier to assist him, Al moved to where Duke lay bleeding. "Oh, Duke," Al managed to say, noting the severity of his injuries.

Duke was jarred awake as the two men lifted him up under his arms and carried him to the relative safety of the beach, which had been secured. *It's hot, so hot on this beach,* Duke thought to himself, or had he said it aloud? He looked up into the face of Al Costella and wondered, *Will I survive? Is this the end?*

As if reading his mind, Al offered his friend hope as he gently placed a hand on his uninjured shoulder and said, "Hang in there, Duke. You're not finished yet!"

Duke focused on Al's smile as he was lifted onto a stretcher and carried away. Next, he was loaded onto an amtrac. A body was placed next to him. Duke couldn't remember his name, but looking at the man's face, he remembered he'd spoken to him before and that he was from Michigan. The guy had a huge hole blown into the small of his back.

The pain in Duke's legs and back broke through his concentration. It was unbearable. Duke looked down at the source of his pain and saw that his pant legs were soaked in blood. Following the length of the pants, his eyes traveled down to his socks and boots, which were also covered in blood. *I must have lost a lot of blood,* Then he lost consciousness.

***

Duke awoke to the dampened sound of "Taps" resounding from the deck of a ship. He was told he was on board the USS *DuPage*. There was a wounded Marine for every bunk on the ship. All that day and through the night that bugle sounded, conveying the deaths of men lost to war. Duke overheard a Navy Corpsman speaking with a nurse, "So many bodies, draped with The United States flag, are being slipped into their seawater graves..." Duke imagined the scene on deck before drifting back into unconsciousness.

When next he awoke, he learned he'd been transferred to the medical ship, the USS *Bountiful*. It wasn't long after he was on board that two attendants entered from the hall. They cleaned him up and placed his clothes, shoes and other belongings underneath his bunk.

Duke wasn't sure how many days had passed before he came fully awake. The aroma of food wafted past his nostrils. Even though he didn't have much of an appetite, the food smelled so good he decided to tell the nurse he would like to try some.

For the first time in six days, Duke ate. It wasn't the usual Marine fare that was served for chow. He ate a chicken breast and boiled potatoes with butter, but left the green beans on the plate. What Duke enjoyed the most was the small scoop of vanilla ice cream that was served for dessert.

He was told the USS *Bountiful* zigzagged its way through the ocean, toward Guadalcanal. At the hospital there, military doctors and nurses would minister to the wounds of the Marines who had survived the Battle of Peleliu.

It was about a week that he laid on that bunk, listening to the muffled sounds of wounded soldiers around him groaning, or sometimes talking in their sleep from fever-ravished brains. He couldn't make out any words; he couldn't really hear anything other than dull tones that seemed very distant. He dozed in and out of consciousness, not certain of which thoughts were born of memory or which were from waking moments.

Finally, one day he managed to focus enough to consider his physical state and wondered where his gear might be. Using the edge of his bunk for support, he pulled himself up a bit, then forward, to look underneath his bunk. His clothes were gone—even his blood-soaked socks and boots. Everything was gone; all the souvenirs he had collected during the battle were missing. All that he had to show for his time on Peleliu now was a busted back, broken ear drums and two very badly wounded legs. Exhausted from the effort of raising himself, he fell back into his bunk and passed out.

***

It was several days' journey on the USS *Bountiful*. After making its way across the waves of the Pacific, the ship arrived safely at its destination on September 29th. Formerly known as the USS *Henderson* (AP-1), the elderly transport ship had been converted to a hospital ship at Oakland, California. Re-commissioned in March 1944, she was renamed USS *Bountiful* (AH-9), and served to carry several casualties from the battles at Peleliu.

The hospital ship docked at Port Cruz, Guadalcanal, as Red Cross nurses and doctors stood on the dock, watching. The ramps were lowered and extended from the ship to the dock. Duke awoke to the movement of soldiers working together to lift a man bunked near him onto a stretcher. He was next to be moved gingerly from his bunk to the awaiting gurney held by two sturdy young men. They proceeded to carry him topside, then down the ramp to the dock.

The familiar throbbing of pain in his legs caused him to close his eyes and grit his teeth. When next his eyes opened, the pain in his legs subsided a bit. He caught sight of a nurse standing next to a doctor.

He couldn't remember the last time he'd seen a woman, and this one was a sight for sore eyes. He could see her profile as she stood next to the man she was speaking to. She had long, blonde hair drawn up into a thick, rounded bun. Her eyes were a bright sea-blue with long, dark eyelashes. She held her hand up across the top of her brows to shield her eyes from the sun as she listened to the man speak, her beautiful blonde head nodding at his words. Next his gaze was drawn to her full, rosy mouth as she asked a few questions, then turned and directed the orderly to the tent that Duke would be housed in. It was not far from where her shapely figure stood, and the soldiers carrying him continued on to the tent indicated.

Just before she turned away, she angled her gaze at Duke and smiled. He thought to himself, *I'm going to be all right.*

Duke glanced around as he was carried through to the front of the hospital compound. They transported him through the door of a tent. The hospital set-up there really amounted to nothing more than adjoining tents that were vented at the tops, with individual cots set-up inside. Surrounding the cots were a thin film of mosquito netting.

He was placed on the right side of the tent in the cot closest to the door. His five roommates would follow him shortly, filling the remaining cots. It felt good to be on solid ground. It was hot, but somehow the warmth felt good right now.

Several hours after he had arrived, lunch was brought into their bunks. Duke sniffed. Back to the standard, tasteless food. Oh, it filled his belly all right, but somehow it always fell short of satisfying.

Over the next several weeks, Duke was examined by doctors often. Some of the doctors were concerned he might not heal well enough to rejoin the war. Duke wondered if he might be sent home. For a moment, a smile spread across his lips as the idea of returning home seemed a possibility. To see his sweet mother's face and give her a big bear hug would be wonderful!

***

He had been told later a letter from the Navy had been sent to his mother in Wagner, South Dakota informing her that Duke had been injured. She later received another letter from a South Dakota senator. It read:

> *United States Senate*
> *Committee on*
> *Agriculture and Forestry*
>
> *October 25, 1944*
>
> *Mrs. Harriet Abdalla*
> *Wagner, South Dakota*
>
> *Dear Mrs. Abdalla,*
>
> *I have just learned from the Navy Department that your son Loren D., has been reported as wounded in action. You probably have heard from the Department already, but I am sending this word just in case you have not.*
>
> *I realize that there is little that I can say under such circumstances, but I do want you to know that all of us who have someone in this conflict, have an abiding sympathy for each other. I cannot relieve your grief, but I do send you my sympathy. I hope that your son will soon be well and fully recovered from his wounds, whatever they may be.*
>
> *Sincerely yours,*
> *Harlan J. Bushfield*
> *Senator, S. Dakota*

He knew his mother was concerned for him and probably relieved to hear that he was alive.

***

It had been two months since Duke had arrived in Guadalcanal. Just a few days ago, he had learned how to make his way around outside on crutches. It felt good to be mobile. Lying still in a cot was not Duke's idea of a good time. He'd walk from one end of the compound to the other, conversing with other patients, getting some exercise. More than one time, he would stop to look up at a soldier who had climbed up a palm tree to try and get a look at one of the six Red Cross nurses who were reported to be on the island.

Duke yelled up to the observer, "Is it the blonde?" The smile on his face was real and could have lit up a candle. It was great to be alive.

Duke continued his ambling toward the end of the compound, then noticed a soldier leaning against the fence of the stockade. The area consisted of several telephone poles adjoined by rolls of chicken wire fencing. The man's fingertips bore the weight of his body hanging on the chicken-wire fence. He was tall and dark, and he looked familiar. His eyes were big and round, like saucers.

"Shade! Shade, is that you?" yelled Duke to the man.

"Yeah, it's me!" Shade yelled back.

"What happened?" asked Duke.

"I fooled 'em!" Shade responded with a conspicuous smile, his eyes rolling in his head. "I'm goin' back to the States, I'm goin' home! I fooled 'em, Duke!" His eyes were glazed as he stared straight ahead of him, no longer seeming to recognize his friend.

Duke shook his head in pity as he turned to complete the walk back to his tent. "He doesn't have anybody fooled," he murmured to himself. So many men he'd met since he first arrived at Pavuvu had cracked up. Shade had joined their ranks.

A few days after his encounter with Shade, Duke was told by the doctor that he was being reassigned to the First Marine Division, to return to his old outfit. The doctor knew he was a fighter, having recovered more speedily than most, and he was needed back on the front line. Duke was headed back to Pavuvu for the duration of his recovery, and to prepare again for battle. He sent a letter home to his mother, letting her know he would not be coming home any time soon, but that he would be alright. His mouth tightly grimaced, his eyes narrowed with determination as he wrote. *I will survive this war!*

When the day came for him to go, Duke was still on crutches. He boarded the LCI that was to take him to Pavuvu, and was led to his bunk. Memories flooded back of having lived on that island, and they weren't pleasant.

The trip wasn't long, and as the ramp was lowered for them to disembark, Duke stood up and headed topside. He looked out to a 'sea of khaki' visible from the top deck. From one end of the beach to the other he could see fully dressed, new recruits. Resplendent in their brand-new khaki uniforms, they had arrived in droves and now blanketed the beach in a sea of dark-green.

He tightened the strings of his knee-length skivvies before he approached the ramp. As he descended the ramp on his crutches, about half way down he hesitated. He could hear a familiar voice calling, "Duke! Duke!"

He looked to his left to see Bucky Walters from his hometown of Wagner jumping up and down and waving his hands over his head. Propping his crutch against his right side, Duke waved back to him and smiled, then continued down the ramp.

He reached the bottom about the same time Bucky approached. "Hey there, Duke!" he said. "What happened to you?"

Holding out his right hand, he waited for Duke to present his hand for a friendly, hearty handshake. Duke proceeded to tell Bucky about his last few months, walking as they talked. Bucky kept rhythm with his crutches as Duke advanced. Listening intently as Duke revealed the details of Peleliu, Bucky cringed noticeably when Duke described his being hit with mortar fire. He explained he had been recovering in Guadalcanal for the past two months at the hospital there, and now he was here to rejoin the war. Bucky couldn't believe that they hadn't sent Duke Stateside, and said as much. Duke didn't say anything, but he wondered what kind of injury did it take to be sent back home?

The serviceman who had been leading them stopped in front of a tent. It was right next to the mess hall. "This one's yours," he said, opening the flap for Duke to enter. The other five soldiers that had been recovering from their injuries followed him into the tent.

They had been given a wide berth on their stroll to the tent. The new recruits had great respect for wounded soldiers. Duke and the other five men were deemed to be heroes, not only for having survived Peleliu, but for returning from their injuries to serve again.

Thereafter, each time the bugle sounded for chow, Duke and the five seasoned Marines emerged from their tent dressed in skivvies. The rest of the troops were fully dressed in khaki, due to the threat of malaria. With mess kits in hand, and Duke and a few of the others on crutches, they would make their way through the parted masses of green khaki to be given first honors for chow.

One of the troops would take Duke's mess gear and get his food for him, then carried the tray to Duke's table. The tables in the tent consisted of long, wooden planks, set atop two wooden saw horses. Two equally long, wooden benches had been placed on either side of the table and rested in the dirt, providing seating. When Duke took his first bite, he noticed the food hadn't changed. He ate as much as he could stomach, then laid down his fork next to the tin plate.

One of the recruits approached him and asked if he had finished his meal. Duke nodded and watched as the man picked up his mess kit, walked to the rear of the tent, and scraped the remaining food into a fifty-five gallon slop barrel. The same recruit then washed his mess gear and the tin plate by dipping the pieces into three steaming hot barrels: the first was filled with soapy water while the remaining two held rinse water. After washing the items, the mess kit was thoroughly dried, and the recruit handed it back to Duke. The honor was duly noted and appreciated by Duke and the other injured heroes.

As happened on the island of Pavuvu previously, the seasoned Marines swapped stories with new recruits. Only this time, Duke was the one telling stories as he had experienced the war firsthand. Duke explained the terrain, how just up from the beach the ground was solid coral. They couldn't dig fox holes to lie in for cover. Every time a mortar shell went off nearby, shards of knife-like coral would fly up from the ground, injuring the men—as much or more than the mortar fragments.

As he spoke of their Japanese enemy, his expression turned fierce. He explained to the men that they had built a system of caves six stories deep into the coral, that had withstood the bombardment of shells and mortars during the three-day strike that preempted their landing.

Duke told the men, "There were as many as five hundred caves, and it was said some of these caves could hold a thousand men. Several entrances were found that had sliding armored doors to protect the Japs that hid there. Most of the caves had more than one entrance and many of 'em served as living quarters for the soldiers. They never stopped coming," Duke reported, shaking his head. "Like thousands of ants coming up through the ground."

He went on, staring at the sand in front of him as though they were about to emerge. The horror of realizing he'd lost so many of his comrades after the explosion of the big gun was evident. Several young recruits listening nearby drew closer to hear the story. He could see they were in awe of his ability to continue moving after having been so badly wounded, and admired his tenacity and cool composure under such unimaginable conditions.

Duke explained they were two hundred thirty-five men strong when A Company landed on Peleliu that day. His friends, Sergeant Aubertin and Stan Bitchell, were two of only six men from A Company left standing. B Company had twelve men left, C Company had nine surviving men. There were a total of twenty-seven men remaining in the First Battalion, over fifty percent of the First Regiment had been lost. General Chesty Puller's First Regiment suffered more casualties on the heavily fortified Bloody Nose Ridge than any other regiments on the island, after only six days of fighting on Peleliu.

Duke had been told more than twenty attempts had been made to take Bloody Nose Ridge, but because of the intense fire from the Japanese on nearby ridges, they were repeatedly forced to withdraw. Finally, the Fifth and Seventh Regiments were called upon to relieve the First Regiment, given that they had lost more than fifty percent of their men. Eventually, the Eighty-First Wildcat Army Division was also brought in to relieve what was left of the injured Marines.

But it was not until November 27th, 1944, that Peleliu was declared to be secure. One of the bloodiest Pacific battles in Marine Corps history was over, after seventy-four days of brutal warfare.

After having been on Pavuvu for a few days, Duke and the others were asked to present in full khaki for an award ceremony. It was here that Duke was awarded a Purple Heart Medal for his injuries, and was promoted to corporal. He was assigned as squad leader of the third squad, in the first platoon of A Company. His friend, John Brady, was assigned as squad leader for the second squad and also promoted to corporal. Stan Bitchell was promoted to corporal and was assigned as acting platoon sergeant for the first platoon, since he had attended V12 officers' training school. Sergeant Frank Aubertin had finished his duty as a Marine and platoon sergeant at the Battles of Guadalcanal and Peleliu returning home to the States.

***

By early March of 1945, Duke was finally able to get around without his crutches. In a matter of weeks, he was running again. He participated in the maneuvers on Pavuvu in preparation for their next battle. This time he trained with the knowledge and experience of having survived the tactics of the cold-blooded Japanese soldiers. He tried to prepare the twelve men in his squad as best he could for the brutal warfare that was ahead of them. There was no question in his mind that focus kept a man alive. As in any fight, maintaining focus was crucial to the outcome.

Near the end of the month, the First Marine Division left Pavuvu and was shipped back to Guadalcanal to get supplies and ammunition for the next battle. Recollections of the bloody Peleliu landing flooded Duke's mind. When they landed on that beach, there was no place to hide from the perpetual onslaught of machine guns and rifle fire. It was kill or be killed. The anxiousness took hold in his body, and he felt an overwhelming desire to charge forward. The muscles in his legs twitched as he sat on his cot, remembering. His palms were wet with sweat as he imagined his trigger finger coiling around the metal lever, squeezing it in defense of his life. He was emboldened by the experience—and he planned on preparing his squad to face the realities of aggression in war.

Tensions were high, and he relayed to the men in his squad as best he could—the Japanese didn't give any ground, they had to take it. They had only two days on the island before they were to face the enemy again.

While on Guadalcanal, Duke was asked to obtain supplies from the Army Supply Depot. Forbes was the jeep driver, and after they'd gotten what they needed from the depot, Duke noticed some tents that had been erected just behind it. They had vented canopies, and he was also curious to see what else was there.

"Hey, Forbes," Duke said to the driver. "Let's take a ride over there to see what's behind those tents."

Forbes drove the jeep closer and Duke got out of the jeep. As he walked up to the opening, Duke could see that the deck the tents were built on was three steps up off the ground. There were eight tents built over frames that housed a doorway for each one, with a vented top on each tent. It was quite a set-up. These Army men were living high on the hog.

Duke and the driver looked behind one of the tents. They could hardly believe their eyes when they saw a huge, beautiful garden! It was about two acres in expanse, and was chock-full of tasty-looking fresh vegetables and fruits. Gardening in the tropics certainly was rewarding. The warm temperatures and moist soil made for ideal conditions to growing. There were watermelons the size of five gallon drums, carrots as long as his forearm. zucchinis, tomatoes, cucumbers, lettuce, green beans, and even fresh corn-on-the-cob.

Duke's mouth watered as he eyed a large watermelon. An Army first sergeant stepped out from a tent and approached Duke and Forbes.

Duke politely asked the first sergeant, "Could I buy some of those vegetables from you? We haven't had any fresh vegetables for a long time."

The first sergeant responded, "No, they're not for sale! Now, you bums get out of here! I'm tired of you guys coming around begging."

"Hey, it was our division that took this island!" Duke insisted.

The first sergeant responded, "Yeah, I know. But we're on it now!"

Duke retreated, then Forbes and he returned to the jeep and drove back to camp.

As Forbes was about to jump out of the jeep, Duke put a hand on his arm, "Forbes, you go over to the motor pool and get a five quarter truck." Duke continued with authority in his voice, "Get it, and bring it back here immediately!" A five quarter truck was a flatbed truck with side rails about eight inches high, and Duke had a plan on how to use it.

Forbes jumped to the task while Duke gathered fellow Marines around him to report the insult they had just received from the Army sergeant. He revealed his plan for revenge to the remainder of his cronies.

When Forbes returned with the vehicle, Duke hoisted a light machine gun into the truck, then secured it to the center of the bed with ropes. Next, he had as many Marines as would fit, jump into the cab and onto the back of the truck. The rest followed in the jeep. Duke directed the men where they were to go. He had them pull the truck up to the end of the garden where all eight tents were visible. They were lined up like sitting ducks, awaiting obliteration.

Pointing to the vented tops of each tent, Duke told the machine gunner, "You're going to shoot off the top of each one of those tents!" To the surrounding men he said, "If any heads pop up, you boys fire over their heads!"

Then he ordered the machine gunner, "Open up on 'em!"

As the machine gunner fired, pieces of green canvas flew everywhere. They'd teach these Army men to respect the Marines.

Army canvas continued to rain on the compound. Not one head popped up as they fired. While the tent tops were being cut off, Duke's men swarmed the garden and gathered as many fruits and vegetables as they could get their hands on. They filled their ponchos and burlap bags full of food, then carried it back to the truck. It took a matter of minutes to empty the garden.

Duke gave one last order before they headed back to the truck. "Smash anything that's left," he growled. "I want this place leveled!"

When they had finished loading their spoils, there was a huge mound of food on the back of the truck. Not a single piece of fresh fruit or vegetable was left in the garden. The Army men in the tents stayed conspicuously absent.

The men transported their newly acquired goods back to camp and Duke's men feasted. There were carrots and green beans, baked potatoes and, one of Duke's favorites, corn-on-the-cob.

Lieutenant Burke, A Company's executive officer, was one of many company men that ate well that night. Seated not far from him, Duke smiled as he took another bite. The officer smiled back and said, "Sure is good to have 'The Indian' on my side."

Duke saved the watermelon for dessert.

***

Aware that it was a countdown now, but unsure of the number of days before they would move out, the men in Duke's company became somber. Their rifles were cleaned, Ka-Bars were sharpened, pack supplies were checked and rechecked by each and every soldier.

Colonel Kenneth B. Chappell gave the order for the First Regiment to assemble. The men gathered to listen to his appeal for their patriotism in the upcoming battle. Duke listened to the words of his commander as memories from the Battle of Peleliu raced through his mind. The words of General Chesty Puller reverberated in his head as his thoughts flowed, "They're ruthless, they'll fight you to the death! Take no prisoners!" He hadn't heard all of what Colonel Chappell had said, but the message he needed to hear was clear. He knew what he had to do, and he was ready!

The following morning, the First Battalion was ordered by their battalion commander, Lieutenant-Colonel R. P. Ross, Jr., to board a ship bound for their next battle destination. He didn't know where it would be, but Duke knew plenty. He knew the difficult terrain and the jungle-like conditions, and he understood the brutality of his enemy. As squad leader for twelve men of the third squad, he understood how to direct his men. And as always, he was ready to fight, and he was going in to kill again.

From the deck of the ship, Duke looked out across the expanse of ocean and attempted to envision the landing ahead of them. Nothing could be as chaotic and deadly as his first landing at Peleliu, could it?

The memories that invaded his mind were uninvited but nevertheless they came. Standing alone for the moment, Duke remembered the sounds of guns and mortar shells and bombs. In his mind, he could see flashes of light, a telltale sign that bullets or shells were on their way. Amidst the flashes and deafening noise, he had descended the cargo nets that were thrown over the side of the ship, then jumped into the undulating amtrac that would carry his comrades and him to the beach.

The first obstacle he had encountered after entering the knee-high water was the body of his Indian friend, Case. It was not something he would ever forget. The man had been a good friend.

With bullets flying over his head, he had turned to watch as boats were being blown out of the water. The terrain itself was unforgiving, deadly even, due to the projectile shards of coral from nearby blasts.

In his mind now, he steeled himself for the onslaught that was ahead of him. He was as prepared as he would ever be for what he knew was balls-out fighting with the suicidal Japanese enemy.

A fellow Marine approached him where he stood. Duke turned to the man and smiled. He knew the younger recruit was scared. Hell, they were all scared!

"When it's our turn to land, you get in off that beach as quick as you can, hear? Move fast and always focus on your next move."

The man nodded. It was good advice from The Indian.

The ship continued on its zigzag course and Duke continued to watch. Everything was on the Q.T. aboard ship. Orders were given at the latest possible moment to ensure the security of information. As the days passed, Duke saw more and more ships on the horizon in any direction he looked. A Company's executive officer, Lieutenant Burke, ordered the men on deck to receive their orders and learn of their destination. It was expected that the First Marine Division would be marching into the heat of the battle on an island called Okinawa. They were told this battle was not going to be a short one by any stretch of the imagination. A fierce fight was expected on the beaches when they hit the island.

The men were apprised of a secret weapon being transported in limited numbers on their ship under the mysterious tarp on the deck. It was a bevy of M3 rifles with infra-red scopes attached. The rifle was smaller than the Thompson sub-machine gun that Duke would be carrying. Its range was also limited to about seventy yards. The gun was to be used at night, hopefully to detect any Japanese infiltrating through American lines. It allowed the shape and form of a body to be seen in a yellow-green light through the sniper scope.

Duke remembered how the enemy soldiers had moved during the night on Peleliu. He remembered how still he had remained in the swamp so as not to be detected by them. The technology gave some of the men, especially the newer recruits, hopes of an advantage with night vision now a part of their defense. Duke was interested to see how the gun would work in a real combat situation, and he didn't have long to wait.

Okinawa was very close to the larger islands of Japan and would be used as a base for air operations once they had secured it. From there, the United States military could successfully attack the mainland of Japan.

The code name for the battle was 'Operation Iceberg'. He had heard that together Duke and his company were traveling on one of fifteen-hundred ships that had been amassed to attack the Japanese. It was the largest U.S. amphibious force ever assembled to date in the Pacific Campaign and consisted of over one hundred eighty-three thousand troops. It was as if a massive iceberg had detached from the United States carrying an expanse of armed troops and landed on the doorstep of Okinawa.

The First and Sixth Marine Divisions would join with five divisions of the U.S. Tenth Army, the Seventh, Twenty-Seventh, Seventy-Seventh, Eighty-First, and Ninety-Sixth, as well as a British Commonwealth Fleet of Allied Ships to be part of an organization commanded by U.S. Army General Simon Bolivar Buckner, Jr.

Several days before Duke's ship would arrive, U.S. Naval ships had begun shelling of the island and would continue the bombardment for the next week. Unlike his previous journey to battle, Duke and his company were called on more frequently to assemble on deck. Orders had been repeated to the men throughout the week as the ship plowed through the rough, salty waters to the precipice of the battle.

The day finally arrived. Their ship hovered at the edge of Okinawa. Concentrating on being the predator and not the prey, Duke prepared himself for battle. He understood the savage determination of the Japanese soldier to win at all costs. But, as a member of the United States Marine Corps, he was just as determined.

April 1, 1945 was Easter Sunday that year as well as April Fool's Day. The morning of the invasion, "Reveille" was played loud and clear. The men were called to the traditional breakfast before battle of steak and eggs. The steak was thick, the eggs were fluffy and scrambled, and he even had a pile of potatoes this morning. It tasted better than almost anything Duke had eaten in the past year. He knew to fill his belly before battle. In Peleliu, he had experienced a total of six days passing before he would eat again.

***

After chow, A Company was called again to the deck. Duke looked out at the horizon and saw ships as far as his sharp, grey eyes could see. He'd never seen anything like it in his life. It was a force larger than the one that had been amassed at Normandy, France nearly a year before.

The men were ordered to board the amtracs bound for shore. Fully dressed in his combat gear, his helmet in place and pack on his back, Duke climbed down the ropes of the cargo net that ended in the amphibious landing boat. As the amtrac headed for shore, no opposition was encountered, but he watched the horizon continuously.

He waited with the rest of the Marines in the amtrac while the commanding officer ordered the LVT to continue to circle in the water until all of the amtracs were in place, and the signal to advance was given. U.S. Naval ships were continuing to bombard the island with shells in preparation of their landing. The sound was comforting, somehow.

The amtrac smoothly advanced through the water without opposition until it pulled up on shore. At approximately 0830 hours, Duke and his comrades arrived on the sands of Okinawa. There was no resistance, no mortar fire. The ramp of the amtrac was lowered at the back, and Duke was one of the first men to jump off and turn toward the beach. He took a few steps out of the ankle-deep water and onto the beach before dropping to the sand on his stomach along with the other men, rifle poised to target and kill the enemy.

The silence was deafening.

There was no sniper fire, no enemy there to greet them.

Rising gradually from the ground, he continued to scan the tops of the trees, hills and ridges, expecting to see the reflection off the barrel of a rifle or the flash of a bullet being fired. *Nothing.*

Duke stood up slowly, still scanning the horizon. He could not believe he was walking up the beach with the rest of his company, standing fully upright.

Having landed unopposed, the First and Sixth Marine Divisions moved quickly to the north and across to Yontan Airfield to secure it. Two Army divisions moved inland and south to take over Kadena Airfield near the Bishi Gawa River. Both divisions arrived at their destinations in a matter of hours.

They knew the Japanese still had guns trained on the center of Yontan Airstrip, even though the First and Sixth Marine Divisions had surrounded the airfield. They had lost radio contact with headquarters, but somehow word got to the Marines on the other side of the strip that the First had secured their objective and to cease firing toward their position.

Just then, Duke saw Forbes jump into his jeep and start it up. He revved the engine, then gunned it by flooring the gas pedal and peeled out onto what was left of the pavement.

Almost immediately, the enemy shelled the field with mortar fire. The Japs were closer than they thought. A blast would hit, leaving a large hole in the ground and a huge puff of smoke in the air.

Momentarily, their vision was obscured. Duke and the other men watched, then cheered as Forbes made it through to the other side of the smoke cloud. The men monitored Forbe's progress as he zigzagged in a diagonal path across the airfield, intermittently watchful, then jubilant as he survived yet another blast.

Duke gasped as he watched his friend gain the other side of the airstrip, shaking his head and wondering if anyone back home could imagine what he'd just seen, let alone believe it. Before noon that day, Okinawa's two major airstrips were truly and finally secured and in the hands of the Americans.

With the airfields taken, the Sixth Marine Division continued north while the Army divisions moved south. With no appreciable defense from the Japanese, the First Marine Division moved on toward the east, across the center of the island. It was eerily quiet as they progressed.

That first night, A Company stopped in a small village that had a cobblestone street running through the center of it. The men separated on either side of the street and bunked down for the night.

Sometime after they'd bedded down, Duke was awakened by the clamor of metal against the cobblestones in the street. A Japanese soldier with hobnailed shoes was running down the middle of the road as the men of A Company looked on. Faster and faster he ran, shoes tapping on the stones in a frenzied pace as he passed by Duke and the rest of the men.

They watched him run, understanding what the outcome would be. Not one of them reached for his rifle, but a few of them exchanged knowing looks. Some of the men even lay back down on their bedding, apathetic to what was about to take place.

As the soldier ran past the end of the line of Marines, several rifle shots rang out. The man collapsed to the ground, dead. Duke and the rest of the men went back to sleep.

The next morning, A Company journeyed on in single file, heading straight across the island. No opposition was encountered, other than sporadic sniper fire. It felt strange to the men that there was only a sparse resistance. It took them a total of three and one half days to travel the fifteen miles to the other side of the island. *The Japanese had to be here somewhere, didn't they?*

Duke was on the point of a peninsula with the men from the First Marine Division awaiting further orders. He was standing in a rice paddy that had dried up. Always at the ready, Duke heard a droning noise from above and looked up in time to see a plane coming right at them.

As he and every other man hit the deck, the plane opened up and fired on them. But it was one of theirs!

With all men assigned their own duties, Bob Stedronsky from Lake Andes, South Dakota, was the radio man, and he got on the band and radioed their position to HQ. Steadily but repeatedly, Bob continued to radio the message that they were being attacked by a U.S. Navy fighter plane.

As the first plane was turning around, a second plane joined it to prepare to strafe the ground they were now lying on with machine gun fire. The planes lowered in unison, the sound of their engines gearing down, and just as Duke and the men expected the firing to begin, the low-flying aircraft pulled up and veered away from them, engines roaring.

Bob's call must have gotten through! Duke's heart was racing in his chest as he watched the planes fly away. It wasn't the first occasion of friendly fire in this war, but Duke sure hoped it would be his last association with it.

The day dragged on, and Duke heard a commotion from further out on the point. As he approached the noise, he saw the fuselage of a Japanese airplane. The men were stripping it for souvenirs. By the time Duke got close enough to take a look, the plane had been stripped bare. Anything and everything that could be ripped off of that plane was gone. Gauges, mirrors, gear shift, pieces of the dash or seat, any piece that could be pried loose. He took a moment and sat in it, considering how many Americans might have died at the hands of the Japanese pilot who once sat there.

***

The morning of April 6, Duke awoke to the sounds of bombs and guns sounding off from the battleships in the distance. He looked out over the water, and even though he couldn't see the ships on the other side of the island, he could see the gray, black and white clouds of smoke that were left in the air following the strike from U.S. Naval ships against Japanese airplanes. He could hear and see the Kamikaze pilots as they made their deadly dives towards the ships floating on the sea, and watched on in helpless amazement. Occasionally he could see the flash of fire as a plane hit its mark.

Duke had learned Japanese pilots were coerced to step forward and volunteer for the suicidal mission of crashing their well-fortified planes into an American or Allied ship. By diving from a height that would allow a steep yet nearly stealthy approach, the pilots could be successful in sinking or damaging many vessels. Duke heard that once asked, it would have been cowardice for a member of the Japanese Imperial Forces to refuse the mission.

Throughout the morning and into the night, the droning noises of the battle at sea could be heard as clouds of smoke floating in the air could be seen above. The sky was filled with Japanese Zero's manned by maniacal, suicidal pilots intent on sinking U.S. and Allied War Ships, so as to cut off and strand the more than one hundred eighty thousand troops ashore.

Over and over again the enemy planes attacked! The ominous flock of Japanese Zeros rained almost certain death on the destroyers or smaller vessels, like merchant ships. The decks of the air craft carriers, battleships or cruisers were made of reinforced steel, so none were sunk, but many, Duke imagined, were heavily damaged.

At that moment Duke felt safer on land. He and the rest of the men he was with wondered how many ships had been sunk or destroyed by the crazy Kamikaze pilots, and how many fellow servicemen had died. They had heard some news come over, but nothing was certain.

The men had been ordered to wait on the peninsula until their next assignment was given. All that they had to eat were C-rations. It was a slight improvement from the K-rations they had eaten on Pavuvu, Duke thought, but not by much. The C-ration was limited to a few canned meals: stew, hash, peas, cheese, or pork and beans. Canned heat or C-4 explosives for pack charges could be used to heat the food. C-4 was a little trickier, since it wasn't contained and men had to be careful handling it, but Duke managed well using either.

The food was palatable, but the problem was that their rations ran out very quickly. Duke managed to survive on roots, or anything looking like a vegetable that he could dig up using his Ka-Bar. They all foraged for vegetation whenever they could find it.

Frequent, heavy, tropical rains fell and were a trial to endure, but at least they softened the ground somewhat. Sometimes a stray chicken or pig would wander their way, but for the most part the men were starving.

One day one of the men spotted a cow not far from their camp. It wasn't long before it had been shot by a rifle. A few of the men ran out to where the cow lay, including a soldier named Wedell, who had been a butcher back home. He made quick work of cutting up the cow using his Ka-Bar and a machete knife, proportioning sections for each company.

The men in Duke's company raced to prepare a spit to cook their hind quarter on. After cooking the meat over the fire, they ate like barbarians due to their severe hunger, but still savored every bite of the beef as they chewed. Duke didn't know when they might eat like this again.

A few weeks had passed with minimal enemy contact to contend with. Looking for food was one of their greatest tasks for a while. A ritual that had survived, even flourished on that peninsula, was the making of jungle juice. All of the men participated by sharing whatever ingredients they could and handing them over to the jungle juice preparer.

The wait for the juice to be ready to drink was excruciating for the men. But once sufficiently fermented, the juice was consumed by all. It was the only means of escape they had from the cold reality of the war, or from the uncertainty of their future.

One night, Duke was lying on his back, gazing up at the stars in the sky and listening to the sounds of blasts, just a few miles south. That night became one of many nights full of fireworks made up of flares. When those flares lit up the sky, so close yet so far away, it reminded the men of the eerie presence of war. Knowing that death was nearby, and that they could be called to duty at any moment to face it.

This night, Duke knew almost instinctively his call would come soon. Every night the flares moved closer to where the First Marines slept. "Will it be tonight?" Duke wondered.

***

When the word came from HQ at the end of April for the First Marine Division to relieve the Army, they were ready. After having experienced some good weather and having had a chance to rest, Lieutenant Colonel Ross gave the order.

Duke shoved his .45mm handgun into the front of his trousers, threw his pack on his back and slipped the strap of his Thompson sub-machine gun over his shoulder. The gun was prized for its high rate of firepower. His "Tommy" was his best friend now.

On April 30th, the First Marines moved out in a truck convoy to relieve the Army. The Marines occupied a line from the beach, north of Kuwan, running south of Machinato Airfield. As they attached themselves to the Twenty-Seventh Army, who were exhausted from battle, Duke noticed a light gray canvas pack on the ground to his left. He knew what it was, even from this distance. Every Army man made a wide arc as they passed by the object on the ground. They were obviously afraid of its potency and gave it a wide berth.

Duke eyed the gray material and headed straight toward it. He strolled over, picked it up gently and opened the bag. It was a pack-charge full of C-4 charges! Each pack came with sixteen sticks. Each stick was about two inches square and twelve inches long with a wick or fuse in the center of it so it could be ignited. With great concentration and with a firm hold on each fuse, Duke began yanking out each one with a practiced hand until he had four of them.

The Army men just stared. Duke was exposing himself to C-4 explosives, but he knew what he was doing. He knew the C-4 was like gold out here, and it could come in very handy having the extra sticks. He rolled them into a ball and stored them in his pack, continuing the march with his division, never once glancing back at the Army that was leaving.

With every step forward, Duke strengthened his resolve, not just to survive the war—but to do his part to win it. The terrain here was a bit different than on Peleliu—the climate, too. The average temperature was about 72 degrees Fahrenheit. The ground, however, was reminiscent of Pavuvu in that the mud was ankle to knee-deep, depending on where he stepped. He looked ahead of him as he trudged on, feeling the weight of his pack on his back and the security of his Tommy gun over his shoulder.

On May 1st, heavy firing caused the dirt to rise from the ground just ahead of them. The First Regiment stopped near a long, hogback ridge, a Japanese fortress near Dakeshi. It guarded the entrance to a draw, which was a lengthy, flat expanse of a path that extended to Shuri Castle. The First Battalion readjusted their front lines, as they had reached the high ground looking down onto Kuwan Draw, and relieved the Twenty-Seventh Army Division.

Upon their arrival, Major General del Valle, commander of their division, had learned the details of the combat taking place. The Twenty-Seventh Army Division had been spent for the entire month of April, from the intensive attacks of the Japanese defensive.

This ridge was a deadly killing ground, surrounded by towering cliffs and pocketed with machine gun nests that housed two to three men each. It was about one and one-half stories high and was fortified not only with several machine guns, but with spider traps as well. The enemy soldier dug small holes in the ground and covered the top with sticks or thatching for camouflage. Each spider trap housed a Japanese soldier armed with a rapid-fire light nambu machine gun. They were strategically located both at the base of the ridge, and up all along one side. There were also snipers, hidden on branches of trees or hiding behind dark-green vegetation or bushes.

The worst of their defense was a large cannon, housed in a cave and located at the mouth of the ridge. It was mounted on wheels, which rolled on a track and carried it out to the edge to fire on the advancing Americans, or deep, back into the cave to be protected. One of the things the cave protected the big gun from was American battleships firing sixteen inch cannon rounds into the ridge in an attempt to destroy it.

Lieutenant Colonel Ross ordered his battalion to attack the ridge that sheltered the enemy and take it!

On May 2nd C Company made their advance, making their way up a ravine, across the deep draw, up to its front, to attack the ridge when they received the order to take the large gun. Japanese artillery and mortars had every inch of the several ravines that extended toward them, zeroed in on, from their mutually supportive positions. C Company was receiving heavy fire on their left flank and equally perilous fire from caves in the north side of the draw. They experienced severe casualties due to their precarious position, and were forced to withdraw under the cover of heavy smoke.

As Duke and his squad "glassed" the ridge with their binoculars, a platoon from F Company, which was now attached to A Company, could be seen making their way up another one of the ravines, moving toward the northwestern outskirts of the ridge. It had begun raining, making the ground a muddy, slippery mess. Duke and his squad watched as the last man from the platoon entered the ravine.

Within seconds, the ground shook all around them as the Japanese opened up with artillery and mortar fire that created a brown haze of smoke. It filled the air surrounding them and obscured their vision of the platoon's progress.

Duke kept his binoculars focused on the last position where he had witnessed movement. His heart pounded heavily in his chest as he waited. Finally, he saw three Marines exiting the ravine, waving their hands in front of their faces to clear the smoke, and moving toward them. Three Marines! Out of the entire platoon, only three men had survived.

Focusing more firepower on suspected locations that shielded the enemy, C Company took an even closer note of specific harbors of machine gun nests and spider traps. Still, they were pushed back.

During the light of day on May 3rd, B Company moved up to attack the ridge. The gunfire, grenades, shells and cannon fire spewing from the face of the ridge proved to be too much for them. They were pushed further back.

On May 4th, A Company was informed it was their turn to attack the ridge. After reviewing the information supplied by C and B Companies, and having witnessed the annihilation of an entire platoon from F Company, Duke and the men knew what they were up against. They knew the locations of most nests or traps, and needed to form a plan to take out the big gun in the cave, without the support of tanks.

First Lieutenant Burke met with his platoon leaders of A Company to devise a winning plan. He decided to hold the second platoon in reserve. The first, third, and mortar platoons would attack the ridge that evening, under the cover of darkness. The third platoon was to draw their fire with a frontal attack from the broad side of the ridge. The first platoon would attack and take the ridge from the base.

Lieutenant DeLong, platoon leader for the first platoon, gathered his platoon sergeant, Corporal Stan Bitchell, and the three squad leaders together to share with them the plan of attack. He explained the third platoon was going to draw fire with a frontal attack while the first platoon attacked the ridge from the ravine closest to the base. Duke's third squad would attack the machine gun nests from the base to the top of the ridge, making the way clear to the cave, where the big gun was housed. The first squad, along with the second, was to take out the spider traps around the base of the ridge, then move up to destroy the big gun once their way had been cleared by Duke's third squad.

John Brady was the squad leader for the second squad. Duke and John were two of the more experienced men in the platoon. Not only had they survived Pavuvu together, they both had managed to survive Peleliu. After being dismissed by the lieutenant, the two friends nodded at one another. Their jaws, and intentions, now firmly set. They were ordered to attack under the cover of darkness.

That evening, it was pitch black and pouring rain. Wearing ponchos, A Company traveled along the edge and top of the ravine, making their way toward the base of the ridge. The Japanese continued to pummel the ravines with mortar and artillery fire, their vision obscured by the smoke they created, along with the darkness and the sheets of rain pouring from the sky.

As the third squad got closer, they were thankful for the rain and crawled together, where they gathered behind an embankment about three feet high and eight feet wide. Duke told each one of the men in his squad what they had to do to reach the top of the ridge.

"Watch for anything that moves, anything!" he said. "If you have a doubt about any object, you throw a grenade at it. If it moves, throw a grenade then shoot! When I tell you to throw your grenades, I want to see the air filled with 'em. Do you hear me?" Over the sounds of the downpour and heavy fire, he screamed at his men.

"Yes!" they responded in unison.

Duke wanted the men to understand their intent clearly. "We have to wipe out these nests to get to the top." Every man's head nodded in understanding.

Due to the severe weather, their attack had been postponed until the morning. Vaguely aware of their position, the Japanese continued to bombard the area with shells. Duke's ears were ringing from the noise of the big gun sounding off every time the Japanese fired it. He told his men to find cover wherever they could until the signal was given to assemble.

The torrential downpour had created ankle-deep mud that the men kept sliding in as they searched for a place to bed down. Duke felt along the side of the embankment below his feet and tried to look through the downpour of water rolling off the bill of the hood of his poncho for a hole or breach in the rock. After several minutes, he was successful. Cautiously he entered the opening, reaching out in front of him with his left hand, while keeping a firm hand on his .45.

He crouched as he entered the small opening to avoid hitting his head on the low, rocky ceiling, then crouched further, still, to a kneeling position. After determining that the small space was unoccupied, he removed his poncho, shifting his position until he could reach the exposed breach in the rock. He used the poncho to cover the opening of the crevice to avoid detection, and to keep the rain from penetrating the hole, while the enemy was still firing. He then reached into his pack for the C-4 charge that he had picked up along the way, making sure that his striking hand was dry. He pinched off a piece of the clay and rolled it into a little ball, just smaller than a golf ball. He set the ball of clay on the ground and surrounded it with small rocks before lighting it by striking his Zippo as he rolled his thumb over the wheel on top, and held it to the clay-like form. It sputtered, then caught fire. After burning slowly for a few seconds, it flared up into a fireball of white flame. The burning C-4 created an intense heat he would use to heat his dinner.

Placing his canteen cup onto the small circle of rocks, he began to heat the cup filled with soup mix and water directly over the flame. As the light revealed his surroundings, an eerie feeling came over him. He noticed urns lined the walls of the small cave. After carefully examining them, he realized he was in a tomb.

Looking more closely at the urns, he examined the contents. He picked one up and dumped the ashes onto the ground. Using the toe of his boot, then bending over and using his hand to spread the gray powder, he looked for gold teeth in the dust of the remains. After checking several more of the clay containers, he found nothing of value and gave up his search.

Returning to his food, he cautiously lifted the still-warm cup, then reached into the leg of his right boot to pull out his spoon. He rubbed it on his shirt sleeve, then knelt on the ground and ate his dinner with it. After finishing his meager meal, he managed to sit on the floor in the tight space. The stream of rain falling from the pitch black sky on the other side of his poncho relentlessly pummeled the ground. He hoped that the men from his squad could rest in the few hours left until daylight. They would need their strength for the attack.

Duke leaned back against the wall of the tomb, relaxed his muscles, and sat still while he warmed up. He never actually slept, knowing that the enemy was just above him.

USS *Bountiful* Hospital Ship docking at Guadalcanal with Duke onboard, injured.

Duke and shirtless comrades.

Corporal Roland James' second drawing of Duke.

Forbes driving Jeep.

Chapter 7

May 5th, 1945. It was The Indian's turn to fight. Sometime during the hours before dawn, while darkness still loomed, the rain had continued to stream. The almost rhythmic sounds of the big gun in the cave boomed in eerie harmony with the cadence of shelling and gunfire, muted only by the constant downpour. Duke pulled his poncho down from where it had afforded protection from the deluge during the night, shook it out, then rolled it up tightly before shoving it into his backpack. Crawling out of the tomb, Duke called his squad together behind the embankment at the base of the ridge. Every man knew what he was supposed to do, and adrenaline was flowing freely.

Before the third platoon gave the signal to begin firing at the ridge to divert the Japanese' attention, Duke heard a loud blast, followed by a piercing scream. He knew instantly it was his friend, John Brady, leader of the second squad. Duke peered over the embankment to locate his friend, then jumped over it and ran to John, who'd been hit by a phosphorous grenade and was literally burning up. The phosphorous ate away at his skin and left a pungent smell. Duke could only imagine the pain John was feeling as the acid burned away layers of his flesh.

Amidst the heavy firing, and despite the peril to himself, Duke carefully lifted his injured comrade over his shoulder and began running, hoping to bring John to the safety of the ravine behind them. As he ran, the unearthly lights created by tracers from machine guns firing blindly, shells exploding, and flares being lofted into the pre-dawn sky unwittingly aided him in his task. He passed Charteur, from the second squad, and saw he had a large hole blown through his side and was using his hands to try to cover the bloody mess. Charteur looked up at Duke with eyes as big as saucers, and Duke knew the man was in shock. Gauging the amount of blood pouring out of his wound, Duke also knew there was nothing to be done for him. With a heavy heart and the weight of John Brady hanging over his shoulder, Duke moved as fast as he could toward safety.

As Duke ran, he passed Green, from the third platoon, who had just been shot and was lying injured in a ditch.

Green yelled to Duke, "Don't go past the wall; it's covered by machine gun fire!"

Duke ignored the warning and ran until he could pass his friend off and into the waiting arms of Al Costella from the mortar platoon, near the other ravine.

"Get him outta here!" he yelled to Al.

With his head ducked low, Duke then ran back to join his third squad, keeping a close eye on what was happening in the battle. More than twenty minutes must have passed.

Duke looked up at the clouds and saw the rain had stopped. As the sun peeked over the horizon, it left a pinkish-yellow hue in the sky. At that moment, the third platoon initiated their attack from the broad side of the ridge, drawing the enemy's fire.

Duke glanced quickly over the embankment to see that the attack had been signaled. Great streams of smoke snaking into the air made it difficult to see anything, but he was certain he saw Bonneville, platoon sergeant from the third platoon, standing and firing his old M1903. It was a bolt-action rifle that he'd used on Guadalcanal.

Suddenly, Duke saw him go down. The entire third platoon was being wiped out from the top of the ridge, and smoke poured from the broad side of the ridge as the Japanese emptied their guns on the exposed platoon.

The Indian knew what his squad had to do and what they were up against. He had prepared his squad beforehand, giving them specific orders prior to their advance. He motioned for the men to ready themselves, then bellowed, "Grenades!"

After hurtling a grenade of his own, he looked up in the sky above him and saw a mass of green, egg-shaped missiles flying through the air toward the enemy. He watched as the Japanese infantrymen that had been protecting the machine gun nests scattered as the grenades exploded. As he launched himself forward, Duke screamed "Let's go!" and immediately, on either side of him, bullets began whizzing by his face.

Lernahan and Christiansen were both shot through the head and killed instantly. Constant machine gun fire was coming from the top of the ridge while rifle fire spewed from Japanese infantrymen hidden in the hillside brush. Keeping his head low and eying his targets, Duke and his squad advanced. Whenever he saw movement, Duke grabbed a grenade from his belt and yanked the pin off the top. Then he launched the grenade toward his target with a forceful throw, immediately following with rapid machine gun fire from his Thompson, expeditiously killing several enemy soldiers.

With no time to waste, Duke moved further up the ridge, repeating the process as he went. The Japanese had strategically built pill boxes, using concrete fortified by steel rods to house several machine gun nests over the expanse of the ridge. Grenades were like gold to him right now, as a means to demolish these fortresses.

Meanwhile, behind him, Duke's squad was disappearing.

The familiar sounds of battle invaded his senses. The loud *boom* from the big gun maintained a slow rhythm in the background, while the *brrrrrrrrrrt* sounding off from the quick-fire nambu machine guns filled the air all around him. Duke responded with a promenade from his Tommy, silencing yet another Japanese machine gun nest. With sweat dripping down his face, he could smell the gunpowder hanging in the air and all he could see was smoke, but Duke counted four machine gun nests he and his squad had destroyed together. Several Japanese infantrymen had been killed as well.

Intent on his mission, Duke strove forward to reach the top of the ridge. He turned sharply in response to the cry of, "Duke, I'm heet!" It was Ralpholito Cruse Altomarino from California, imploring him in his heavy Mexican accent. He'd been shot through the leg, and it was bleeding badly.

"Can you move?" Duke yelled over the noise of gunfire.

"Yes!" the injured Marine cried.

"Then get out of here!"

In that moment, Duke realized he was alone in his task now. He was the last man standing in the third squad; all twelve of his men were either dead or wounded.

The Indian moved stealthily up the slope, hand on his Tommy. Determined to complete the duty single-handedly, Duke searched the hillside for the next machine gun nest. A flash of sunlight glinting off of the barrel of a gun gave it away. In a fraction of a second, Duke hurled his grenade toward the sight. In the same movement, he rolled his Tommy gun into place in his hand, squeezed the trigger with a steady finger, and pummeled the nest with machine gun fire. All three Japanese soldiers were killed.

Racing forward with purpose, eyes scanning the terrain, he spotted the final nest. Jumping as he threw his grenade, then spinning to one side to avoid the return fire, he landed squarely on his feet. With a firm grip on his Tommy gun, he began to finish off the last nest. After slaying two of the occupants, he knew the last Jap had to be killed! Duke fired on him, but the Japanese machine gunner ran and jumped off the edge of the ridge sideways, eluding his fire. Immediately there was a loud boom! Duke heard the blast emanate from just below him. Calliqurei from the second squad had blasted the Jap from the base of the ridge with his sawed-off shot gun, killing him in mid-air.

Running forward, Duke reached the top of the ridge. Turning slowly, he looked out at the draw. The vast expanse of the mostly flat, wide valley toward Shuri Castle was laid out in front of him. This was what the Marines had wanted, and there it was.

At the same time, the first and second squads had been advancing, as the third squad had cleared their way. They had taken out the spider traps around the base and were just nearing the cave that housed the big gun. Standing just below and to one side of the mouth of the cave were Corporal Bitchell and Second Lieutenant DeLong. The lieutenant called for a flame-thrower to come to the entrance of the cave. He would pull the trigger on the flame gun, first holding it level then rocking the flame from one side of the cave to the other to cover the interior and destroy any lurking enemies.

The flame-thrower moved quickly up the ridge, then jumped stoically in front of the opening, landing in a firm stance with his gun held at the ready. He pressed the lever to ignite the flame to fire the cave, but there was no flame. The gas had not been turned on to fuel the flame gun! Standing with the flame gun in his hand and a look of complete astonishment on his face, the flame-thrower was shot repeatedly through his chest by the enemies in the cave. He fell to the ground, dead.

Second Lieutenant DeLong braved the fire of the hostile machine gun as he led his group of Marines around the hostile position of the enemy. The Japs' fire was constant, and though he moved quickly with his men, DeLong took several shots to the leg. Although severely wounded and knocked to the ground by the enemy fire, he picked himself up and relieved the now deceased flame thrower operator. Crawling to the side of his dead comrade, he succeeded in removing the flaming apparatus, turning on the gas, hoisting himself up to stand and shooting the flame into the opening of the fortified cave.

DeLong fired several rounds from his BAR deep into the cave then peeked around the wall of the cave from the other side, to see if it was clear. As one eye cleared the wall, he tried to focus so that he could discover if there were any Japanese survivors. *Blam!* A Japanese rifle exploded and a bullet blew through his eye and out the side of his temple, wounding him badly and knocking him unconscious to the ground.

Realizing their predicament, Corporal Bitchell and Private First Class "Buck" Davis remained one on each side of the cave mouth behind the cover of the cave wall. They raised their BARs, aiming the noses of their rifles deep into the cave and shot rapid fire in hopes of killing any of the remaining enemy concealed there.

The return fire caused Buck painfully dire wounds in his leg, but he continued to advance toward the slope of the cave, climbing it with great difficulty and while under heavy sniper fire.

Bitchell spoke hurriedly to Buck, the demolition man who hovered on the cave top, and told him to set up a couple of C-4 satchel charges to throw into the still-occupied cave. Buck worked quickly, attaching long ropes to each of the charges so that he and Bitchell could each launch a forty pound pack into the cave. In a synchronized movement, the two men pulled the pins on the charges, then hurled them into the cave by swinging the ropes and releasing their weight deep into its belly. Bitchell ran for cover under some nearby rocks. Buck hunkered down and waited a matter of seconds until the charges exploded. He then slid down the hill, entered the cave with blood running down his pant leg, and killed the surviving members of the enemy gun crew.

Meanwhile, on top of the ridge, above the entrance of the cave, the ground shook violently underneath Duke's feet, knocking him to the ground with the force of the explosion, and Duke knew it was over. The big gun below him had been silenced. A Company's mission was accomplished.

Duke retraced his steps down the ridge. He first passed his squad member and friend, Gallagher, whose bloody form still held his machine gun to his chest, eyes staring at nothing. He saw men from his squad strewn along the path, some being tended by corpsmen. Others were being loaded onto stretchers with blankets drawn over their still faces. There were also Japanese soldiers lying dead and bloodied on the ground. It was an ugly sight. Duke's satisfaction at the team effort that had secured the ridge sank rapidly into sorrow at viewing his comrades dead or morbidly wounded along the way.

Al Costella from mortar platoon came running up beside him. They walked together silently awhile before Al spoke, gently placing his hand on Duke's shoulder. "I saw you, Duke. I saw you up on that ridge, standing alone. I want you to know, it is an honor and a privilege to be fighting by your side."

Duke, choked up by the loss of his squad, nodded his head in appreciation.

The First Marine Division was now able to enter the draw. The successful attack from A Company had made their way clear. It was B and C Company's turn to advance, and they did so immediately. Working their way through the rough terrain, they faced intense Japanese mortar and machine gun fire. The fight was constant every step of the way. By the end of the first day, the First Battalion's total casualties had mounted to more than one hundred twenty-five men. Thus, the draw was renamed by the Marines. It would now and forever be known to them as 'Death Valley'.

May 6th, Lieutenant Colonel A. C. Shofner of the Seventh Regiment took command over the sector vacated by the First Battalion, First Regiment and a new boundary line between the regiments was established.

A Company received a new company commander, Captain James Duffy. Duke also received replacements for his third squad. They were all new recruits—greenhorns, every one of them and hadn't seen a day of battle. Duke passed by the line of men in front of him, eying them individually as he progressed. These men had no idea what they were going to face in battle against Japanese soldiers, but Duke was about to tell them.

"These Japs will kill you! That is their sole focus. Kill or be killed. Fight to the death, then move on. Give no mercy to the Japs, because they won't give you any!"

Not a single recruit moved; all eyes were on their squad leader. He knew they saw a hardened jaw, a strong nose and piercing grey eyes full of determination and purpose. Some of them were probably comforted by his presence. Others recognized and wanted to emulate his strength. But they all looked up to The Indian, he knew.

"One last thing," he said, raising his finger in the air. "We are A Company's third squad of the first platoon! We are the tip of the spear!" Duke pointed at the ground in their midst. "We are the front line!"

A Company moved out, always with a plan. By taking turns with two relays of tanks to move forward, they were able to maintain a continuous attack on Japanese forces. One group of men from a platoon or company would advance and secure their position, then the next group would advance ahead of them. The Japanese didn't have a chance to rearm, and Duke's company, with the rest of the First Battalion, was able to advance. They gained several hundred yards at a time this way and had plenty of time to reload their weapons.

Duke and his squad pushed forward, keeping an eye out for any movement. Thinking quickly as he pinpointed a spider trap on the side of a ridge, Duke slung the strap of his Tommy snugly over his right shoulder and pulled his .45mm pistol out of his belt, securing it in the same hand. As his squad members watched, he moved to the left of the raised, thatched roof of the trap, avoiding the nozzle of the nambu machine gun that was just poking out of it. Then, with his left hand, he lifted the roof of the trap, simultaneously raising and pointing his pistol with his right hand.

The Japanese soldier turned quickly to face him, raising his hands high in the air and smiling widely in surprise. *Blam!* Duke's gun exploded point-blank in his face, killing the man instantly. Dropping the roof of the dead man's grave as he stepped over it, Duke motioned with the pistol still in his hand for his squad to move on ahead with him.

As rain began to pour from the darkened skies, Duke and his third squad ferociously held the front line. For three days and nights, no man slept as they continuously attacked the Japanese. Every member of the squad knew it was kill or be killed.

Firing through the downpour at the slightest hint of movement, the first platoon had to stay alert until another platoon was available to relieve them, and they had no idea when that might be.

It was difficult to maintain a steady position in the mud as any shift of a man's weight made him slip or slide. Duke told the men to stay on their toes, to shake off the sleep that threatened to overtake their weary minds. And so they continued, shooting at all the targets that seemed to pour at them more continuously than the rain. When their relief finally did arrive, Duke and his men collapsed, their bodies exhausted, in the very spot they had been battling the last seventy-two hours.

The First Regiment forged ahead, into Death Valley. The rain had finally stopped, but the ground was still wet and unforgiving, making travel difficult at best. As they approached an area where there was a small cart path, they drew heavy fire from the left side of a ridge. Scanning the terrain with an experienced eye, Duke saw a spot on the right side of the path where a tank could move up and fire on the enemy.

He got on the radio and called HQ. "Get a tank up here!" he yelled into the device. "We're drawing fire from the left, and I've got a spot for a tank to fire directly at them from the opposite side!"

To Duke's surprise, two tanks were sent up. After pointing out the small path and directing the tanks to the vantage point from where they could fire, Duke crouched low and waited. The two tanks moved up together then stopped, just short of the path. Duke ran to the lead tank again, grabbing the outside phone and yelling, "What's the hold-up?"

"We think the path is mined," the tank driver said, "and it's only wide enough for one tank to pass at a time."

"Mined?" Duke was incredulous, but he took charge.

"Listen, you watch me. I'm gonna go ahead of you through there. I'll get over to the other side, then I'll wave you across!"

"Gotcha!" the tank driver said.

In full view of enemy fire, The Indian carefully scoured the ground, searching for any signs that mines had been placed there. He could hear an occasional bullet whizzing by his head, but he stayed intent on his purpose, never once faltering.

When he reached the vantage point, he waved the tanks up and showed them exactly where to go. They managed to position themselves side by side, just as he'd explained, then they fired on the Japanese simultaneously, blasting them off the ridge.

It was time to move on, and there was no time to waste as far as The Indian was concerned. The battalion shuffled through the always drenched and muddy draw, shifting forces. The vegetation-strewn, rocky ridges that lined the path they traveled through were laden with an intimidating number of Japanese soldiers. Shifting a two-tank unit with a squad of men seemed to be reducing their casualties, but the enemy fire was relentless. As they traveled across Okinawa, constant torrents of rain fell from angry skies, and the mud-soaked terrain threatened to engulf the tanks, as well as the soldiers who marched in its snagging mire. Though the temperatures were cooler here than on Peleliu, the rain continually hampered their vision.

The regiment was also advancing through myriad spider traps and machine gun nests. Sniper fire rained from the trees and scant bushes. When caves were detected ahead, the men knew the drill. Soldiers had to steel themselves to face the unending gunfire and to move forward through the limitless miles of uneven terrain in Death Valley. They had to keep their wits about them just to stay alive, but Duke did not allow fear to settle in his mind. He strode forward with a purpose, and the men who moved forward with him gained courage from his savage determination and unflinching strength.

They encountered many peasants along the way, looking for food or medical assistance. Sometimes Japanese officers hid amongst the peasants, infiltrating American lines. Other Japanese soldiers sneaked into the rear of the lines when they found gaps. Some of the infiltrators killed by Americans turned out to have large stocks of American supplies hidden on their person— American cigarettes, chewing gum, chocolates and other candies, as well as the finest C or K rations to be had.

Duke heard that the officers determined they not only needed to increase their security measures in guarding supplies, they also needed to be more alert in defending against pillagers at night. Rear defenses were beefed up during the darkest hours to maintain secure lines.

As night fell, the Marines took turns resting behind the cover of trees, bushes, and rocks, as best they could. Duke stayed alert to the sounds around him. His turn to rest came in the early morning hours after midnight, when the night was at its darkest.

***

One night, Duke leaned back against a rocky ledge, closing his eyes for only a moment. Suddenly, the sounds of screaming, gunfire, and running footsteps filled the air.

Duke jumped up and readied his Thompson machine gun. Mortar platoon fired flares from behind into the black sky, lighting the faces of the yellowish-gray forms that were yelling crazily and running right at them, shooting. At least one hundred-fifty Japanese soldiers raced at them in a line—it was a banzai charge!

Duke went down onto one knee, pumping rifle fire into the screaming faces in front of him. He kept his rapid-fire Tommy moving, finger on the trigger, shooting a deluge of rounds at the maniacal stream of the enemy that ran toward them in what seemed an endless flow. He steadily fanned left, then to the right of the banzai charge, as the pile of dead bodies in front of him began to grow, stacking up like cord-wood in a pile near his feet.

Adrenaline raced through his blood as the line of Japanese men clashed with the front line of the Marines. Not a single Japanese soldier got within three feet of The Indian as he fired. But in the peripheral left of his vision, Duke saw a Japanese officer with his razor-sharp samurai sword raised high. At that moment, the man's sword just beginning to slice through the air, the officer was shot and killed by another Marine. Benovites, a member of Duke's squad, had raised his hand to ward off the falling sword, not realizing the momentum of the dead man's final swing or the sharpness of its blade as it continued to swipe through the air. The sword cut between his thumb and forefinger, down through the inside of his forearm, slicing all the way to Benovites' elbow.

The men on either side of Duke were now engaged in hand-to-hand combat. Some of them stabbed the enemy with their bayonets and Ka-Bar knives. Duke continued to fire his machine gun, never allowing the enemy to get nearer than a few feet away. He battled with his company against the Japanese for what seemed an eternity, until the last of the Japanese were dead. In reality, the chaos and resulting tragic wounds and deaths had occurred in just a matter of fifteen minutes.

Breathing heavily and still holding his machine gun steadily in his hands, Duke replayed the scene of the last bloody moments through his mind. He'd never seen anything like it in his life; he couldn't even have imagined anything like it. The Japanese had deliberately, openly attacked American front lines, knowing they were going to be killed. It was unnerving to experience such a fierce, crazy, suicidal attack, let alone to have survived it.

Duke turned to look at his friend, Benovites, who with adrenaline flowing, apparently hadn't felt a thing since the fine slice of the samurai blade. He watched as Benovites looked down at where the better part of his thumb and forearm had been and saw the man's face register realization, followed by horror and pain. Benovites began screaming in agony at the blood squirting out of his arm and pooling in the dirt. He grabbed at his arm and fell to his knees. Corpsmen were called to him quickly, and they wrapped the bloody appendage tightly to stem the flow of blood. Duke detached himself from the grisliness and watched as they carried his friend away on a stretcher. He never saw Benovites again.

The survivors, though many, had lost a lot of comrades, too. Duke had learned to get used to the scene—the bodies of friends, wounded, dying or dead on Japanese soil. There were times when he made an effort *not* to learn the names of the men around him, because it was easier that way. Somehow, death was less heartbreaking if you couldn't put a name to a face. Still, it was always gut-wrenching to see another Marine dead at the hands of a Japanese soldier. The bodies of the Americans who had died were removed from the scene by corpsmen, ultimately to be returned home to their families.

Duke stayed alert through the rest of the night, but it remained relatively quiet, giving him more time than he would have liked to reflect on the night's events. He wondered how many enemies were still on the island, and how many more times he and his Marine comrades would have to face a banzai charge from them.

When morning broke a few hours later, the piles of Japanese soldiers' bodies littering the ground was horrendous. The stench of their maggot-ridden bodies was strong and permeated his nostrils. Cautiously, Duke rose to a sitting position and looked around him. All was quiet as the sun began to rise on the horizon. He heard a scuffle, then noticed to his left a body crawling on all fours on the ground, moving toward where the dead Japs lay. It was H.T. Clark, the hulking Georgian.

Duke saw his buddy creeping slowly, rifle in hand. He watched Clark draw himself up and onto his knees over the body of a dead Jap lying face down in the mud. Duke watched further, as Clark rolled the body over and raised the butt of his rifle high in the air over the face of the corpse. Flies were staking their claims on the bodies that had already begun to stink with death, and a circle of them surrounded Clark's head as he smashed the butt of the gun forcefully into the dead man's jaw. A dull thud rang out as he hit his target. Dark-red blood pooled out of the side of the dead man's mouth as Clark turned the head this way and that, searching for gold teeth. Intent on his purpose and eying something shiny, Clark raised his rifle again. This time when he brought the butt down, he broke the jaw apart, ripping two gold teeth from the now loosened gum tissue with his Ka-Bar knife, and placing them in his shirt pocket.

Duke watched him for a while and considered whether or not he should expend the energy to collect his own souvenirs. He shook his head, lowering it into his hands. *Let it go,* he thought to himself. *Just let it go.* Sanity had won this battle, as he closed his eyes to rest.

After a short time, Duke's stomach rumbled with hunger. He looked in his pack for the small, inch-sized wrapped package, opening it slowly so as not to drop its contents in the mud. He placed the chunk of chocolate inside his cheek, savoring it as it slowly melted. He didn't know when they would have a chance to eat or rest again, so he leaned back against a rock and tried again to relax.

Unfortunately, A Company was ordered to move to take advantage of the daylight. A handful of soldiers stored their new-found valuables in the pockets of their shirts or in their packs for safety. They trudged all day in the muddy earth, more alert now that they had experienced the lesson of the banzai charge. Every man kept his eyes scanning the ridges ahead and to the sides of them, looking for the slightest movement. The day was fairly uneventful, but the men remained vigilant, continuing their march until nightfall. The same pattern was followed for sleep, men taking turns resting for a time while others kept watch.

Suddenly in the darkness, there was an eruption of shooting bullets, Japanese soldiers screaming, and quick, heavy boot steps on the ground. In his mind, Duke saw the crazy figures running straight at them even before the mortar platoon could light up the sky. He'd already begun fanning his Tommy gun left and right in a slow, steady stream of rifle fire, killing as many of the enemy as he could. There were so many Japanese it didn't seem he could miss. It was like a human wave, crashing into the line of American soldiers. If the Japanese got close enough, hand-to-hand combat ensued. Again, Duke never let the enemy get close to him.

With one knee on the ground, he pummeled the enemy with continuous gunfire, dropping the bodies a few feet from his stance. When the shooting stopped, there was not a single Japanese soldier alive. Duke saw them stacked up like logs, dead, bloody forms in the light of the flares. This banzai charge had lasted only a matter of minutes, but the number of dead men, Japanese and American, lying on the ground was incredible. While corpsmen tended to the wounded and removed the bodies of those Marines who'd been killed, Captain Duffy ordered the remainder of A Company to rest.

And Duke spent another night surrounded by the putrid, dead corpses of Japanese bodies.

Chapter 8

It was May 13th, almost two weeks since the real fighting had begun for the First Marine Division. The First Regiment was still fighting their way through Death Valley, clashing daily—and nightly—with the Japanese enemy. With each battle, lives were lost and Marines wounded, depleting the ranks of men. Squads needed to be replenished. The only available men were either unseasoned young recruits or middle-aged Marines who had spent most of their time in service sitting behind a desk.

Duke learned from Captain Duffy, who'd been briefed by Headquarters, that First Battalion Commander Lieutenant Colonel Ross resumed the duties of Regimental Executive Officer.

The next morning brought more rain and havoc for the tanks and vehicles traveling with them. Waist-deep mud on the only trails available to travel caused many vehicles to be abandoned, and that meant sometimes supplies had to be left behind, too. Whatever supplies soldiers could carry with them were hoisted over the flooded roads and muddy grasslands.

And there was another issue. Duke had only one replacement soldier in his squad who had endured the same battles as he since the second banzai charge. His name was Ace Adams, a young man from Michigan. All the other recruits he'd been sent had either been killed or wounded.

On this morning, Duke was given seven new recruits, every one of them a greenhorn. He walked in front of them and eyed them, sizing them up as he assessed each man. One man in particular was a weightlifter, and Duke thought he would do well in combat. There were other men that didn't look much like fighters, but he'd seen men like that before, and they'd done well when it came to the actual fighting.

Either way, he never got too friendly with the new recruits. He never knew how long they would last. These were the men he had to work with, though, so he would do what was needed to prepare them for their next task.

Over the next few days, A Company traveled through Wana Draw. As they neared the branch of a river, Captain Duffy formulated a plan to get his company across. He knew the enemy was on the other side. To get across, he needed to get a fire team down to the river where they would give cover for the rest of his company to move down to their position. The captain called on his right-hand man, The Indian, to start the process.

Duke got his squad together and gave them their orders. They were to cross through a rice paddy that was four to five feet deep at its deepest point. Duke got in first and moved all the way in and up to the edge of the paddy, where the ground began to slope down and the grass was about thigh-high or a little higher, going down to the river. The rest of the squad followed him in. He ordered Ace to take a few men and start down toward the river. They would be the fire team that would give cover for the rest of the squad to follow.

Just as Ace started down the slope, the Japanese opened up on him. Machine gun and rifle fire spewed from the bushes and rocks, where the enemy was hidden on the other side. Ace took a shot in the leg, and Duke saw he was limping.

Duke yelled, "Get back here, Ace!"

Captain Duffy was positioned behind an embankment not far from Duke. He saw the trouble. "Abdalla! Get 'em out of there!"

"Move out!" Duke yelled to his squad.

But they didn't move; they froze where they were, crouching in the rice paddy. It was as if they'd all gone into collective shock as they were being fired upon.

Duke knew he had to get his men out himself. *These damn greenhorns are gonna get themselves killed, and me along with them!* he thought to himself. *I can't believe they won't budge.* Duke shook his head in disbelief, but he was determined to get everybody out, and quickly.

The Indian jumped up onto the top of the slope that bordered the rice paddy and walked right down the edge. He began with the first frozen figure, "You!" he pointed to the man, demanding his attention, "Out!" He motioned for him to move back to safety behind the ridge. The soldier snapped out of his trance, and did as he was told. Then the next man, "You!" pointing to the man's chest, "Out!" motioning him back. The second man nodded, then followed the first man back. Walking tall while the enemy continued to fire, Duke continued down the line this way, repeating the process until there was only one man left to move.

Just as he was about to order the last man back to safety, he heard Captain Duffy yell, "Abdalla, you crazy fool, get down!"

Duke dove in front of the last man, just behind a ledge, yelling behind him, "Let's go!" Then he rolled to a crouching position and led his men out, all of them staying bent and low as they moved.

They regrouped with A Company where Duke let his men have it. He noticed the weightlifter sitting on a tree stump, shivering. Seeing a blanket on a rock, not knowing or caring where it came from, Duke grabbed it and threw it in the weightlifter's face. He'd watched the man before, flexing his muscles, trimming his mustache...but now Duke was disgusted with him. "Get yourself covered, then get out of here!" he yelled.

Duke turned to Captain Duffy and growled, "Get rid of all of them, they'll get us all killed."

Duffy nodded his head in agreement, knowing he could take Duke's word. Duke had never spoken up before, but the captain knew he was right. He gave orders to move the men out, and radioed to get Duke new replacements immediately.

Duke received replacements that same day. There were not enough men to supplant the positions in his squad, but it was a start. From their location behind the ledge next to the rice paddy, A Company moved more center than where they'd attempted to approach the river on the right side. From their vantage point on the high ground, they could see down the steep grade to the water they still had to cross.

Night was coming on, and darkness had begun to fall. They received orders from behind to stay there for the night and cross the river the next morning. Headquarters had specifically ordered, "The smoking lamp is out," which meant not to light any fires, so as not to draw attention to their position.

Duke couldn't believe his ears. He knew this river was shallow, and the enemy could easily wade across it during the night to infiltrate their troops. Duke wasn't about to let that happen. He could see a series of eight thatched-roof huts along the river bank.

After formulating a plan, he moved to share the details with his friend, Corky Bernard, who hailed from Michigan and was the leader of the second squad. Corky was about ten years older than Duke, but he respected his experience and natural prowess both as a leader and as a fighter. As Duke came up alongside him, Corky nodded a welcome.

Duke leaned toward his friend and spoke softly, "You see those huts down there, by the river bank?" Duke didn't know what was in them, but he knew the thatched buildings would burn. Corky nodded his head, then turned to look at his friend questioningly.

"Let's go down and set 'em on fire," Duke suggested.

Smiling broadly, Corky nodded and said, "Good idea!"

That evening, just as night fell, he and Corky crawled along through the tall grass, cradling their rifles in one hand and a Zippo lighter tucked into their front pants pocket, as they moved forward and down to the bank. Corky worked his way through the middle while Duke worked his way down one end. Once they'd made their way to the huts, each of them ignited four of the eight huts, then high-tailed it back to where their squads were waiting.

All the men watched as the huts went up in flames. The plan had worked beautifully, and it turned out the huts were storehouses for crates filled with highly flammable water filters. Even better, the filters were packed in dry wood chips. Not only did the ensuing blaze keep the enemy from sneaking into their ranks that night by lighting up the night sky, but it allowed the hungry, weary men to heat and eat whatever food rations they had without fear of detection. The fire raged all night long and allowed them to relax a bit, knowing that any Japanese soldier attempting to wade into their camp would be easily discovered and promptly killed.

The next morning, Duke watched as a jeep raced up a muddy road to their camp and stopped abruptly. An officer from HQ was riding in the front seat and looked madder than hell. He jumped down out of the jeep with Captain Duffy following. .The officer strode over to Duke's men. "Who set that fire?" he yelled as he approached the first man.

"I don't know," the man replied, shrugging his shoulders. "It just happened."

The officer asked the next man and received the same response. He walked up to Duke and asked again, "Who set that fire?"

Duke shrugged his shoulders. "I don't know. Maybe a Jap sneaked up last night and set the fires."

"Well, so long as one of ours didn't do it!" the officer huffed. "When I say *no fires*, I mean *no fires, dammit!*"

Duke knew that Captain Duffy, who was standing nearby, highly suspected that he had been the perpetrator, but he respected the fact that the fires had kept the enemy from crossing the river during the night.

As the two men returned to the jeep with the driver, Duffy turned his head and looked at Duke. He smiled broadly and gave a short nod as the officer hopped up into his seat in the vehicle.

Duke turned back to his task of replacing the supplies in his pack, shaking his head and smiling as he reached down to feel the familiar form of the lighter in the front pocket of his trousers.

***

A Company waded through the knee-deep river that day. Each squad took its turn advancing while the other squads gave cover. They encountered no opposition as they crossed the river, and eventually they surmised that the enemy had scattered and moved on sometime during the night.

After crossing the shallow river, they moved on. During their advance, Duke noticed one of the men in his company stoop to pick up a samurai sword that lay next to a dead Japanese officer. The officer had forfeited the sword in battle, and it was to become a souvenir for the lucky Marine. The man stuck it in his belt, undoubtedly feeling fortunate as he continued moving along with his squad.

Duke got more replacements for his squad over the next few days. They traveled toward an area of land that had three distinct, high ridges surrounded by a myriad of smaller ones. The Marines had named the landmark area The Three Sisters. The ridges were heavily occupied by Japanese forces, and the first platoon was there to flush them out. As they arrived at their position, it began raining heavily. It rained all day and throughout that night, making the terrain the mess that had become a common phenomenon on Okinawa. Captain Duffy relayed orders for the first platoon, and Duke prepared his squad to attack the the enemy.

It was difficult to keep a good footing in the sloppy mud as they advanced, shooting at anything and everything that moved ahead of them. A perpetual stream of gunfire surrounded them on three sides. Keeping his eyes trained to detect movement, Duke spotted a grenade spiraling through the air towards him. He knew it was a Japanese grenade because of its color—black—and size; it was smaller than American grenades, and it had a smooth surface.

He hit the deck to try to protect himself from the explosion as the grenade landed close enough to send a large glob of mud spewing up from the ground and into his left eye, temporarily blinding him. It hurt like hell, but he remained concentrated on his task, using his unaffected eye to hone in on the direction the explosive had come from.

Instinctively, Duke knew his enemy would shortly be following the grenade, aiming to finish his kill. Duke jumped up to his knees, then followed the path the grenade had taken. He spotted his target climbing up a bank on the ridge opposite himself. Before the Japanese soldier could gain position, Duke fired his M1 rifle three times, killing his enemy.

When the Japanese soldier went down, Duke used a hand to quickly wipe the mud out of his injured eye. Then he looked over at their platoon sergeant, Stan Bitchell, and motioned with his head to move back. Bitchell nodded his agreement. They both knew their platoon was surrounded, and they had to move back if they were going to survive.

They jumped from shell hole to shell hole as the Japanese continued to bombard them with gunfire. Duke looked around him as they went, noticing a figure hidden underneath a jutting rock. It was H. T. Clark, hiding just under an embankment, shivering violently.

Duke knew Clark had seen too much combat, and that combat had taken its toll on him. Clark was helpless.

Motioning to Bitchell, then indicating Clark's location, they worked their way to Clark, relying on the shallow shelter of holes blown out of the ground by mortar fire to protect them from the heavy gunfire.

Several men from their platoon fired over their heads to give them cover as they made their way to Clark. Duke grabbed Clark by one arm while Bitchell grabbed the other. Keeping a firm hold on the man, Duke pulled a smoke grenade out of his pocket, yanked the pin out with his teeth, and threw it behind himself at an angle. He knew the enemy would fire at the center of the smoke cloud before they sprayed the area with machine gun fire.

Duke and Bitchell began working their way back, shell hole to shell hole. Bitchell threw the next smoke grenade, and Duke threw again after that.

After they handed Clark off to be tended by corpsmen, Duke found a small water hole and rinsed his injured eye. He didn't notice any blood, so he didn't bother reporting the injury to the Navy corpsman. They had enough severely wounded men to tend to. He didn't need to be one of them.

The first platoon headed back toward The Three Sisters the next day, intending to take it from the Japanese. After hours of intense combat, the platoon succeeded in forcing the Japanese to retreat. As the Marines scoured the area for casualties and wounded men, they came upon the body of the Marine who had acquired the samurai sword as a souvenir just days before. Somehow, he had managed to wander into a heavily wooded area to the left of their offensive. The Japanese had captured him and sliced off his head, but not before they impaled him onto a sharpened bamboo stalk and bayoneted him more than twenty times, according to the corpsman who assessed him.

It wasn't the first time Duke and his comrades had found a Marine who had been transpierced onto jutting bamboo, sharpened for the purpose of torture. One such man they found had had his toenails pulled out. Most often, the bodies of the fellow Americans they found had been decapitated—it was a common scene on Okinawa. It reminded the Marines of the ruthlessness of their Japanese enemy. It gave Duke greater resolve to survive and to annihilate the Japs.

Once The Three Sisters area was secured, A Company passed through and continued fighting their way through Death Valley, which had certainly earned its name in Duke's mind, as well as in the mind of any other Marine that passed through its wicked terrain.

It wasn't long before A Company came across another barrier of Japanese soldiers. Duke's platoon was on the front line at the top of a ridge, taking heavy fire from a Japanese infantry that was well-equipped with nambu machine guns. The battle was intense, and all of Duke's attention was on firing his M1 with the power and precision to kill one enemy soldier at a time. Next to Duke, Red Bottomly was firing with quickness and accuracy.

Noticing a movement behind him, Duke looked back and down and saw a crawling figure in brand-new camouflage khakis with a matching helmet. The man was dragging a pair of binoculars and a camera around his neck. "Where's the front line?" the man yelled over the firing.

Duke, wearing his faded and well-worn "salty" uniform, pointed to the ground where he was lying and said, "Right here!"

The man was obviously a war correspondent. "I've got to get some pictures!" he shouted nervously.

"Don't go out there, they'll get you!" Duke shouted back.

The cameraman repeated shakily, "I gotta get some pictures!"

Duke thought it seemed as if the man was trying to convince himself.

Before Duke could stop him, the man snaked his way past the line, advancing some ten to fifteen feet down the slope. The Japanese opened up on him, and Duke heard the guy screaming as he got hit. He watched as the man lay on his back with his knees in the air, screaming and moaning.

"Lie still!" Duke bellowed. "You'll draw another burst!" But the man kept moaning and swaying his knees back and forth in the air. Duke turned to Red and said, "Let's go get him."

Red nodded his head in agreement. "Okay!"

Duke and Red each threw a smoke grenade as they readied themselves to move forward. Once the room-sized clouds were formed, they jumped up and over the ledge of the small ridge, searching for the nearest shell hole for cover. They repeated the process as they moved down to the injured man.

Once there, each of them grabbed him underneath an arm, then simultaneously threw smoke grenades to obscure their path. Again and again, they jumped forward together into the nearest shell hole. The last hurdle was a small ledge of dirt that topped the ridge. Still under fire, they jumped over the ledge, just as the dirt was cut out from under their feet with the precision of a nambu.

In the final moments of the rescue, Red's exposed hand was shot up badly by Japanese machine gun fire. When they made it back to the platoon, they handed off their shell-shocked companion to the corpsmen, and Red sought medical attention for his hand.

The Indian ran back to the front line. Like so many Marines he'd served with before Red, it was the last time Duke saw his companion.

***

Following a long and difficult battle, they were able to move their lines forward. After what had been a horrendous, never-ending journey through Death Valley, the First Marines finally arrived at Shuri Castle. As they approached the plaza from the west, they saw the magnificent building before them. Shuri Castle was a huge and beautiful construction of brightly painted stone bricks, topped by a layered, pagoda-style roof. The rooftop was made of fiery red ceramic tiles that matched the color of the four columns supporting the entryway. A person had to ascend to the building's entrance via a course of narrowing gray stone stair-steps. The plaza, or parade ground, that extended squarely in front of the castle was now vacant, having been emptied before the Marines' arrival.

As Duke was admiring the building, a shadow emerged from the right side of the plaza and began racing across its expanse. Duke raised his M1 rifle in the air, honing in on the Japanese soldier running for his life across the stone ground. Duke could see the man was running toward a couple of buildings standing on the other side.

He fired three times, watching as the soldier stumbled after the third shot but was still able to move on. Once it was concluded that the Japanese had moved out, they verified by radio to headquarters that the castle and surrounding area were secure.

Ancient Shuri Castle, the one-time seat of Okinawa rulers, and a modern symbol of Japanese defense, fell to the Americans. The Regiments Executive Officer, Lieutenant Colonel R.P. Ross, Jr., raised the American flag over the castle. It was now in the hands of the United States Marines Corps.

On June 21st, the men heard through word of mouth that all fighting had stopped on Okinawa. They had battled for the island, and they had taken it. The Battle of Okinawa was over, and it was time to celebrate. They stayed in the area near Shuri, then received orders to travel back north, back the way they had come. It seemed a shame to have to travel back through the memories of battles that they had completed, of comrades killed, or wounded—of friends who were lost—but the Marines followed orders and headed north.

When they finally arrived at the entrance of Death Valley, Duke looked over at the long, hog-back ridge, and remembered his squad of men that had been wounded or lost in taking it. He thought about his friend, John Brady, and wondered how he was recuperating from the severe burns he'd gotten there.

They moved on, and after a few days of traveling, when they came to a flat expanse of land, they stopped and set up camp. The tents they pitched were supported by four sturdy corner-posts, atop which lay a pitched roof. Each tent-side had a flap that could be raised to let in cool air. It was a nice set-up, and the men appreciated it.

New supplies were received that provided a ten-in-one ration for food; that is, it provided one day's food for ten men. It was the best food Duke had tasted since the hospital ship USS *Bountiful*. His favorite meal included the meat that looked and tasted like glazed ham with biscuits and canned green beans on the side, and a chocolate bar for dessert.

Near the camp, some men found a fifty-five gallon drum they cleaned out and began using to prepare jungle juice in order to celebrate that the fighting had stopped on Okinawa. Now they had some ingredients available to them, some valuable ingredients. They had sugar cubes, canned biscuits (for yeast), powdered juice drinks, raisins, cherries, honey and fruit preserves— all of which made their way into the fifty-five gallon container. Sugar cane, pineapple, and papaya were locally grown produce that could be found to add to the growing pungency of the juice. After all the ingredients were added, the Marines waited for the juice to ferment.

August 6th, the atomic bomb was dropped on the city of Hiroshima, Japan.

August 9th, a second atomic bomb was dropped on the city of Nagasaki, Japan.

August 15th, word came that Japan had announced its unconditional surrender to the Allied Powers.

The Marines didn't wait until the papers were officially signed. To Duke and the men in the first platoon, the announcement meant the Pacific War was over, and back on May 8, Germany had already surrendered. World War II was finally over!

For the first time in a long time, Duke allowed his thoughts to wander Stateside. He wondered how things might have changed over there. He contemplated whether or not he could get his job at the factory in Chicago back—he loved living in the city. Then he thought about how his mother might be faring in South Dakota. *Boy, it'd be great to see her again! I can't wait to taste one of her homemade apple pies,* he thought to himself. It was one of the first times he had even allowed himself to consider that he would actually be going home.

The war was finally over! That meant there was really something to celebrate. In seconds, each man had his canteen cup in hand, ready to dip into the drum filled with jungle juice and enjoy!

Duke dipped his own tin cup into the drum and joined his comrades in drinking the slimy, green juice filled with cherries. It didn't taste so great, but it served its purpose. The men of A Company shouted "Hallelujah!" all around him, laughing with each other in celebration of the end of the war.

For the next several hours it felt like they were free—really free! Duke and his comrades talked about going home, about seeing family and friends. He told the men in his tent about his mother's fried chicken and that he planned to eat a whole plateful of it when he got back. He could almost hear it sizzling and smell it frying in the pan. He wore a wide grin for the rest of the afternoon, remembering and sharing the best of his recollections of home.

It was finally over. No more fighting. It gave The Indian a sense of relief, of peace. Every man in the camp got drunk that day and reveled in the knowledge that they would be going home soon. After several hours of celebrating, several of them began throwing up the vile, still-raw beverage. It didn't help that they hadn't eaten a square meal since they'd left the States.

Watching other men get sick made Duke's stomach queasy. He began vomiting up the foul, green juice as well. At one point he could not control the spasms or the heaving, and he spewed bright red cherries onto the ground like a machine gun. "Have another one!" was the chorus heard 'round camp. It wasn't until the drum was empty that Duke managed to make it back to his cot to lie down before he passed out, exhausted…but victorious and smiling.

Chapter 9

The morning following the news of Japan's surrender, Duke and the other men heard about the celebrations back home in the States. News traveled fast when President Truman announced he'd received a message from the Japanese government saying they were willing to surrender unconditionally. People all over America were cheering and enjoying festivities. In New York, Times Square was filled with men and women in uniform—dancing, singing and shouting with happiness.

At Pearl Harbor, in Hawaii, where it all began for Americans, there were parades and cheering in the streets. All over the United States, servicemen were seen kissing girls in jubilation over the news that the war was finally over. When the men on Okinawa heard about the celebrations, excitement permeated the camp. Duke and the rest of the soldiers couldn't wait to get home to join in the festivities.

Two weeks later, on September 2th, 1945, on board the USS *Missouri* in Tokyo Bay, General Douglas MacArthur, senior officer present, accepted the Japanese surrender to the United States and its Allies. World War II was officially over they heard, but no orders had been given yet on Okinawa as to the First Marine Division's next assignment. Duke bided his time with the rest of A Company.

One day seemed to roll into the next as they waited. Stories were swapped between men who had survived the war, and many hopes were revealed concerning the journey home. It was one such afternoon, when the men were relaxing in their tents, that the breeze suddenly turned cooler. The skies darkened and the winds stirred, a forewarning of what was to come. The heavens seemed to open up all at once, depositing torrents of rainwater on the camp.

It was a typhoon!

The wind gusts from the storm ripped all of the tent-posts right out of the ground as men struggled to remain under the cover of their tents. Duke's tent collapsed, pinning his tent-mates and him where they lay. Water poured so heavily from the skies, it felt like five-gallon buckets were being dumped repeatedly onto their backs underneath the canvas. Their clothing was drenched, and they were soaked through to their skin.

Just then, Duke noticed some fidgeting under the tent. It was his friend, Calliqueri, fumbling with an object on the ground. Suddenly, music streamed from under the tent where Calliqueri lay, cranking a pint-sized record player. The strains of the "Marines' Hymn" could be heard throughout the water-soaked tent. All of the men laughed at the ludicrous situation. Then they began to sing along with the music. "From the Halls of Montezuma, to the shores of Tripoli, We fight our country's battles, in the air, on land, and sea; first to fight for right and freedom, and to keep our honor clean; We are proud to claim the title, of United States Marine!"

Amidst the howling winds and violent rains, Duke listened to the voices around him and drew comfort from the familiarity of the men, as well as from the words they sang together.

As he joined the chorus, chanting in a low voice, he thought about the endless days he'd spent away from home, away from friends and family. He thought about the lucky men and women who'd already gotten a ticket back to the States, and it gave him hope that his turn was not far off. He and these men had weathered many violent battles together.

But many of his friends had paid the ultimate sacrifice of giving their lives to win this war. He sang on behalf of those men who had died, and in brotherhood with the soldiers who had survived. When the storm finally passed, the soldiers cleared the area of debris, then set to the task of putting the tent-posts back into the ground.

***

The next few weeks were uneventful, as the First Marine Division settled into monotony. While he was resting in his tent, Duke received a message that Captain Duffy wanted to see him. It seemed Corporal Bitchell's hand had been wounded somehow, and he required medical attention that couldn't be provided in the camp. Captain Duffy offered Duke the position of platoon sergeant. "Corporal Loren Duke Abdalla, I'd like to offer you the honor of becoming acting platoon sergeant of the first platoon." He went on to say, "This is not a formal promotion, but you would be serving your Country well to accept."

"Then I accept, proudly, Sir!" Duke answered with a smile and a salute.

Captain Duffy further informed Duke that the First Regiment was being sent to Tientsin, China, to maintain law and order. Following their surrender, the Japanese were no longer to have a military presence there. Duke relayed the news to his platoon concerning their next assignment. He informed them that it wasn't yet their time to head home. They spent the next week awaiting orders to move out.

The days wore on as the men sought ways to pass the time. During the middle of one lazy afternoon, the tell-tale darkness of another typhoon crept into camp. The wind followed quickly, making the tent-flaps clap rhythmically from its force. Then the rain began to fall, heavily and all at once. The wind came, dancing the rain sideways through Duke's tent, from one side to the other. Within minutes, everything and everyone under the tent was soaking wet. Gusts of wind carrying buckets of water splashed their way through the camp for another twenty or thirty minutes, then stopped blowing abruptly. The tent posts had remained intact this time, but there was debris scattered everywhere on the ground.

Clean up was the first order of business, followed by hanging up shirts and pants on a line to dry. In the late summer sun on Okinawa, that didn't take long.

With so much time on his hands, Duke had plenty of time to consider his journey thus far. He'd gone from being a strong, young athlete from a small town in South Dakota to an eager young man intent on earning his way in Chicago. After enlisting in the Marines, he'd been tagged as one of the best and trained as a rifleman and machine gunner. Then he experienced Pavuvu, which he had managed to survive, enjoying the friendships he'd formed there.

Next came Peleliu, a horrible massacre of his friends and comrades. The wounds he'd received had nearly killed him, but he had survived to fight again on Okinawa. He had even survived Death Valley. It was a strange feeling, sitting on his cot, at the age of twenty, to be at ease with his surroundings. It was good knowing there wouldn't be any more Japanese soldiers racing at him in the night, illuminated by flares that lit up the night sky. But what was next for him?

A Company tents.

115

Chapter 10

They were on their way to China; Captain Duffy told Duke to have the men pack up and move out that morning. It wasn't long before they were aboard a troop ship, grateful to watch the coast of Okinawa fading from their vision. The trip to China was relatively short, just a few days' travel. The Chinese banks were lined with dark-haired Chinese peasants, wearing dark, almost uniform-like clothing. They were there to cheer on the Marines as they passed in their boats. When the boats arrived in Tientsin, all the Marines disembarked.

The First Regiment was ordered to march in parade formation to the British barracks. They marched four abreast down the narrow Chinese streets, made narrower by the hordes of people lining them. Duke led his first platoon proudly through the streets of Tientsin. There were Chinese musicians and local civic organizations, dancers on stilts and school children, all gathered to celebrate as the Marines passed by. Some of the groups wore masks and colorful costumes, but they all cheered wildly as the members of the First Marine Division marched by.

As they reached the British barracks, their lines were down to single file due to the happy, smiling crowds pressing in on them and narrowing their path. When they arrived, Duke was given the duty of Sergeant of the Guard. He was told there were twelve Japanese sentries yet to be relieved from their duties at the local airport, and he wasted no time in attending to the task.

He went to the motor pool and got a bright yellow flatbed truck. There were no windows in the truck, and the steering wheel was oddly placed on the right-hand side of the vehicle. Next, he ordered the Corporal of the Guard to ride with him to the airport, along with twelve Marine guards he motioned to hop up on the back of the truck for the ride. He and the corporal were each armed with a Thompson sub-machine gun, in case they encountered resistance.

When they reached the airport, he relieved one Japanese sentry at a time, replacing each man with a U.S. Marine Guard. After loading the Japanese sentries onto the bed of the truck, he took them back to the barracks and placed them behind bars in the guardhouse where they remained until further notice.

The next day, the Japanese government agreed to surrender in Peking, China, so they would no longer have a military presence there. This meant Duke had performed his last duty of World War II. Corporal Bitchell had returned to A Company earlier that day but was assigned to a different platoon with A Company. Still, it wasn't long before Duke, Bitchell, Calliqueri, Bureau and a greenhorn they called Chick joined forces and headed toward town to enjoy their liberty.

At the edge of the barracks, Bitchell and Bureau motioned for a few rickshaw drivers to stop. Duke saw what he was told by Chick was a rickshaw. It was a small carriage-like seat set on wheels and powered by a single man lifting two oar-like handles which were attached to the seat. The young man carrying this particular rickshaw was running down the narrow street with two Marines as passengers. Next, he saw a carriage that was attached to the back wheel of a bicycle. The ride looked a bit smoother this way, Duke thought to himself, and it certainly moved faster. He thought this was a great way to travel the rough streets of the city.

Duke chose a bicycle-driven rickshaw for himself, whose driver's name was Koda Lung. He was a strong young boy with an eagerness to work, but then, it seemed all the Chinese people were dogged workers. They had the greatest intentions of accomplishing their tasks to perfection, and somehow, they managed to do it by working hard and remaining solely focused.

While Duke and his friends were stopped, several Chinese men approached each of them individually to exchange currency with the American soldiers, which at the current rate was one American dollar to eighteen-hundred Chinese dollars. He and his friends made their exchanges quickly, each leaving with a wad of Chinese cash that amounted to about ten American dollars.

Once these details had been handled, the men urged their drivers to town to celebrate. They chose the finest restaurant in Tientsin, a landmark restaurant that had been boasted about for its fanciness and also came highly recommended by Koda.

The double-front doors opened into a large, ornately decorated entryway that was bordered by fiery, bright red walls. Glass shelves along the walls held ornamental statues of Chinese maidens coquettishly half-covering their painted faces with fans. As the men entered the dining area, the painting on the back wall grabbed Duke's attention. The entire back wall of the restaurant was an enormous mural, resplendent in its color and detail, of Custer's Last Stand, which evoked memories of his home in South Dakota. The latest American musical hits streamed over the loud speakers in the room. Songs like "I Love You" by Bing Crosby, "Till the End of Time" by Perry Como, "On the Atchison, Topeka and the Santa Fe" by Johnny Mercer, "Sentimental Journey" by Doris Day, and a personal favorite of Duke's, "Besame Mucho" by Jimmy Dorsey.

Girls with brightly painted faces were brazenly dressed in skimpy, beaded red, orange and yellow colored dresses. They lined both side walls of the establishment. Most of the girls were young, Duke surmised. Their doll-like faces were garishly covered with makeup. They wore a bold rouge on their cheeks, bright blue eye shadow on their lids and their lips were a glaring red. Duke hadn't had a woman in over two years, and he and the other men were beyond excited. The girls were chittering and smiling at the Marines. The men didn't have to choose; all of the girls were available to please them.

Duke knew what a gold mine they'd found. He and his buddies convinced the owner of the restaurant to close the front doors if the five of them would pay him for their privacy. The owner agreed. The dinner selections were elaborate. Duke had a nice, big juicy steak and a good-sized piece of fish. The chef served the fish by slicing neatly underneath the steak-sized fillet, eliminating the skin and bones, then gently laying the fruit-glazed fish onto Duke's plate. Bitchell had two orders of steak-and-eggs; he couldn't seem to get enough of fresh eggs as far as Duke was concerned. For the next several hours, Duke, Bitchell, Calliqueri, Bureau, and Chick ate all the food they could, drank all they could of the Chinese beer and Russian vodka, and "socialized" with the girls.

Duke noticed daylight cracking its way into the room through small slits that opened between the heavily lined drapes and realized they had to get back to the barracks. He called the owner to the table and asked what their total bill for the night was.

All of the men were drunk from having imbibed through the night, but Duke paid close attention as the owner set a wired rack with little black balls floating on each of several wires in front of him on the table. The man proceeded to push the little black balls this way and that for what seemed a minute or two, then slapped his hand on the table when he'd finished. He informed Duke that the total bill was a little over 27,000 Chinese dollars.

It took the men several minutes to figure out that 27,000, divided by five men was 5,400 Chinese dollars. And with the exchange, that brought the grand total to three American dollars apiece for the bill. Duke and his buddies thought it was the best deal they'd ever been given!

Duke settled in to his life in Tientsin well. He had a little over eight-hundred dollars on the books about now, and he took in approximately fifty-five dollars a month. He made arrangements with Koda to be his permanent driver, to be available to take him anywhere he wanted to go in Tientsin for eight dollars a month. Having assimilated how things worked in China, Duke set about hiring a Number One Boy to clean the barracks for the entire first platoon. He offered the position to a young boy recommended by Koda. The boy's name was Dewey, and he was eager to accept.

Within a matter of minutes, Dewey had assigned boy number two, boy number three, and as many other boys as were needed to clean the entire platoons barracks. In China, no Americans performed the daily chores. The boys cleaned the rooms, made the beds, did the laundry, shined the men's shoes, ran errands, and after being shown how to do it once or twice, even cleaned the rifles. The total cost for Duke to provide the complete service for his platoon was six American dollars a month, and the whole platoon appreciated it.

Duke felt like a king. He had Dewey performing all of the cleaning duties at the barracks and running errands whenever he was needed. Koda kept the bicycle-driven rickshaw polished and looking brand-new, and he chauffeured Duke wherever Duke needed to go. *This is the life!* Duke smiled to himself.

Fruits and vegetables and other fresh foods were available in town for a pittance. There were also carts selling fine silks, hair ornaments, jewelry and other souvenirs. Anything the men wanted was readily available. What made it difficult for Duke to enjoy the luxuries was witnessing the starving Chinese men and women who hovered around the barracks daily, waiting for their chance to grab remnants of meals from the slop buckets that were put out at the end of each meal. Or the civilians dressed in rags, trying to survive in an economy that had been severely depleted.

One afternoon Duke asked Koda to drop him off in town near a local market. As Koda rode off to run errands, Duke noticed a young woman near one of the vegetable carts. She was beautiful. Her wide, almond-shaped brown eyes were fringed with long, dark lashes in her porcelain face. Her hair was wound tightly into a knot at the back of her head and kept neatly in place by a hand-painted comb. She stared down at the ground and smiled when she noticed Duke looking at her. Her mother looked up then, to see why the young woman had stared down, and gave Duke a nod and a smile.

Immediately, Duke moved closer to the cart and asked the ladies if they spoke English. They looked back at him with blank expressions.

Duke yelled to the townspeople around him, "Anyone around here speak English?" Frantically he looked for someone to respond to his query, but no one replied to him.

"Does anyone here speak English?" he asked again.

Finally a young man stepped up to him, "I speek Eenglesh." The young man spoke with a heavy Chinese accent, and Duke guessed he was hoping for an opportunity to earn some money.

"Ask her what her name is," Duke ordered the young man.

After making the inquiry, the man turned to Duke and said, "Liuchen Ling."

"Tell her my name is Loren Duke Abdalla."

The man did as he was asked. With the help of the Chinese man, Duke, the young lady, and her mother had a pleasant conversation. Duke and Liuchen exchanged information and made plans to see each other again, with her mother's approval. When they had said their good-byes for the day, Duke turned to his interpreter and thanked him for his services, pressing a dollar bill into his open palm.

Duke noticed that Koda had returned with the rickshaw, and supposed that he'd been waiting on him awhile on the side of the street. Smiling broadly as they made their way back to the barracks, Duke relayed the story of his afternoon encounter with the lovely Chinese girl and her mother. He told Koda that he had made an appointment to meet the two again the next day, and gave him the address. When they ate at mess that night, Bitchell kept asking him why he was smiling like an idiot. Duke hadn't decided whether or not he would share his encounter with his friends quite yet. They might get ideas of their own to interfere. Duke held the picture of Liuchen's beautiful face in his mind's eye as he slept restlessly that night.

***

The next day in the afternoon when Duke visited Liuchen and her mother, he found that the two women lived in a small, cubicle-like apartment with a single cot for them to share. After Duke and Liuchen had been seeing each other awhile, Duke found he'd begun to care for her very much. He was determined to set the women up in a nicer home. With Koda Lung's help, Duke found out that he could rent an apartment, with daily meals included, for eight dollars a month. Liuchen and her mother were very pleased and appreciated his generosity. Any time that he had available, Duke spent visiting with Liuchen in her new apartment.

One morning after mess, the regiment was called to formation. A replacement platoon leader had not yet been assigned, so as platoon sergeant, Duke stood proudly in front of the first platoon. An awards ceremony had been arranged, honoring Marines who had made extraordinary efforts during the battles on Okinawa. Acts of heroism and remarkable devotion to duty were to be rewarded and duly honored. The speaker addressed the regiment with words of honor and reverence for the First Marines' feats in their extended history. He reminded them that they were the oldest outfit in Marine Corps history and held the reputation of being the best.

Second Lieutenant Robert A. DeLong, as Rifle Platoon Leader, was announced to have received the Navy Cross for relieving a mortally wounded flame thrower operator by retrieving the apparatus, and though he was severely injured, shooting the flame into the heavily fortified cave that housed a large cannon. He fought until he was wounded again, this time being rendered unconscious. The announcer shared with them that Second Lieutenant DeLong was not in attendance, as his injuries had forced him to return to the States to recover.

Milton Gilbert "Buck" Davis was awarded the Navy Cross for constructing two forty-pound satchel charges, one of which he managed to swing into the cave after having received painful leg injuries which bled profusely and still climbing the cave wall to complete his task, then continuing down the wall of the cave and firing into its depths to kill any remaining enemies.

Corporal Stanley L. Bitchell received the Navy Cross for his efforts in destroying the big gun in the cave on the long, hog-back ridge in early May of 1945. He also destroyed an additional three machine guns and demolished several more caves, killing twelve of the Japanese.

Joseph Bureau and Clarence Bleau each received the Silver Star for gallantry in action by knocking out several spider traps around the base of the same ridge that Duke and his squad had cleared. Duke waited anxiously to hear the words that he believed he deserved to hear.

But they never came...

He received no citations, no awards. No recognition for extraordinary efforts of heroism, no recognition for the extreme devotion to duty throughout so many battles he had been witness to and participated successfully in. They hadn't even mentioned that Duke's third squad had completed their mission to clear the path for the other two squads to reach the big gun in the cave, him clearing the last two machine gun nests himself. It didn't make any sense *not* to award him.

Then it dawned on him that there could be an underlying indifference, an unwritten law, motivated by an unspoken prejudice against Native Americans. The Indian, after all, was not just a nickname given to Duke. It was his heritage.

Duke never said a word. He never complained to anyone about not receiving recognition. It wasn't politically correct to talk about these things…race or creed. He was happy to have been part of the team that made the effort to take the ridge and silence the big gun. But they all knew, all the rest of A Company.

For Duke, it was enough to know that the men who had served with him knew his abilities and his motivation. They'd seen him at war, and they'd seen him fearlessly kill the enemy. They'd also watched him risk his own life, under heavy fire, to save another man's life—more than once. And they admired him for his skills, as well as for his loyalty. Medals were not the reason why the Marines fought for their country; they were proud fighting warriors defending the Constitution of the United States of America.

After the ceremony, Duke and the attendees returned to their barracks. There was no discussion regarding the awards that had been given or those that had not been received.

Duke writes a note to his friend, Stan Bitchell on his Marine photograph.

Duke and his #1 boy Koda Lung in Tientsin.

Bicycle-driven rickshaw.

Liuchen Ling, Duke's girlfriend, in China.

A Company.

Blue Diamond 1st Marine
Division Patch.

OK Bar in China.

Night on the town in China, Left to Right: Duke Abdalla, Corky Bernard, Joe Bureau,
Chic Alfonzo Calliqueri, Stan Bitchell, and newly assigned Lieutenant (name unknown) in
Center.

Chapter 11

Several weeks passed before a lieutenant arrived at the barracks and was assigned as platoon leader for the first platoon. The man hadn't seen a day of fighting and was not familiar with life in Tientsin. Noticing some debris on the grounds of the barracks, he ordered Duke, "Have the men fall out for police duty!"

"I can't do that, Lieutenant," Duke said, shaking his head at the same time.

"Why not?" the lieutenant responded indignantly.

"Because that's Chinese work; they do all the work around here and get paid for it. That's their way."

Duke watched as the lieutenant stormed off to Captain Duffy's office and strode through the door after giving a quick knock. He proceeded to complain about Duke to his captain.

Duffy turned on the man. "If there is anything you need to know about A Company, ask Duke Abdalla!" He towered over him as he reprimanded him in voice and posture until the lieutenant had no option but to back into the wall of the office in complete defeat.

Returning to the barracks, the new platoon leader immediately apologized to Duke and made quick friends with him. Duke knew Duffy had his back, and everything returned to normal.

***

Barney Rourke was a Mohawk Indian from New York who was assigned to Duke's platoon, following his service with the Fifth NE Aircraft Unit, where his targets had been Japanese planes. Duke made an easy friendship with him when Barney arrived at the compound. Their heritage paired them into an unnamed category they both understood, and they shared many a card game, as well as heartfelt conversation.

While Duke was resting on his bunk on an early afternoon in March 1946, he heard Captain Duffy's voice as he made his way to his room. He invited Duke and Barney to town for drinks. The three of them piled into their rickshaws and were carried to town in minutes. Rosie's Bar was located on a street corner not far from the restaurant where Duke had eaten when he'd first arrived in Tientsin over six months ago.

The three men sat at the bar on bamboo stools, and they each ordered a beer. It wasn't long before Barney began telling his stories of shooting down Japanese Zeroes. Captain Duffy regaled him with the story of how Duke had jumped up on the edge of a rice paddy near a river, amidst heavy enemy fire, demanding that his fear-stricken squad members scuttle back to safety behind a ridge. Duffy also shared the story of the "no fire" order that had been given that night, and after much needling, and a lot of prompting, Duke finally shared the story of how he and Corky Bernard had crawled down a hill on their bellies at night, with Zippo lighters in their pants pockets, to set fire to the Japanese storage huts.

"That fire lit up the sky all night long!" Duke chortled. "We cooked our food over open flames—no Japs would've dared to cross the river that night."

"I knew it was you!" Duffy pointed a finger at his friend, then smacked his knee with his free hand. Duke and Captain Duffy laughed until they were out of breath, remembering the look on the face of the officer who was trying to determine who'd set the huts on fire. Barney laughed just as hard with them. Beer flowed freely for the remainder of the evening, and it was a night Duke would not soon forget.

***

Duke knew the order was imminent, but when word finally came that he was to be shipped back to the States, his heart was heavy. There was no way he could bring Liuchen and her mother with him; it wasn't allowed. He had come to love Liuchen, but felt their fate had been decided by their circumstances. Still, he was eager to go home and return to his life in the States.

The week before Duke was to ship out, he went to see Liuchen and her mother. After drawing all of his money out of the bank, he gave most of it to the beautiful Chinese girl. It amounted to about three hundred American dollars. Duke knew it would be enough money to cover their living expenses for at least two years.

Liuchen was not only beautiful, but intelligent, and Duke trusted she would be all right. He told her that he cared for her deeply and always would. He tried to explain why he had to go, but she silenced him by putting a finger gently to his lips.

After she walked Duke to the door of their apartment, she threw her arms around his neck with a sob. Holding her face in his hands, Duke kissed her long and hard.

Using his thumbs, he gently wiped her tears away, promising that everything would be alright. She smiled weakly, then nodded her head in resignation and acceptance of their situation.

Duke walked out the door and down the steps to the street, plunging his hands deep into his pockets and walking slowly back to the rickshaw.

He stayed on the grounds of the barracks the next day. The afternoon was spent playing cards with his buddies. The evening passed slowly, with thoughts of Liuchen plaguing his mind. Al Costella noticed Duke's reticence and invited him out with a few of the boys for some drinks at Rosie's bar in town. Duke went along with his friends, and by the end of the evening, had managed to drink himself into a state of oblivion.

He tried to remember the words to the songs his buddies were singing, but couldn't quite focus his thoughts. So he hummed along, slapping his hand on the tabletop, in what he thought was keeping time with the music. When Rosie kicked them out of the bar in the early morning hours, Koda was there to help a stumbling Duke climb into the rickshaw for the ride back to the barracks. When they arrived, Duke stepped clumsily out of the rickshaw and made his way to his bunk. He plopped himself down, fell back onto his pillow, and snored loudly until late morning.

Marine recruitment officers approached Duke later that day in his barracks. The officers told him that if he chose to re-enlist for an additional six months after his tour and stay in China, he would receive a promotion to gunnery sergeant. Duke considered it for a moment, but he had already made his decision to return to the States. He thanked the officers for the opportunity, then respectfully declined.

All of Duke's bags had been neatly packed by Dewey the morning he was to ship out.. The boy carried them to Duke's waiting carriage, and Duke handed him a hearty tip and shook his hand in thanks. When they arrived at the dock, Koda lifted Duke's bags from the rickshaw, then set them at the foot of the gangway. Duke also tipped Koda generously and thanked him for all of his help in getting around Tientsin. He waved him off before boarding the ship, but when he turned back to look at Koda after exiting the ramp, he saw him smile broadly and swing his arm in a wide arc over his head in a friendly good-bye. Duke smiled back and waved vigorously.

As the ship left the bay, Duke stood out on the stern of the deck, watching the land disappear. He gave himself up to the sounds of the engines powerfully pushing the ship toward home. No evasive zigzag maneuvers were required on this trip across the Pacific.

The wind ripped through his hair and pushed his cheeks back as he smiled at the thought of returning to the States. He hadn't seen his mother in a long time, and the thought of seeing her again brought a big grin to his face. The newsreels he and the rest of the platoon had watched at the barracks had shown soldiers celebrating and being greeted at the piers by beautiful women upon their return. Duke looked forward to docking in San Diego, and to his welcome home.

Chapter 12

The trip home was the longest trip Duke had yet taken. Not because of the distance, but because his destination was a world away from how he had been living for so long. He had difficulty remembering what it was like to spend an evening in the city lights and sounds. He couldn't remember the last time he'd talked to a girl from the States or watched a live ball game. He was curious as to what was happening at home, all at once—and he couldn't wait to find out!

Duke spent many mornings on the deck of the ship, looking ahead at the expanse of blue ocean, willing the sight of land into his vision. On the morning he could finally make out the silhouette of the bay on the horizon, his excitement was overwhelming.

The energy on the ship was electric as they neared the coast of San Diego. Duke made sure all his gear was packed and ready as the ship's crew made preparations to dock. Their peaceful travel across the deep blue waters of the Pacific Ocean was about to end. They were home!

He took two steps at a time, as he made his way up the narrow steps to the deck. He, and every other Marine returning home on the ship, climbed up as far as the crowded gangway allowed. They all wanted to see the people gathered at the docks to greet them as they landed—like they had seen in the movies back in the barracks at Tientsin.

As the ship came to a complete halt, the crews tied the massive ropes up to the pier.

But where were the crowds? Where was the welcoming committee? Except for the ground crews dressed in naval attire, no one was there to greet the men returning home from war. There were no women, no photographers, no parades to welcome these fighting men home. Nothing could have prepared Duke and the other Marines for the disappointment of their silent return.

Duke saw the letdown evident in the slumped shoulders and dropped chins of the men on board surrounding him. They couldn't even look at one another as they grabbed their duffel bags and headed to the ramp to disembark from the ship.

Duke looked around for a familiar face on the pier but saw no one he knew. He continued to walk to the main drive where a bus was waiting to take him and some of the others to Camp Elliot. When he arrived at the camp, he stepped off the bus and scanned the grounds with wizened eyes. A sense of distant familiarity mixed with sadness filled his mind. He'd lost many friends in this war and at that moment he felt very alone.

He watched as new recruits assembled, their eyes forward, shoulders back, standing stiffly at attention as orders were barked from the wide mouth of the drill sergeant.

What a long way away they were from the place he was now. Had he ever been that young?

Duke continued on to the barracks, contemplating his future. He still had some months left on the books before he could apply for an honorable discharge, but at least he was able to finish his tour in the States. He wasn't sure how long he would have to wait until he received his next orders. Still, he wanted to write to his mother and let her know that he was home and safe. In her last letter, she had explained to Duke that she didn't have the money to get a phone installed yet. Duke would have loved to hear her voice just then.

Instead, he stowed his pack, pulled out a piece of paper and a pen, and sat down to write a letter to his mother in South Dakota. His mother had also explained that she'd developed a relationship with a man from town. Duke didn't know much about the man, and he hadn't really cared until this moment. He only hoped the man was the right one for his mother.

After penning a few lines, he finished with his signature *Love, Duke* and addressed the envelope. It'd be a few days before she received the letter, but Duke could imagine her happiness when she read the news.

A few weeks later, Duke received the transfer to Camp Smalls at the Great Lakes Naval Base, located on the north side of Chicago, Illinois. They sent him on a bus to the train station in San Diego.

Throwing his bag onto a seat, he sat down and weathered the bumpy ride to the station. When he arrived, he tossed his bag over his shoulder and jumped off the bus. He looked around to see if anyone he knew was taking the same train. He couldn't find a familiar face, so he sought out a car that had empty seats available and boarded the train. Promptly finding a window seat, he stowed his bag underneath, then sat down and settled himself for the ride.

He watched the other passengers as they were boarding. Not one of them gave him a second glance as they searched for a seat to occupy; he was just another man in uniform.

Duke leaned back and closed his eyes. This certainly wasn't a Pullman car, but it was taking him where he needed to go. Strange, how once he'd experienced the finest of amenities, the comparison still lingered.

There were a handful of stops along the way, but Duke didn't bother to get off until the train stopped in Chicago. He recalled the soft, cushioned seats of the Pullman car. The beginning of an adventure, he had thought then. Randomly, memories of war pervaded his psyche. Images flashed into his mind, and it took a conscious effort to replace those horrible, haunting images with happier memories. He thought of his mom with a smile on her lovely face. He thought about his friends in Chicago and all the good times they'd shared, and how much he was looking forward to seeing them again. As the disturbing images faded and were replaced with more positive hopes for the future, Duke drifted off to sleep, lulled by the rocking movement of the train.

When he arrived at the base, he was told he had earned a ten day furlough. It didn't take Duke long; he'd never even unpacked his bags. He found a train headed to Sioux City, Iowa which was the closest he could take the train to Wagner, South Dakota. When he stepped off that train, he spotted his mother right away, there at the station to pick him up and take him home.

She smiled at him and waved her hand over her head, then as he broke the distance between them, she ran forward and embraced him with a big squeeze. Duke kissed his mother's cheek and hugged her back, finally feeling the welcome home he'd been waiting for.

She pointed out her old, red truck parked on a side street, and they walked quickly toward it to get out of the cold. Remnants of snow lingered on the streets from a late blizzard that had hit in the middle of April.

Duke opened the passenger door and helped his mother into the truck. He threw his gear into the bed of the truck and slid into the driver's seat. They shared lively conversation on the way to her new home in Wagner. He no longer considered Wagner to be his home; you couldn't earn a decent wage here. He planned on making a living in Chicago once he received his discharge.

His mother and her boyfriend, Melvin Kranig, lived in a small shack of a house made up of one bedroom and a decent-sized kitchen with a small wooden table surrounded by four chairs. There was no porch, but they had set two chairs out in front of the house where they could sit and watch the setting sun or the slow-moving waters of the Missouri River passing by. The view of the river from the house was stirring. The sun was sitting low in the sky and its yellow-hued light reflected off the shimmering water.

Duke stood there a moment, soaking in the scene before turning to go inside. He brought his gear into the house and set it down on the kitchen floor behind the door, hanging his jacket on the hook protruding from the wall. His mother set to making a pot of coffee as he took his hat off and, running a hand through his thick, dark hair, he sat down at the kitchen table.

He wasn't prepared for what came next.

As his mother set a steaming cup of hot coffee in front of him on the table, she placed a hand on his shoulder. Duke turned toward her before she spoke and saw the look on her face was the one she wore when she had unpleasant news to deliver. Shaking her head as if in self-reproof, she faced him squarely.

She asked him if he'd heard about what happened to Dusty Harrington, from town. Duke shook his head and watched his mother's facial expression change from sadness to concern. And then she said, "He was killed on Okinawa."

She embraced him before she went on. "We lost Wayne Bridge, too," she said somberly. "He's been missing in action since his ship went down." Her hand remained on his shoulder for support.

Duke nodded his head in understanding, looking down at the floor as the grief took hold. "War is a terrible thing, Mom," he managed.

"Well," she said, "why don't you relax a bit, while I start supper?" She walked to the cupboard to take out a few pans and a cutting board, then grabbed a knife out of a drawer.

Duke sat back to watch his mother prepare dinner. It was almost like old times again. They conversed lightly about changes that had taken place in town, the weather, and any other light-hearted subjects they could focus on. His mother set to cutting up a chicken while the fat boiled in a black, cast-iron skillet on the stove.

Duke watched as she rolled the chicken pieces in egg wash, then into a floury salt and pepper mixture that she coated the meat with before dropping it into the hot grease. The aroma in the kitchen made his mouth water. He was about to enjoy the first home-cooked meal he'd had in a long, long time.

Mel walked in while Harriet was finishing preparing the meal, and Duke stood to greet him. The two men shook hands as Duke looked Mel in the eye and smiled. Mel grinned back and shook his hand firmly, then said, "It is nice to finally meet you, Duke; welcome home."

Duke returned the greeting. "It is nice to meet you, too. Thank you."

Mel turned toward the kitchen sink to wash his hands for supper. Duke sat down slowly in his chair, watching as his mother neatly set the table. Harriet placed a large bowl of mashed potatoes on the table, followed by a bowl of hot, sweet-smelling corn-on-the-cob. Finally, she carried a platter piled high with golden, crispy fried chicken and set it in the center of the table. As soon as she sat down, the three of them began to eat. After enjoying several pieces, Duke chewed every last piece of meat off the bone of a large chicken leg, then set the bone on the pile on the plate in front of him.

It was the best fried chicken Duke had ever eaten. He smiled a broad grin and thanked his mother for a wonderful meal. She grinned back, clearly happy to see that he had enjoyed it. Next, she went to the refrigerator and pulled out a round, tin pan. As she carried it to the table, Duke saw it was some kind of pie covered with a layer of homemade whipped cream. After setting three dessert plates on the table, she cut into the pie and lifted a large slice onto the plate in front of Duke.

It was banana cream pie! His favorite.

"Wow!" was all Duke could say.

His mother smiled at him as she served the pie, placing a slice onto Mel's plate, and then one on her own. By the time she had retrieved the coffee pot from the stove and grabbed mugs, Duke had already finished his first piece. Slicing another piece of the pie before she sat down, Harriet set it on Duke's plate and settled into her chair with a happy sigh. They spent the early part of the evening conversing and enjoying each other's company.

After dinner, Duke decided to see what was happening around town. He borrowed the truck and drove the few miles to Wagner. Seeing the bar at the edge of town, he pulled up near the door and parked. Still wearing his uniform, as required while on liberty, he removed his cover (hat), and walked in the door.

The bartender stood behind the bar and called him over to the counter. "What's your name, fella?" he asked Duke.

"Abdalla," Duke replied.

"I can't serve you any alcohol."

Duke looked at the set, grim expression on the man's face and decided not to argue with him. Raising his hand between himself and the bartender, he shook his head as if to say there was no need for an explanation. He didn't want it to be said out loud—he was an Indian. He knew it had to do with his being an Indian.

He walked out of the bar back to the truck, jumped in, and drove back to his mom's house. He told her what had happened, and she told him Indians were not allowed to be served any alcohol. It was the law now.

Duke pursed his lips in disgust and slapped his hand on the kitchen table. "I can't even have a cold beer!" He shook his head in disbelief. He had fought to protect the freedoms of America yet Indians weren't allowed to enjoy all of those freedoms, it seemed.

At that moment, there was a knock on the front door. Duke turned sharply and walked toward the door to open it. Standing in the doorway was a face he hadn't seen since he was seventeen years old.

Buzz Bastemeyer took a step forward and threw an arm around his childhood buddy, slapping him on the back with his other hand.

"Why don't you come in and sit down?" Duke invited him in.

Buzz removed his hat as he entered, nodding his head towards Harriet in greeting. The two men moved to the kitchen table and sat down.

"Would you boys like some coffee?" Duke's mother asked sweetly.

"That'd be nice, Mom."

"Good to see you home, Duke." Buzz looked across the table at his friend. "I heard you just got in a few days ago."

"Yep, and glad to be back," Duke answered.

"You hear about Dusty Harrington?" Buzz asked carefully.

"Mom told me he was killed."

"He was killed on Okinawa, fighting with the Ninety-Sixth Army Division on April 7th last year," Buzz said.

A jolt went through his body as Duke remembered the fierceness of the battles there, and now he'd learned that he'd lost his buddy Dusty on the same island. He proceeded to enlighten his friend Buzz as he told him about his fighting experiences on Okinawa, particularly how he'd lost his whole squad in a regimental battle to secure a hogback ridge near an open draw. He began to describe for him the banzai charges made by the crazy Japanese. Aware that his mother was listening from near the stove, Duke didn't explain in gory details. He didn't want her to imagine the horrors he had gone through.

When Duke finished talking, Buzz let the air pass slowly through his teeth in a low whistle. "I'm sorry, Duke. I didn't know." He shook his head and looked down at the embroidered cloth that covered the tabletop.

"What about Wayne Bridge, did ya' hear about Wayne?" Buzz finally said.

Duke responded that he knew only of his being MIA.

"You knew that he was in the Navy." Buzz's voice was grave as he continued, "He was on the USS *Indianapolis*. His crew was responsible for delivering the first atomic bomb to the United States air base on the island of Tinian, near Japan. It was horrible, Duke. The Japanese torpedoed the ship on its way home, and his body was never found. The sailors that survived the blast were left with very few lifeboats, as most went down with the ship. They had almost no food or water for four or five days. Of a crew of twelve hundred men, three hundred went down with the ship. The rest of the men, nearly nine hundred of them, waited for help while they were exposed to the salt water and intense sun. They suffered from dehydration and were even attacked by sharks. No one knows for sure how many men were lost to the sharks, but apparently there were swarms of them in the water. It must have been terrible. So many men died. They said that only three hundred-seventeen men lived," Buzz finished, wiping his hand down over his eyes.

"Poor Wayne," Duke uttered, shaking his head in disbelief of the gruesomeness his friend, and all those men who'd died, must have suffered. Even the ones who survived would have to suffer the memories of that horrific experience the rest of their life.

Duke knew about suffering the memories of comrades being injured and killed around him. It would never leave him, the tortuous visions that plagued a man and drove him mad. He'd seen it happen on Pavuvu with men who'd gone Asiatic. He'd seen it in the hospital at Guadalcanal, where he'd seen his friend Shade hanging wild-eyed on a fence after Peleliu. And he'd seen it on Okinawa, where he'd watched H.T. Clark, "The Killer," become a shivering mass of immobility.

Mentally shaking himself, Duke changed the subject to ask what was happening in town.

Buzz was happy to oblige and told Duke that Bucky Walters was due to be shipped home soon, which was good news. Buzz would let Duke's mom know when Bucky was back in town.

The limited days of his furlough slipped away quickly, and Duke prepared himself to return to Camp Smalls. His mother took him to the train in Sioux City, hugging him tightly before she watched him board. She was happy to have spent time with her son, glad to know he was home safe, he knew.

Once settled in his seat, Duke slept most of the way to Chicago. A short bus ride from the station landed him back at the barracks. He was still getting used to being back in the States. Even though he had made a nice set-up for himself in China, the amenities available in America were unique, and he was glad to be home.

***

Every other weekend he was given liberty to leave the naval base, and each time he got the pass, he would head into the city of Chicago to enjoy it. His first weekend out, he took the Green Line bus to the downtown area. He wanted to buy a new suit to wear when he went out on the town. He headed into a department store on State Street by the name of Marshall Field & Company. It held the distinction of being able to claim itself the world's largest department store.

The building encompassed the entire square city block bounded by Washington, State, Wabash, and Randolph Avenues. It was a beautiful building with intricate and ornate décor. The Tiffany ceiling was the first and largest ceiling ever built in favrile glass and contained over a million and a half pieces of brilliant, deeply-toned, jewel-colored glass.

Duke dropped his gaze to the aisle in front of him, then looked left and right for a sign overhead that would indicate where he would find the men's department. Once he spotted the sign, he headed straight for that department.

A salesman approached him and asked if he could be of assistance. Duke told him that he was looking for a new suit, and it wasn't long before the man had him outfitted in one of the finest sport-suits Duke had ever worn. He looked handsome in the dark brown wool gabardine jacket with double-breasted styling, accented by six shiny buttons that trailed down its front. It had peaked lapels, a rayon lining, and a fitted silhouette that complimented his lean physique. His starched white shirt and short, wide, blue-patterned tie (held in place with a gold stick tie clip) brought out the color in his steel grey-blue eyes. His pants were a pleated tan wool gabardine, with dropped belt loops, suspender buttons and full-cut, slightly tapered legs. The suspenders were worn in place of a leather belt, since leather was still difficult to get so soon after the war's end.

The next three items on Duke's list were a good-looking hat, a soft pair of trouser socks and a comfortable pair of shoes. After trying on several hats, Duke chose a wide-brimmed fedora made of brown felt with a wide black ribbon hatband. It was comfortable, and it looked good on him. Next, he chose a nice pair of light brown cotton socks which were soft on his tender feet that were still recovering from the jungle rot that had formed between his toes and on the sides and bottoms of his feet. Almost everyone wore wingtip spectator shoes now, so Duke found a pair that didn't scrunch his feet in any way. The pair he chose was made of a soft, dark brown leather with brown string ties.

He stood and walked to the three-way mirror located near the moving staircase leading to the next level. He stood tall in front of the mirror, turning first to the right, then to the left, then all the way around. He liked the suit and accessories he'd chosen, and asked the salesman to wrap them up.

After changing back into his uniform, he paid the man for his new clothes and accoutrements, then walked out the door and onto the streets of the city.

His gaze was drawn to the ornate clock that graced the corner of the building on State Street. Duke had seen the cover of a magazine where

Norman Rockwell had immortalized "The Great Clock" when he drew a picture of it for the cover of the November 3, 1945, issue of *The Saturday Evening Post.*

The day wasn't over yet, and Duke felt like exploring. Deciding to tour the area, he scanned the names of the businesses as he passed the individual shops on the street. Duke walked two blocks south, then three blocks west before he spotted a store he wanted to investigate. It was a Fannie May Candy Store on North LaSalle Street.

He inhaled as he entered the shop, and the smell was heavenly!

Duke's eyes widened as he scanned the rows of chocolates. The lady working behind the counter had been watching him, and the minute he looked up at her, she smiled and asked what it was that he would like to buy. He had already decided what he wanted. He grinned and nodded back, then asked for twenty-five cents worth of cashews and twenty-five cents worth of fudge. Then he picked up his packages from Marshall Field, grabbed the two bags of goodies, and sauntered out the door.

He decided to head back north and traveled two blocks before heading east toward Lake Michigan. About two and a half blocks later, he found what he was looking for, The Oriental Theatre. The matinee showing was a newly released film called *The Postman Always Rings Twice,* starring Lana Turner and John Garfield. It was a thriller that had absolutely nothing to do with war—exactly the kind of film Duke was looking forward to enjoying.

He found a seat in the near center of the theater and placed his packages on the seat next to him. Then he made himself comfortable, placing both the bag of cashews and the bag of fudge in his lap on his handkerchief, as he waited for the movie to begin.

Lana Turner's character was so beautiful and insidiously evil that Duke's attention was riveted throughout the movie. His eyes never left the screen as he popped handfuls of nuts, followed by bites of fudge, into his mouth. Nearly two hours later, the film was finished and Duke had enjoyed himself thoroughly. Picking up his packages, he exited the theater and headed for the bus that would take him back to the naval base. He wasn't hungry for dinner anymore, and he had accomplished all that he had wanted to do for the day.

Two weeks later, when he was given liberty again, Duke headed to a place called Mike's Restaurant. It was located directly across the street from the factory where he used to work before he turned eighteen, the Stewart Die Casting Company, on Diversey Avenue.

It was a nice restaurant with a bar and a dance floor, and they served good food. Duke ordered a burger, fries and a beer. There weren't any laws in Illinois that prevented him from having a cold beer. He sat at the table waiting for the waitress to return with his drink.

The bell on the door sounded as another customer entered, and Duke turned his head in time to see Neil Fox, whom he'd worked with at the die casting company, enter the restaurant.

Neil walked over to Duke with a big smile on his face, as Duke pushed his chair back from the table and stood to greet his old friend. They hugged each other warmly, and Duke invited Neil to sit with him. After calling the waitress over, Neil ordered a chicken sandwich with fries and a cold beer. They sat and talked while they waited for their lunches.

Duke couldn't say enough how happy he was to see Neil. He felt more at home now than he had since he left his mother's house. As they neared the end of their meal, Neil leaned forward and invited Duke to come to his house the very next weekend he had liberty.

Duke smiled big and said, "Oh, I'd like that!"

Neil slapped his back as he nodded while saying, "Good, good, Duke. The girls will be happy to meet you. You haven't met my daughters, have you?"

"No, I don't believe I have," Duke replied.

Then Duke got an idea. The smile on his face widened further before he spoke to his friend, "You know, Neil, I know the cook at the base real well. I'll bet he could get me some steaks for dinner. How'd you like to have some big, juicy T-bones?"

"If you could do that, Duke, I can guarantee you a homemade peach pie."

They laughed together, sharing in their conspiracy.

The bus ride back to the base passed quickly while Duke was lost in his thoughts. Neil Fox was a good man, and Duke was glad he'd run into him. He could remember when he'd worked with Neil at the plant, how Neil would talk continuously while he moved the arms of the spider machine that was used to cast mortar shells. He would tell story after story of his family and friends, and of his life in the city. Hot metal would pour into the casting cups, plungers would be pulled, then the casts released to reveal the perfect mortar mold. It had been amazing watching Neil work. On top of all this, he'd given good advice to Duke about working hard and saving money for the future.

Duke thought about plans for his visit during his next liberty the entire ride back to the base. If all went well, he would make a grand impression on Neil and his family.

When he got back to camp, he sought out his buddy, Charlie. Duke had made friends easily when he arrived at the naval base, and one of the good friends he made happened to be the head cook from mess hall. The head cook was in charge of ordering and rationing all the food that entered the base. Duke held rank as Sergeant of the Guard; that came in handy when he wanted to get his hands on something tasty and hard to come by. Meat was still being rationed in the States, and Duke wanted to know what the odds were of his obtaining some good cuts of beef.

He explained to Charlie how he had met up with his old buddy, Neil Fox, and how he had been invited to dinner there with his family on his next liberty.

"Do you think you could get me six nice, thick, T-bone steaks to bring for dinner?" Then, wanting to make sure that Charlie understood, Duke showed him by spreading his fingers and thumb about an inch and one-half apart. "I want them this thick—can you do it?"

Charlie responded with a broad smile, then shook Duke's hand saying, "Yeah, Duke. I'll take care of you."

"Good, good," Duke said. "Thanks!"

Over the next two weeks, Duke performed his duties methodically. He couldn't wait to visit Neil and his family. When the afternoon before the appointed dinner arrived, he took his time with his shower and shaved carefully. Then he put on his full dress Marine uniform. He liked what he saw in the mirror in his room. Taking one more swipe through his hair with the narrow-toothed black comb, he stuck it in his inside pocket and stepped out the door. He made his way to the mess hall, where his buddy Charlie was waiting with the neatly wrapped package of steaks.

"Whit-woo!" Charlie whistled as Duke entered the kitchen.

"If you weren't giving me these steaks, I'd knock your block off!" Duke growled back.

"You look good, Duke," Charlie stated in a matter-of-fact manner. "Here's the booty." He handed off the package to his friend.

"Thanks, again!" Duke shook his hand.

"Have a good time!" Charlie waved good-bye and Duke hurried out the door.

From the Great Lakes Station, Duke took the Green Line train to Western Avenue. There he got on a streetcar going to North Avenue, and then another street car to Central Park Avenue. The Fox family lived near the intersection of Central Park and Armitage on McLean Avenue. Duke walked the few blocks to Neil's house and started up the front steps. He noticed the curtains on the front windows flap a few times before he rang the doorbell. It hadn't reached the second note before Neil opened the door and swung it wide in welcome.

"Hello, Duke. Come right on in!" Neil invited.

Duke shook his hand heartily before removing his hat and placing it on a coat rack in the entrance way. Neil led him into the front room, where Grandma Edith Cole was seated in a wide tub chair. Duke approached her first, greeting her with a friendly hello.

Then he turned to Eunice, Neil's wife, giving her a quick hug and a smile, while their dog, Brownie ran around Eunice's legs in excitement. Neil's two teenage daughters were standing side-by-side next to Eunice, staring at Duke in uniform.

Duke turned to shake each of their hands as Neil introduced Jeanette and Virginia. He thought they were both very pretty young ladies.

All of a sudden, Duke remembered the bundle of meat under his arm. "I brought you a gift!" He handed the package of steaks to Neil.

He and Neil had already spoken about the steaks, but they wanted it to be a surprise for Eunice and the girls. Finding that cut of beef was a rare and expensive thing so soon after the war.

Neil opened the package as though he didn't have the faintest idea of what was inside. When he saw the six, thick, juicy-looking T-bones he spoke loudly, "Well, I'll be! If those aren't the tastiest-looking steaks I've ever seen, Duke!"

"Ohhhh!" the girls cried happily in unison.

Eunice took the steaks from her husband and said, "I'll get these on the grill right away. And since peaches are in season now, I've baked a peach pie for dessert. I'm sending a jar of homemade peach jelly home with you, Duke." Her smile was emphatic before she turned to go into the kitchen.

Dinner was delicious, and everyone took turns telling stories about their week. Duke felt very much at home here in the company of this warm family. Neil was the best storyteller, and he had a great sense of humor. He shared stories from when he and Duke had worked together at the factory. Once Eunice and the girls had cleared the dishes from the table, Eunice brought out her peach pie. Then, she retrieved a box of ice cream from the freezer while Jeanette and Virginia set the table for dessert.

The pie was scrumptious, and Duke ate every last bite of it with delight. It'd been a while since he'd had such a delicious dessert.

Long after nightfall, Duke made his good-byes to the family and promised to visit again soon. Before he walked out the door, Eunice handed him the jar of peach jelly and thanked him again for bringing the steaks. He kissed her on her cheek good-night and thanked her for her kindness. As he turned to walk down the steps to the sidewalk, he couldn't help grinning. He'd had a wonderful time, and it would be a long wait until his next liberty, when he could visit the family—and Jeanette—again.

Engagement picture of Duke in suit with teal blue tie and Jeanette in matching teal blue dress.	Loren Duke Abdalla and Jeanette Bernadine Fox married on September 3, 1948.

Neil and Eunice Fox.

Chapter 13

Living at the naval base was a fair living, but Duke was ready to make his move back into regular society. One thought that kept hounding him was the fact he'd never completed high school before heading off to Chicago. He spoke to Charlie about it, and he suggested Duke speak to one of the counselors on the base.

Duke was informed he was eligible to take a short study course and an exam to obtain his diploma from his old high school in South Dakota. Thinking it was an easy enough situation to remedy, Duke signed up to take the exam and passed on the first try. On the second day of December 1946, he received his high school diploma from Wagner High School.

Along with the diploma, the high school also sent the school yearbook, titled *The Raiders Yearbook*. As Duke browsed through the book, looking at photos of the students he had attended school with, it occurred to him that it seemed a very long time ago. Some of those friends were now married with children, others had lost their lives in the war, and then there was him— waiting to finish his tour in the Marines.

He was proud to show his diploma to Neil and his family at their next dinner gathering, and they congratulated him for his achievement. He wrote to his mother to share the news with her as well. She sent a letter back from her and Mel of how proud she was of him.

In January, Duke knew his service in the military was almost up. Several weeks before Duke's discharge would be final, Neil spoke to his cousin, Bud Fox, about arranging a room for Duke to rent when he got out of the military.

Duke was looking forward to living in a place of his own. Bud and Frieda Fox owned a store on McLean Avenue, not far from Neil's house. If Duke wasn't opposed to having a roommate, Bud Junior would share and rent the room with him. Duke agreed, and was all set up with a place to live by the end of the month, which left Duke feeling again that it was good to have friends looking out for him.

***

During that same month, on a Saturday afternoon, Duke arrived in the city a bit early to visit the Fox home, so he headed over to Mike's Restaurant to kill time with a sandwich and a beer.

Sitting at the counter, he struck up a conversation with the man sitting next to him, who introduced himself as Dick Kleist. After sharing some stories,

Duke informed the man that his duty with the Marines was nearly up and he needed to find a good job.

Dick was more than happy to oblige, telling Duke that he would ask his boss at the Kercher Company, where he worked, if they had room for another masonry man. That sounded good to Duke and he nodded his approval of the idea.

Dick arranged a meeting with the owner of the business, and invited Duke in for an interview. The man liked Duke so well he ended up giving him a job as a tuck-pointer, repairing bricks and mortar on buildings in Chicago and the surrounding area.

Duke couldn't help feeling he had been in the right place at the right time. His life was all falling into place—running into Neil Fox, Neil's cousin offering him a place to rent, landing a good job in the city, and being introduced to a lovely young lady, Jeanette.

A few weeks later, on February 18, 1947, Duke was honorably discharged from the United States Marine Corps. In a way, his time in the service had shaped him to be the man he was. After leaving the barracks for the last time, he saluted the base. He'd never forget his lost comrades or the dear friends he had made.

That day he moved into the apartment above Bud and Frieda's store. He didn't have much to move—just his duffel and a few boxes and before long he was settled into his new room. The next day he started his job with the Kercher Company.

He and young Bud took their meals with Neil and Eunice and their family, visiting their home regularly. Duke paid Eunice for the meals he ate, which allowed him to enjoy the company of Grandma Cole, Virginia, and especially Jeanette. Soon, it was as if he were part of the family.

Duke knew Neil and his family respected him. Sometimes Neil would arrange with Duke to meet him for lunch at one of their favorite hangouts, a chili mac joint on Montrose and Kedzie. It was a short ride, and the place was always packed.

Neil and Duke took their spot in the long line to the counter. The aromas alone were enough to make their mouths water. The chili was served in a long, paper boat. First, the boat was filled with plump elbow macaroni noodles, which were then covered with a meaty, red chili sauce, and finally, everything was smothered with a layer of melted cheddar cheese.

Duke and Neil placed their order with a short, stocky man wearing a white paper cap over his dark, curly hair. He yelled the order over his shoulder to the cook in the kitchen, who was also sporting a pleated white paper hat. In a matter of minutes, the order was completed and handed off to them.

They found a table that had recently been cleared and sat down on the shiny chrome bar stools to enjoy their meal. Duke was content to listen to his friend tell stories about his morning while they devoured the contents of the chili mac dish.

Over the next year, Duke worked hard, as he'd always done, and he was well-respected by his boss and co-workers. Duke grew closer not only to the family, but also to Jeanette. She was maturing as a young woman, and he took notice. On one particular weekend in 1948, as the evening was winding down, Duke managed to pull Jeanette aside and ask if she would like to go with him to see a movie sometime. She immediately said yes.

Although he suspected Neil and Eunice would approve, Duke still spoke to Neil about taking Jeanette out, as she was only sixteen. He respected Neil as much as he would if he had been his own father. Neil put his arm around Duke's shoulders and told him that he thought it was a fine idea for him to ask Jeanette out.

Duke couldn't wait until Friday night. The work week passed slowly until the night finally arrived. He couldn't resist a wide smile as he ambled up the stairs to the house to pick her up.

Jeanette met him at the door. "Hi, Duke."

"Are you ready?"

She nodded. "Yes, let's go."

He and Jeanette took a street trolley to the Armitage Theatre. Duke had chosen this particular theater because they were showing a romantic film by the name of *The Kissing Bandit*, starring Frank Sinatra and Kathryn Grayson.

During the show, Duke reached over and put his arm around Jeanette's shoulders and she snuggled closer. The movie ended up being only so-so, but there were a few dance numbers that were fun to watch. The real fun came after the movie when Duke led Jeanette outside. They held hands as they exited the theater, smiling as they swung their hands back and forth as they walked. Then Duke turned Jeanette slowly toward him, using their handhold as a rudder behind her back to steer her into his arms. He pulled her against him ever so slightly, placing his hand on her dark-brown hair. Then he pressed his mouth to her upturned lips and placed his first kiss there. When they pulled back from one another, they both gasped at the intensity.

It was the beginning of a beautiful relationship.

***

He and Jeanette continued to spend time together. Whenever they went out on a date, they always dressed up. Everyone did in Chicago. Duke would wear either a sports suit or double-breasted suit with his wing tip dress shoes and brown fedora hat. Jeanette would wear a nice dress or a two-piece suit with matching hat, and she always wore white gloves that buttoned at the wrists.

They often took a trolley to a nearby theater to watch a show. The downtown theaters were a bit fancier, so on occasion, they would make the trip all the way downtown. There was always some kind of entertainment before the show. Sometimes it was a singer, like Frank Sinatra, Dean Martin, Benny Goodman, Louis Armstrong or Sophie Tucker. Other times it was a comedian or two, like Jack Benny or George Burns and Gracie Allen, who would perform before the movie was shown. The dates became fairly regular, and they enjoyed each other's company very much.

Duke sensed that he had found a home of sorts, spending so much time with the Fox family. He felt very much at ease with Jeanette, and he could tell she was comfortable with him as well. Most nights he joined the family for dinner, and afterward they would all sit at the kitchen table and play cards or chat about their day.

One evening they got to talking about their family histories, and Duke shared with them how his great grandfather was Chief Running Bull of The Yankton Sioux Tribe. Duke was proud of his heritage, always had been, and of the fact that his great grandfather had been a member of the group that had traveled to Washington D.C. to sign a peace treaty in 1858 with the United States of America. The girls were especially impressed when Duke told them that his grandmother was Princess Minnie Running Bull, and what a fine cook she had been.

Eunice encouraged Jeanette to tell Duke of some of their family history. Jeanette was proud to tell him that she and Virginia often wrote poetry, as it seemed to be a family trait.

"You see," Jeanette explained with great pride, "Grandma Cole's maiden name was Emerson, and she is a second cousin to the poet Ralph Waldo Emerson!"

Her cheeks were flushed Duke noticed immediately and smiled at her in appreciation. Jeanette was a lovely, young woman, and he relished her response to him.

"Would you like to hear a poem that Grandma's cousin, John, wrote during the Civil War?" she asked Duke.

"Sure," he nodded.

"I think you may appreciate this particular selection," Jeanette said, as she stood near the fireplace. She held the page from the book in her hand and read "'My Father's Musket' by John H. Emerson, Jr." She glanced at Duke then continued.

"I am fond of guns and like to shoot them,
I like the best and latest kind,
Of shot or rifle Automatics,
The very best that I can find.

I have a gun that I prize highly,
It hangs at home above the door,
Although it's old I wouldn't trade it,
For all the guns in any store.

The musket my old father carried,
(And like it too, his voice is still),

142

It bears the furrow of a bullet,
A rebel shot, who meant to kill.

He had the gun on his left shoulder,
With stock and hand before his heart,
A bullet came and hit his gun-stock,
And tore the hand and gun apart.

We've relics old that we prize highly,
And some that will tell of recent strife,
Above them all I prize the musket,
That saved my dear old father's life."

Duke stood and applauded her performance—and the poem. "That was wonderful, and you read it so nicely," he said, smiling warmly at her. It had meant a lot to him that she had found a piece that brought forth memories for him.

Later that evening, as Duke stood to take his leave, Jeanette motioned for him to come over. He walked to where she was standing near the coatrack and she pulled his head down, so that his ear was next to her mouth. He could feel the warmth of her breath as she spoke into his ear. "Would you like to take me to the beach tomorrow?"

He spun slowly to stand in front of her, grinning. "I would love to take you to the beach tomorrow. Should I pick you up at ten?" Duke asked eagerly.

"Ten would be nice." Jeanette flushed, then raced up the stairs, bidding him good-bye from the landing.

***

The warmth of June had crept up on Chicago that morning and Duke was glad to be doing something fun with Jeanette. She was standing with the door open at the top of the steps, looking pretty in a flowered blue-print dress with cap sleeves. Her dark-brown tresses were neatly coiffed, and as Duke's gaze traveled down the length of her trim figure, one brow raised as he noticed she was wearing a pair of white heeled sling-back shoes with open toes. Not very practical for the beach, he surmised. But she did look lovely. She grabbed her matching white purse and beach towel from the chair in the entryway and stood in the doorway, waiting for Duke to greet her. "Are you ready to go?" asked Duke as he stepped up to her door.

He had combed his thick, black hair back neatly from his forehead. His trousers were a medium-blue and fit his trim, athletic figure well. He wore a crisp, white cotton shirt, opened at the neck.

"All ready!" she replied with a giddy smile.

Eunice handed her a red-checkered cotton blanket, along with a large wicker picnic basket with wooden handles, to take to the beach with them.

143

"Thanks, Mom," grinned Jeanette, giving her mother a quick kiss on the cheek.

Duke grabbed the basket with one hand and with the other took Jeanette's hand as they descended the stairway. He didn't let go until they reached the streetcar stop. Her hand was so small and delicate in his much larger, calloused hand. He helped her up the steps and into the streetcar, finding a seat for them to share on the ride to North Avenue Beach. They shared a pleasant conversation on the way there, but all the while Duke was imagining the bathing suit that was underneath her pretty flower-print dress.

When they arrived at the park, Duke took her hand in his as she descended the steps. They walked together hand-in-hand through the sand until they found an ideal spot to lay their blanket. After placing her purse on a corner of the blanket to keep the breeze from blowing it away, Jeanette unbuttoned the front of her dress.

At the same time, Duke removed his tie and was unbuttoning the front of his shirt—all the while keeping a watchful eye on Jeanette.

She slipped the dress off her shoulders and stepped lightly out of it. Then she stood, neatly folding the dress before placing it on the blanket beside her purse. She turned to face Duke. He could feel himself grinning from ear to ear. Not able to hold back, he said, "Wow! What a doll. You look beautiful, Jeanette!"

At the sight of seeing her in her bright blue swimming suit, he was in love! But keeping his cool, he placidly invited Jeanette into the water.

She grabbed his hand, following him into the chilly waters of Lake Michigan.

"Ohhhh!" she shrieked as her feet hit the water.

"You'll get used to it," Duke assured her.

After wading more deeply into the lake, he felt his body getting used to the feel of the cool water on his skin. The sun was warm on their shoulders and faces as they continued to swim for a time, playfully splashing at each other, and oblivious to the people around them.

Making their way back to the blanket a little while later, Duke hurriedly gathered a towel to wrap around Jeanette's shoulders before he reached for his own towel. They sat, huddled close together, warming each other in the sun as their suits dried.

After some time had passed, Jeanette asked Duke if he was hungry enough to eat. He nodded, anxious to see what Eunice had packed. He had experienced firsthand her delicious cooking. Jeanette raised the lid of the picnic basket and lifted out an aluminum foil wrapped package. Duke could smell the savory aroma of fried chicken before Jeanette could open the bundle. Eunice had also included two small bowls of a flavorful egg-and-potato salad for them to enjoy. They ate and talked for hours, laughing at each other's stories and sharing interested glances. As they ate the last of the delicious sugar cookies that Eunice had baked for their picnic, they watched together as the sun set low on the Chicago skyline. Neither of them wanted the day to end, but it was time to gather up their belongings and head for the streetcar that would take them home.

They sat in a comfortable silence, holding each other's hand, and occasionally gazing into each other's eyes. Duke suspected it was evident to everyone riding the street car that he and Jeanette were in love.

Duke soon realized he wanted to marry Jeanette. She had talked to him about marriage before, and he did love Jeanette and wanted her to be happy. On the night he decided to propose to her, the only thing he told her was to dress fancy for their night out.

She chose a teal-blue dress that had black trim and black lace cuffs on the short, capped sleeves. Her dark-brown, red high-lighted hair was curled back from her face and worn just below her ears, which were adorned with earrings embellished with pearls in a star shape. She wore a complimenting double-strand pearl necklace. Duke thought she looked lovely.

He had chosen a dark-brown suit with a starched white shirt and teal-colored tie that just happened to match Jeanette's dress. He sported a thin mustache on his upper lip and wore a white linen kerchief in his pocket.

That night he took Jeannette to the Aragon Ballroom in Chicago. It was an extravagantly decorated ballroom located on Lawrence Avenue. Built in 1926, it was designed to resemble a Spanish village. Wayne King and His Orchestra were playing, and the sultry sounds of The Waltz King's saxophone lent just the right atmosphere to the evening. When King's signature song conversion of "I Love You Truly" floated across the dance floor, Duke got down on one knee and presented Jeanette with what he hoped she thought was the most beautiful diamond ring she had ever seen. It was a gorgeous antique design of platinum with a half carat diamond set in the center that was surrounded by tiny diamonds all around.

"I love you, Jeanette. Will you marry me?" he asked Jeanette.

She leapt out of her chair and into Duke's arms, sitting herself on his extended knee and wrapping her arms around his neck. "Yes!" Extending her hand so Duke could slide the ring onto the appropriate finger, she then looked at it appreciatively, turning it this way and that to watch it catch and reflect the lights in the grand room.

She followed up by placing a soft kiss on Duke's mouth, and then looked into his eyes with happiness. Duke was overjoyed.

They spent the rest of the evening dancing in each other's arms, listening to a myriad of waltzes, including "Dream a Little Dream of Me" and "Goodnight Sweetheart."

The week after Duke proposed, he went to work finding an inexpensive apartment that the two of them could afford. As luck would have it, an apartment opened up on Eddy Avenue in Chicago. It wasn't far from Duke's work, and it had a driveway where he could park his work truck.

Duke called and asked his mother to come to the wedding, but because she and Mel had recently purchased a large farm just outside of Wagner, South Dakota, and had much work to do, they were unable to attend. They didn't have anyone who could watch the farm for them and it had a lot of cattle to attend. His mother wished them well in their marriage, and asked him to be sure to call, now that they had a phone, following the wedding. And perhaps they could arrange for him and Jeanette to visit South Dakota soon.

Duke and Jeanette were married on September 3, 1948, with Grandma Cole and the Fox family in attendance. It was a small ceremony, conducted by Pastor Lavergne at the local Methodist Church.

Duke smiled broadly as his lovely wife-to-be was walked down the aisle by her father. When they neared the altar, they stopped, and Neil hesitated briefly before placing a kiss on Jeanette's cheek. He then handed her off to Duke, who wrapped her arm in his.

Duke and Jeanette turned together to face Pastor Lavergne, who was standing with his back to the altar, The Holy Bible in his hands. After sharing several verses with the bride, groom, and congregation, the pastor remarked on the seriousness of the commitment of marriage, and then he addressed Duke and Jeanette directly.

"You will repeat these words after me: I, Loren Duke Abdalla, take thee, Jeanette Bernadine Fox, to be my wife, to have and to hold, from this day forward, for better, for worse, for richer, for poorer, in sickness and in health, to love and to cherish, till death do us part, and thereto I pledge thee my faith."

Duke repeated the vows flawlessly, and then Jeanette took her turn repeating the same vows to Duke.

When the pastor offered, "You may kiss the bride," Duke had already wrapped both arms around Jeanette's waist and was drawing her into an exuberant kiss to seal their marriage vows.

Following the ceremony, Duke took Jeanette out for a steak dinner. The restaurant was close to their new apartment located on Eddy Avenue in Chicago. They didn't have the funds to travel anywhere for their honeymoon, but neither of them seemed to mind.

After climbing a flight of stairs hand-in-hand, Duke swung Jeanette up off her feet, as tradition commanded, unlocked the door to the apartment and carried her over the threshold of their new home.

She giggled nervously until he finally put her down, and then they kissed and held each other into the small hours of the morning. Duke and Jeanette looked forward to their future together.

***

Their apartment was small but quaint. It was a one room studio with different areas sectioned off by furniture. It wasn't very large, but the walls had a fresh coat of paint to spruce it up. Jeanette had been given as a gift some fine lace curtains to cover the numerous windows that surrounded the apartment. Duke knew she loved the light that illuminated the room and made it more cheery. The kitchen was clean and the appliances fairly new. Their life as newlyweds was a busy one. Jeanette had a job at Illinois Bell working the switchboard, and Duke continued to work for the Kercher Company as a tuck-pointer. During the week, Jeanette prepared dinner when she got home from work. She learned how to stretch the grocery money and make meals last. Dinners were simple but tasty.

On one particular evening, after clearing the dinner dishes from the kitchen table, she told Duke she'd decided to call her new mother-in-law and become more acquainted with her. His mother was happy to receive word of how well their marriage was going, and the women spent nearly an hour talking about recent events before they finally ended the call. Duke had promised his mother he'd come for a visit soon.

But marriage wasn't all happy times. Life had difficult moments for them as well. Jeanette was still young, and Duke had spent the better part of his youth in the war. Duke often woke during the night, his bedclothes soaked in sweat. His nights were plagued with nightmares that held images from the war. In those dreams, he often imagined he was still in battle.

He was standing in a swamp, the water reaching up to his waist as he crouched low to avoid detection by the Japs. Hearing crackling and rustling sounds along with the roar of a tank, he immersed himself up to his chin and waited, motionless. The tank stopped just fifteen feet from where he hid behind the bamboo stalks. It was hot, so hot in the jungle...

Duke sat up straight in bed. He pushed the covers back gently, so as not to awaken Jeanette. He padded to the bathroom sink and turned the cold water handle just until the water trickled out, then he splashed his face and neck with the cool water before wiping himself dry with a small hand towel.

From the bed he heard his wife call out to him. "Duke, are you okay?"

"Yeah..."

Jeanette had stayed in bed. "Do you want to talk about it?" she asked.

Duke considered her offer as he walked back to the bed and sat down. "Do you really want to hear about it?" he asked cautiously.

"If it'll help you sleep, I'd like to try."

Duke took a deep breath then released it in a long sigh before he began. "It was awful, Jeanette, that first day and night on the island of Peleliu. I won't go into the details, but so many men were killed that day. I didn't think I would get off that beach alive, let alone in one piece. Guys I'd lived with on the island of Pavuvu, men I had suffered terrible living conditions with, young men my age—blown to pieces on that beach in front of me!"

He ran his hand through his coarse, black hair. "How do I forget?" he asked, staring straight ahead. "When will it go away?" he added.

Jeanette reached out to him, shaking her head, and murmured, "I don't know, Duke. I don't know."

He laid down on his pillow, holding her in his embrace until he fell asleep. The warmth of her body and the sweet fragrance of her hair helped his mind to settle as he slept.

147

***

Since Jeanette had opened the door on communicating memories of the war, every week or so, he regaled her with stories of his travels and experiences. He told her about the Pullman car he rode out to California and talked of taking her on a similar trip some day. He told her about boot camp and the drill sergeant named Crick that he had flattened with a single punch. And he told her about his days on Pavuvu, about meeting Chesty Puller and sharing a conversation with him, and the horrendous conditions they had lived in.

Jeanette listened as he held her close as he told her about jungle juice and H. T. Clark—a clean, condensed version of his friendship with the big Indian. He spoke of Chicken Boyd with his Southern twang and slim silhouette. All the names and faces came flooding back as Duke revealed his stories. He shared with her his boxing status of A-1-1 champion on the island, even with Chesty Puller and Ray Davis in attendance regularly. He also told her about Bob Hope and his troupe visiting Pavuvu before his regiment was deployed to Peleliu.

On one particular night, Duke walked over to the bed and pulled his service trunk out from under it, carefully lifting the lid. He had decided to share with her the souvenirs he had collected from the war. Pushing the Ka-Bar knives to one side, he lifted out an Imperial Japanese flag he had acquired on Okinawa. The flag was made of silk and had a white background with a large red, circle in the center of it. Red stripes, or rays, extended from the red center to the borders of the material, depicting a sun. On eight of the rays, Duke had written in ink the names of each of the ships he had traveled on during the war: USS *Polk*, USS *Howitz*, USS *Warren*, USS *Renville*, USS *Attala*, USS *Butner*, USS *Bountiful*—the hospital ship—and USS *Dupage*. He had crossed over the equator a total of four times. Jeanette was so interested to hear about his adventures, but he had a feeling she knew that he kept the worst of his experiences from her.

Maybe that was why she forgave him for his faults. On Friday nights, Duke would join his friends from the neighborhood for a guys' night out. It wasn't Jeanette's favorite day of the week. Sometimes Duke would become so inebriated that his friends would have to assist him home. She would help him to bed where she would try to help him take off his clothing and shoes before he plopped backward onto his pillow. Then he fell into a deep sleep, snoring loudly the rest of the night.

The rest of their days were spent working and dealing with the mundane details of everyday living. On Saturdays Jeanette loved going out, and Duke made sure to be a charming escort.

They would get dressed up and head to the Aragon Ballroom or the McVeagh or Willowbrook Ballrooms, where Duke would twirl her about the dance floor. Sometimes they would see a movie, either at a local theater or somewhere downtown. Jeanette liked going downtown because they always had a show before the movie started.

Most of the time they were happy, and Duke felt sure that things would be fine between them. Just over a year after they were married, Jeanette gave birth to a son, Brady Neil. The middle name had been chosen by both Duke and Jeanette in honor of her father, Neil Fox. Duke was proud to be a father. He had decided to honor his long-time friend John Brady by naming his son after him. Brady was the man whose life he had saved when he was burned by a phosphorous grenade. It was a day he would never forget, not ever.

That night Duke had a dream reliving the last time he had seen Brady.

The air was filled with tension, the pitch black sky illuminated only momentarily by the eerie light of a flare or the tracer shot from a machine gun. He was ready to fight...he was always ready to fight.

Duke stood crouched behind an embankment, waiting to give the go ahead signal to the men in his squad. Then he heard a scream, a bone-chilling, blood-curdling scream that made his spine tingle and the hairs on the back of his neck stand straight on end. Without a second thought, he was leaping over the embankment and running to save John Brady. He knew it was his friend's agonized scream he heard. He had seen many gory sights since the war had begun, but nothing could have prepared him for the sight of John writhing in torment on the blood-soaked ground. Parts of his clothing had been burned off of his body by the foul-smelling phosphorous acid that had been released from the explosion from the Japanese grenade. It had eaten away through John's clothing and was burning his skin, leaving a pungent odor in the air.

Duke didn't hesitate for a second. He hoisted his friend over his shoulder, ignoring the sound of machine guns and mortar shells exploding all around him. He carried John to the safety of the arms that were waiting behind the cover of the ravine. Then he ran full force back into the battle.

More than three years had passed, but Duke still remembered the incident as though it had happened yesterday. Jeanette chose not to ask him about it that day—he would tell her when he was ready.

Duke suddenly turned, looked at his wife, and smiled. He walked the few steps to where she and their son were sitting on the couch, and kissed his son on the top of his head. Then he leaned in to kiss Jeanette on the lips. They were happy, weren't they? Somehow, he'd find a way to get through these nightmares...

Duke and Jeanette's children: Brady Neil and Raleigh Jane Abdalla.

Duke with his mother, Harriet.

Chapter 14

Duke finished work early on this especially cold Friday evening, feeling the chill seeping through the warm layers of clothing he wore as he walked home. He kept his hand on his hat as he passed the last few blocks to the apartment, fighting the frigid winds that battled to remove it from his head. He stepped through the entryway and took the stairs two at a time to the landing. Removing his hat as he entered, he felt the skin of his ears sting as they adjusted to the warmth of the room. He took off his coat to hang it on the coatrack and turned to see Brady asleep in his crib.

The delicious aroma of stew simmering on the stove was a welcome balm at the end of a hard week's work. Jeanette asked him about his day, and he mumbled that it was all right. He sat down at the kitchen table and waited patiently for Jeanette to fill his bowl with stew.

She placed the dish on the table in front of him, then added a plate of sliced bread with butter next to it. "Are you going out tonight, Duke?" *Why would she ask that?* he thought to himself.

He looked up at her and frowned, then responded, "You know I go out on Friday night."

"Yes," she continued pointedly, "but it's so cold outside. I thought maybe you'd like to stay in tonight?"

"Nope," Duke spoke shortly. "I'm going out!" *Why was she badgering him? She knew that Friday night was his release from the stresses of the week.*

Not another word was said until he finished eating and changed into his suit for the night.

"Be careful," was all Jeanette could manage before Duke gave her a quick kiss good-bye on the cheek and headed out the door.

Duke had always gone out on Friday nights, even though he figured she'd never been fond of the idea. He opened the door at the bottom of the stairs and exited onto the sidewalk. At least he'd taken her out dancing, or to see a movie once in a while. She ought to be grateful that he took her out at all, since the money he was making wasn't enough for them to make ends meet nowadays.

***

Jeanette had decided she would go back to work at Illinois Bell as a telephone operator. She'd already spoken to her mother, she told Duke, and Eunice Fox had agreed to watch the baby so Jeanette could return to work.

At first, Duke was against the idea. But after they fell into a routine, he was glad to have the extra money. He was spending more and more time away from home he vaguely realized, and spending more and more of the money both he and Jeanette brought home. And he was drinking more often. It seemed to help him forget, if only for the evening, the barbaric brutality of the memories of war.

His nights were filled with visions of bodies being flung from the ground by explosions and the constant noise of rifle fire or machine guns reverberating in his head. He was tortured by the memory of the pain that had seized him when he'd been hit by mortar fire that blew holes through both of his thighs and slammed him into the wall of coral behind him when he had believed he was going to die. He wanted to forget the empty stares of the men he'd fought side by side with, the sight of them lying in a bloody mess on the ground. He remembered the killing machine he'd become to survive.

Duke would never forget lifting the top of a moss-covered spider trap, gun at the ready, and watching the smiling face of the Japanese soldier exploding in front of his eyes as he pulled the trigger. He wanted to forget seeing his buddy, H. T. Clark, huddled in a trembling mass of hysteria on The Three Sisters. He wanted to forget, but every night when he closed his eyes, he was trapped in his nightmares.

He would often wake during the night drenched in sweat. On those nights, he would quietly pad to his dresser to grab fresh clothing, then wash and change in the bathroom. Some nights he would share the details of his nightmares with Jeanette if she woke up, too. They would stay up all night as she listened to the memories that tormented him. But Duke knew it was causing her fatigue.

He looked forward to drinking on Friday nights. If he drank enough whiskey or beer, the memories would fade into a blur. He hoped. He didn't talk about the war to anyone other than Jeanette. But it angered him whenever he heard some ignorant fool in a bar talk about how bad the war was when the fool had never even put on a uniform or seen any action. Those idiots had no idea what war was really like, and Duke had been fighting in the jungles of the front lines.

When he'd heard enough, he would stand up, put on his coat, and head out the door to traipse to another bar. By the time he arrived back at the apartment, he could barely make it up the stairs.

One Friday night, Duke didn't even seem to notice Jeanette gently placing the baby in his crib as he walked to his side of the bed and sat down to take off his shoes. He quickly undressed, laying his clothing on a nearby chair, then climbed under the covers to get warm. Moments after his head hit the pillow, he began to snore loudly.

***

Life went on like this for a while. The best times seemed to be when Duke and Jeanette brought the baby to see the family and have dinner at the Fox home. But even there, Duke felt himself withdrawing.

One evening when they were visiting with family, Jeanette stood up to make an announcement. They were expecting their second child. Duke was thrilled, though that meant they'd be spending more money. *And why did she have to announce it here and not privately to him at home?* The thought perturbed him.

Jeanette's cousin Bud was visiting that night, too, and he grabbed Duke's attention by throwing an arm around his shoulders. "Congratulations, Duke!" he proclaimed loudly. Duke took the beer he offered and nodded his thanks. Bud and Duke had become good friends over the years, and Duke felt like he could use a good friend tonight. Somehow the weight of the world felt like it had landed on his shoulders.

The family was delighted to hear that Duke and Jeanette were going to have another baby, and for the moment, Duke was happy, too.

***

On January 1st, 1952, their darling little girl was born. Duke and Jeanette's daughter had a tuft of coarse brown hair that stood nearly straight up on top of her head. Her eyes were a medium-brown and she had plump, rosy cheeks. Jeanette had decided to name the baby after a dear friend of hers with an unusual name, Raleigh Jane.

Duke liked the name as well, and things seemed to calm down for a few months with the joy of a new baby in their home. But it wasn't long before his interests wandered to drinking again.

Maybe it was the pressures of raising a family. Maybe it was struggling to make ends meet. But he was having flashbacks even during the daytime, and his attention would wander mid-conversation. He'd go on and on about the horrors he'd seen at night with Jeanette, the comrades he'd lost. But he knew Jeanette's compassion was wearing thin.

The only solace Duke seemed to be able to find was at the bottom of a bottle. And it wasn't just on Friday nights now that he looked for it. Any night of the week he had money in his pocket was a good night for drinking.

One of Duke's favorite haunts was a place called The Eight O'clock Club in Logan Square. He felt comfortable there and often chatted with some of the regulars who frequented the place. One such gentleman was Joe, a dark-haired man whose suit hung loosely on his light frame. He always seemed to occupy the seat at the opposite end of the bar from where Duke was sitting.

One evening, Duke threw two quarters on the bar counter, asking Luigi the bartender to give his friend a beer "on him". He and Joe engaged in small talk while enjoying their beers together. Joe worked in a nearby office, was always dressed in a nice suit, and was a pleasant guy to converse with, Duke thought. On this particular evening, an Italian man named Big Frank, (also known as The Dago), started giving Joe a bad time. He was a hulk of a guy and was known as the neighborhood bully. Plenty of men had seen his victims sailing through plate-glass windows or through the nearest door.

Unfortunately, this night Frank was determined to get a rise out of little Joe. Duke couldn't help but feel sorry for the man. It must have shown on Duke's face, because Big Frank stopped bullying Joe long enough to ask Duke, "Do you want some of this?"

Duke had just enough alcohol in his blood to consider Frank's challenge, even though the man was nearly twice his size. He looked for a reaction from Luigi, the stout, round, bald-headed bartender. Luigi had seen Duke fight before. "Go ahead, Duke, you can take him!" his friend behind the bar yelled over the din of the room.

So, Duke turned to face Big Frank squarely and said, "I'll take some!"

Duke had barely stepped off the bar stool when Frank came charging at him like a raging bull. Duke was ready with a swift left, "Bam!" then a resounding right, "Bam!" Frank went down on the barroom floor. Then Frank pushed himself up a bit, shaking his head to regain his senses.

Duke allowed him to get up off the floor, but was ready with another combination of punches to rattle the man's brain. The two men were tearing the joint apart. Tables were turned over, lamps and chairs were broken, drinks were spilled. Several patrons were forced to move out of the way quickly as Duke and Big Frank made their way around the bar.

Duke landed more punches on Big Frank before he was on the floor with a split lip and a black eye. Duke had bruised both of his hands from the severity with which he had punched the man, but Duke's face didn't have a single mark on it.

The news spread around Logan Square that The Indian had beaten The Dago. All the way to Fullerton Avenue, near Duke's work. Everyone heard that The Indian was the man to contend with—and nobody better mess around with him.

***

Duke struggled to unlock the door to the apartment; his key didn't seem to fit. Squinting one eye, he managed to slip the key into the lock just as Jeanette whisked the door open widely. She turned on her heel without greeting him, and he watched her as she walked back into the kitchen. With her back to him, she began emptying groceries out of a paper bag and slamming the cans on the countertop.

"Well hello, Duke!"

He thought the voice came from the direction of the couch, and he stumbled as he turned to face her. Eunice had been babysitting and was sitting on the couch with Brady, working on a puzzle laid out on the coffee table.

"Hullo," he managed to greet her. "Howss the mother-in-law?" he slurred with a lopsided smile, raising his hand grandly and nearly crashing into the kitchen table.

"You see, Mother," Jeanette spoke harshly. "It's barely six o'clock and the man is drunk!" She raised her palm and gestured toward Duke.

Duke watched as Jeanette pivoted, then reached up to the top of the cabinet next to the sink to draw down a glass jar. *Oh no,* he thought to himself, *here it comes!* She reached into her pocketbook to pull out the few dollars left from grocery shopping and turned to add them to the contents of the jar.

As he watched from where he stood, Duke wobbled on his feet. He saw the looks of disbelief and horror play across Jeanette's face before she turned angrily toward her mother to speak. "He's done it again, Mother—now we won't have enough money to pay the rent!" she screamed, walking past Duke as though he were not in the room.

"I can't take it anymore." Sobbing, she ran towards her mother and kneeled down into her arms.

Duke turned around unapologetically and traipsed back to the door of the apartment. *He didn't need this harassment.* He turned the handle, walked out and down the stairs, then headed for the nearest bar.

***

Duke and Jeanette were divorced in the spring of 1952. The stupor Duke was living in created a barrier to the sadness he felt at having failed his marriage. He knew it wasn't Jeanette's fault; she'd done everything right. And he hadn't. She took the kids and left.

The alcohol filled an empty space in the pit inside him that nothing else seemed to be able to fill. He began drinking every day of the week to cope.

Since the fight at The Eight O' Clock Club with Big Frank, The Indian of Logan Square was seen as a menace on the bar scene. On one evening stroll through his regular haunts, Duke started at The Bar where his friend Bob tended. He walked in and sat down at the counter, motioning to Bob that he wanted a beer.

Four rednecks were sitting at the far end of the bar. They started mouthing off to Duke. "Hey, Indian! You beat anyone up, lately? Why don't you take out one of us?"

They had big mouths, these rednecks, Duke's blood was beginning to boil. The four men continued taunting him as he drank. They thought they were so tough—four against one.

Duke burned with rage, so he finished his beer with a gulp and set it down firmly on the bar counter. He got up and walked to the phone to call for a cab to get out of there. He told the driver where to take him, and the cabbie drove him to Johnny Nash's.

Duke walked through the door of the bar to the sound of greetings from fellow regulars. He wasn't up for conversation tonight, and he drank a couple of beers in short order. He couldn't stop thinking of those four rednecks at The Bar. He downed a shot of whiskey and one more beer, then made the decision to go back and teach those bums a lesson.

He hailed a cab on the street, and a young, black cab driver greeted him as he entered the car, "Good evening, sir. Where can I take you?"

Duke answered pointedly, "Take me over to The Bar on the corner of Fullerton and Sacramento Boulevard."

The cab driver drove through the traffic deftly. "Here we are, sir," the driver announced.

The driver jumped out of the driver's seat and opened the rear passenger door for Duke.

Duke stepped out of the cab, shrugged out of his blazer, folded it shoulder to shoulder, then placed it neatly over his arm. "Hold this for me," he said, handing the blazer to the cabbie. "I'll be right out."

The driver looked at Duke and nodded his head, then followed him to the entrance of the bar.

Duke opened the door and swung it wide. "I'm back!" he called.

The four rednecks were sitting in the same four seats at the far end of the bar. They turned in unison and stared at him.

"I'm back!" Duke repeated the taunt, leaning toward them.

The fight was over in the blink of an eye as Duke flattened three of them, one right after the other. The fourth man ran around to the other side of the room and out the back door.

The place erupted with clapping and laughter from the other patrons in attendance. Just short of taking a bow, Duke nodded his head and tipped his hat before turning to walk out the door. He took his sports jacket from the cab driver, who was standing next to the cab with the back door open, and asked him to take him back to Johnny Nash's Bar.

When the driver pulled up to the curb, Duke turned to the man and asked, "What do I owe ya'?"

The driver turned to face him, pearly whites shining, and exclaimed, "Mister, you don't owe me a dime. I'd have paid to see that! You have a good evening, now!" He pinched the brim of his cap in tribute to Duke and drove away from the curb.

Duke's reputation was building in the neighborhood and with it, his ego. Some men kept a wide berth from The Indian, but others wanted to be his friend to avoid fighting with him. They'd buy him drinks to keep him happy. Still, others wanted to challenge him. Duke never backed away from a fight, and he always won.

One evening, he was sitting at a bar that was close to the building where he worked. He and the lady bartender were the only ones in the place. Penny was the owner of the bar, and she and Duke conversed often.

Duke bought a drink, and then he bought the lady a drink. They talked awhile longer, but then she began to look at the clock with a worried expression on her face. "I'm going to have to close up pretty soon."

"This early?" Duke asked.

"Yes," Penny said, "The Indian should be coming along pretty soon."

"The Indian?" asked Duke wryly.

"Yeah," she continued, "there's an Indian tearing up bars on Fullerton Avenue."

"Yeah?" Duke responded with a knowing smile. "You don't have to close up." He batted his hand in the air at the idea.

"Oh, yes I do."

"No. No, ya don't!" Duke assured the lady.

"Why do you say that—I don't have to close up?" Penny asked him suspiciously.

"Because *I'm* The Indian!" He raised his glass in the air with a wide smile on his face before downing its contents.

The two of them laughed heartily, then Duke bought them both another drink. For the remainder of the night, Duke regaled the lady bartender with stories of his prowess. She was a rapt audience, and it was an enjoyable evening. The first in a long time for Duke.

***

Duke's drinking spree continued the next three years, until one enlightening summer evening at Conny's Bar. Mixing whiskey and beer, Duke had been pouring drinks down his throat all night when the barroom started to spin. He couldn't focus on a single piece of furniture in the room. He swayed on the bar stool, fighting to maintain his balance.

Seeing that he had an advantage, the younger bartender grabbed the night stick from behind the counter and started to razz Duke about his condition. "Aren't you The Indian? You're the guy that dropped Big Frank a few years back, right?"

Duke's blood surged. He squeezed both of his hands into fists at his sides, and slid off of the bar stool. He turned to look at the younger man behind the bar counter. "What about it?" he asked.

"You couldn't knock a can off of a fence right now. You're a drunkard!"

Duke leaned forward menacingly toward the man and said, "Why don't you come out from behind that bar and let me show you what I can do?"

The bartender swung the night stick down as hard as he could.

The night stick bounced off the side of Duke's head, angering him beyond his limit. Duke glared at the man, pulling his right arm back until his clenched hand was nearly even with his shoulder. Then, like a catapult, he launched himself over the bar, his steel-hard fist smashing into the man's jaw, shattering it. The loud *crack* split the air just before the man dropped to the ground behind the bar. Duke picked up his hat off the counter and headed out the door to walk home to his empty apartment.

His cousin, Corrine, had heard word through the neighborhood about what had happened at Conny's and decided to get Duke out of town. Using the spare key her cousin had given to her she opened the door of his apartment and found Duke passed out on his couch, snoring loudly. He half-awoke

157

and vaguely remembered her and a few male attendants putting him on the train that night headed towards South Dakota. He was still drunk when she dumped him onto a seat in a coach car and handed the money for the fare to the conductor.

In the light of morning, the liquor started to wear off. Duke woke up and looked around groggily. The beat of the coach car on the rails registered in his mind that he was on a train. He had difficulty focusing on his surroundings, and his head and stomach ached horribly.

As he pushed himself up in his seat, he began to shake violently. He was sweating so profusely his clothing was damp.

There were only a few other passengers seated in the car with him. One gentleman watched as Duke curled himself into a ball on the seat. He came to sit beside Duke, covering him with a small travel blanket, "I know what you are going through, son. I went through it myself not too long ago. You're going to be okay."

Duke didn't feel well enough to answer. He simply laid still, willing his stomach to stop churning.

The man stayed near Duke all the way to Sioux City. He explained to Duke that he was experiencing withdrawal from the alcohol. "It's going to be tough to get it out of your system, but once you do—you'll be all right," the man assured him.

Duke was grateful for the man's presence and soothing words. When they arrived at their destination, Duke shook the man's hand before he exited from the train.

It didn't take long to pick out his mother, Harriet, from the small crowd. She wore the long, black shawl that made her stand out and though her hair was beginning to gray at the temples, her face looked lovely to Duke. He walked to her weakly, then embraced her with an appreciative hug and continued to the passenger door of the truck where he leaned a moment before opening the door and slid onto the cloth seat. He didn't feel much like driving; his hands were shaking too much.

Harriet and Mel lived on a farm just outside of Wagner. After taking a long, hot shower, Duke changed into some clean clothes his mother had provided for him and laid down on the bed in the spare room. He stared at the ceiling, talking to himself.

"I could have killed him!" Duke said aloud to the ceiling. "I've gotta quit! I've gotta stop drinking, or I'm gonna kill someone."

Forgetting his life in Chicago, he stayed with his mother for the time being. Jeanette had remarried, and the children were small—they belonged with their mother, he figured.

He would call from time to time to speak with the kids and catch up on their activities. They were part of the reason he knew he wanted to get sober.

It was the end of summer, 1955. Harriet and Mel's farm had progressed quite nicely. Duke helped out on the farm wherever he could, and struck up a friendship with his step-cousin, Dub. They spent many days together, hunting for pheasant, deer and jack-rabbits. The time spent outdoors was soothing to Duke's soul. Somehow, up here in the vast wilderness of South Dakota, he found peace without a bottle.

In March of that year, Duke returned to his job as a tuck-pointer in Chicago. Every morning, he headed to a nearby coffee house for breakfast. When he tried to lift his coffee cup from its saucer, his hand shook so violently that the dark, hot liquid spilled onto his fingers and the white tablecloth beneath.

Cursing under his breath, he took his napkin and sponged up the mess. Then he grabbed his coffee cup with both hands, managing to bring it to his lips for a quick sip. For three months Duke was plagued by the shakes, but he was determined not to let alcohol get hold of him again.

Duke made the decision to move out of Chicago and into Long Lake, which was several miles north and west of the city. Still working as a tuck-pointer, Duke took the train to and from work in the city. Most weekends, he'd have his kids, Brady and Raleigh Jane, out to visit him.

As they got older, they were able to take the train out to see him. It was important to Duke to maintain his relationship with his children, but he was happy to be away from the city and all of its troubling influences. The relative quiet and peace of living at the water's edge gave him the perfect environment to relax and rejuvenate.

Duke eventually bought a small home in Fox Lake, just up a hillside from the water. It had a large lot of land next door, and he started to build a new home on it. He purchased a wheelbarrow and used a pick and a shovel to dig out a basement in the rocky ground. In the time it took Duke to build the home from the ground up, he was able to work through his nightmares, filing the details of the war in the recesses of his mind and vowing never again to reveal their contents.

Every day, after working hard in the city, he would return to the house and work on the lot next door, pouring his energy into making a home for himself, exactly the way he wanted his home to be.

It took him over ten years, and most of the spare time he had away from work, to complete his home. When he finished building it, he had worked through his demons and made the decision not to discuss his service in the Marines. No one in Fox Lake had any knowledge of the horrors he'd endured in the war—he kept it to himself. The only information that he shared was that he had been a Marine in World War II in the Pacific.

And he made a conscious decision to have people refer to him by his first name, Loren, instead of Duke. He was learning how to live again, how to enjoy the simple pleasures of life. He was laughing more, smiling more… and he wasn't drinking.

And Duke decided to pursue other interests. He bought a 1963 Cruiser's Inc., a wooden speedboat to use on Fox Lake. He spent a lot of time there with new friends, water-skiing and swimming off the side of the boat in the cool waters. Duke sought out his old friend, Bud Fox, to accompany him to dance halls in the city since he and Bud had remained friends, despite his divorce from Jeanette. And even though Duke enjoyed meeting ladies and spending time in their company, he made an oath to himself never to marry again. He couldn't go through the loving and leaving of another woman.

Duke had always had fun dancing, not only because he enjoyed the moves, but because it was a great way to maneuver an introduction to women he wanted to meet. Some Friday nights when he'd finish working at the Kercher Company, he'd called Bud to join him, and the two would hang out and dance until the hall closed. Dancing kept Duke busy and physically fit, and he was able to have a good time without drinking alcohol.

He won several trophies for his finesse as a ballroom dancer. The Fox Trot, The Jitterbug, the Waltz—he loved them all. He could always make quick moves with his feet. Developing himself as a boxer, according to the skills he'd read of Joe Louis, had become an advantage in more ways than one.

Duke's love of dancing gave him the idea for a new name for his boat. A silhouette of a black top hat, along with a tilted, black cane, was neatly painted on the sides of his boat, the "Top Hat and Cane." Duke enjoyed the boat more and more often, entertaining friends and close work associates. He'd also take his son Brady and his friends out to go water-skiing and swimming off the boat.

He'd found his niche, a place he could truly call "Home".

Duke with John Brady, at his home in Rhode Island.

Mother Harriet, smiling in front of her red car.

Chapter 15

The sun's afternoon rays sparkled like fireworks on the waters in front of the bridge as colors from passing boats got caught up in their reflection. The air was warm, and the breeze fragrant with the aroma of lilacs as it wafted past Duke's nose where he stood on his deck. He breathed in deeply, closing his eyes and enjoying the serenity.

As he slowly opened his eyes, his smile spread from ear to ear. Everything he had been working for was his. The house of his dreams, built with his own two hands, was his haven.

His companion appreciated the view from the deck, too, and remarked on Duke's choice of setting for his home. "It is a remarkable view, Loren," Bill said.

Duke had become good friends with Bill Buschman, the son of the woman who owned Fox Lake State Bank. Duke took Bill and his friends out on the boat water-skiing and cruising around the lake. The day Duke invited Bill to take a tour of his home, Bill was amazed at Duke's skills in construction.

At the front entrance of the home, Duke had laid out a framework for an impressive winding cement staircase that led to the front door. To the right of the door as he entered the living room was a large picture window that presented a picturesque view of the tree-lined hillside. Further into the room, he watched as Bill appreciated the workmanship obvious in the charming dark red, brick fireplace. Indian artwork and artifacts lined the walls and adorned the mantle. There were paintings of Indians, a hand-carved wooden buffalo, a small, hand-carved wooden canoe, a dream-catcher or two, and a sculpture, as well as a print, which depicted "The End of the Trail," by artist James Earle Fraser. Both sculpture and print showed a lone Native American Indian on his weary horse. Duke kept the images as a reminder of the great and valiant people who lost their rights as members of their native land.

Bill asked about the large picture of Duke's great grandfather over the fireplace.

"The photo of my great grandfather, Chief Running Bull of The Yankton Sioux Tribe, was taken at The White House in 1858. The original portrait hangs in the Smithsonian Gallery. I had this one blown up into a portrait-sized print from the picture my mother gave me. A friend of mine who lives in town, Don Kriz, is married to an artist, Laverne, who had an enlarged print made from the picture and added shading and depth to it with a few strokes of her paint brush. She did a great job, didn't she?" Duke asked his friend.

"It's incredible," Bill replied as he scrutinized the piece. The picture showed Chief Running Bull in a hand-carved wooden chair, his tomahawk in hand. His shirt was dark and neatly-tailored, and resembled the western fashion of the time. He wore a traditional Yankton Sioux blanket robe wrapped about his waist, and on his feet he wore leather moccasins. His face was handsome, with prominent cheekbones and a firm, aquiline nose. His chin was strong and square, and his mouth set with purpose. Running Bull's long braids extended down his shoulders, a quilted cloth woven between the plaits. Duke explained the significance of the headpiece worn on his great-grandfather's head. "Running Bull's headdress had two eagle feathers that extended straight out horizontally on either side, reflecting the deeds he had done in battle. An additional eagle feather stood straight up and reached toward the sky, signifying his status as a warrior—it was considered quite an honor to wear."

Duke expounded to his friend, "Running Bull had been in Washington to sign The Yankton Dakota Sioux Treaty of 1858, to define reservation boundary lines and make safe passage for people traveling through the Dakota lands. He had believed strongly in the mission and wanted peace between his people and the American Government," Duke spoke proudly of his great grandfather.

Bill was impressed by the history, shook his head and said, "That's amazing, Loren! I had no idea."

Duke motioned for Bill to follow him into the small bedroom located off the living room, next to the bathroom on the main floor. On the walls and book shelves were photos of Duke's family, and several books about both The Yankton Sioux and the United States Marine Corps. Duke switched the bedroom light off and led Bill back through the living room, where the two men moved on to the kitchen.

The kitchen was good-sized, and allowed room for a small dining table and chairs. As they entered, Bill asked Duke about the unusual bamboo print wallpaper that lined the kitchen walls. "This wallpaper reminds me of when I was in a swamp at Peleliu. I never thought I was gonna get outa there alive," he continued. "It's a reminder to me of what I've survived."

He took a breath, then continued somberly. "Peleliu was the first place I'd experienced those stiff stalks of bamboo. I'll never forget how hard it was to move through 'em. Most of the stalks were only six inches or so apart!" He held up his hands to demonstrate the distance to his friend. "And I had to move quietly so the Japs wouldn't find me." He finished shaking his head, then motioned for Bill to follow him.

Duke walked through the kitchen door to the indoor porch quickly, deliberately ending the path that the conversation had taken. He didn't want to discuss anything further about the war, and Bill didn't ask any more questions about it, seeming to have sensed his discomfort.

As Bill followed Duke into the enclosed porch warmed by the mid-day sun, Duke showed him an indoor grill made of the same dark red brick as the fireplace in the living room. Duke called it his barbecue room. Much like a fireplace, the grill vented to the outdoors via a decorative chimney. Dark metal grates were suspended in the brick to act as a cooking surface over the flames. There were windows to the north of the room that offered a view of the shimmering water of the lake below. The entrance to the porch was a sliding glass door that led out to a large, two-story deck that had a perfect view of the hillside leading down to the lake. As a special feature, when guests pressed the doorbell off the deck, it played the tune of "The Halls of Montezuma," the "Marines' Hymn". Duke got a kick out of operating it for his friend.

They had returned to their starting point in the tour, and Duke was getting hungry for supper. He had built another staircase, this one a wooden one, that had a small landing place between the two sets of steps that led down to the driveway. He led his friend down the staircase, and the two stood conversing for a few more minutes on the gravel drive.

Duke could see Bill was very impressed at both the level of skill and the amount of work required to complete such a task as single-handedly building his home. He offered to take Duke to dinner that night at a local restaurant to chat.

After a pleasant dinner, the two of them got to talking about living in Fox Lake. Bill admired Duke's abilities as a carpenter, electrician, and general handyman and told him about the new bank building he was planning. He told Duke quite frankly that he appreciated his working skills, and then offered him a position with the bank as a general handyman, of sorts.

"Loren," he said, "come work for me at the bank." He knew Duke could conquer just about any problem that arose in the bank—electrical, structural, or simply keeping up with the general maintenance of the building.

In good humor, Duke told Bill in no uncertain terms, "You couldn't afford me, Bill."

"Well, I don't know about that. What are you currently taking in?"

When Duke told him, Bill smiled and extended his hand. "I'll offer you the same salary you're making now, and you'll only have to drive a few blocks to work."

Duke couldn't believe Bill was offering the same money he was making at Kercher Company. Suddenly, he was glad to take the job.

"I accept," he answered, shaking the hand of his new boss. "Just give me time to give notice at Kercher. I've been there a long time."

"No problem, Loren. Take all the time you need," Bill replied.

***

Duke was an integral part in the building of the new bank. The new building was much larger and more modern, and the project totaled about a million and a half dollars. It was a large building, with many offices and even a small room for Duke to use as an office.

Duke liked working at the bank and in the town he lived in. Commuting in busy traffic to Kercher had never been easy. With the time saved from not having to travel so far to work, Duke was able to enjoy more leisure time. The extra money he saved was put to good use, as well. Not only did he have the full use of a Chevrolet 4x4 pickup truck as a company car, but he had been able to purchase a sports car, too, a brand-new, bright white, 1976 Chrysler Cordoba. It came with a white vinyl landau roof that extended over the back top end of the car. It had luxurious pillow seats made of a deep, burgundy-colored knit cloth. Under the hood was a 400hp, 4 barrel carb engine that vented to dual exhausts in the rear. It was the sweetest ride Duke had ever owned!

Late one Sunday afternoon, Duke decided to take a walk before the sun went down. He made his way down the steep, wooden staircase with his dog, Luke, panting at his heels. Luke was a five-year-old Basset hound that had large black, brown and white spots haphazardly coloring his furry mid-sized form. His ears hung down to his feet, but he had managed to learn to keep his head up as he ran so as not to step on his ears as he tried to keep pace with Duke.

Luke jumped and barked loudly at Duke's side as they made their way down the sharply angled hillside to walk the short distance to the lake. Continuing down the road as it wound its way around the bay, several people greeted Duke, many of them stopping to chat. He really liked living here in Fox Lake, away from the city.

Duke had maintained relationships with many of his fellow Marines. He corresponded with many of them often, or spoke with them on the phone regularly. He and General Ray Davis spoke every few months to keep in touch concerning their comrades in the First Marine Division.

Duke also made several trips over the years to attend reunions that included his friends from A Company, including Frank Aubertin and Stan Bitchell. The reunions took place across the country from San Diego, California to Boston, Massachusetts; to both Pittsburgh and Philadelphia, Pennsylvania; to New York, New York. It was always good to see the friends who had survived with him. The bonds he and his fellow Marines had developed were stronger than any other bonds Duke developed in his life.

Duke's good friend and Marine comrade, Corporal John Brady, had never been able to attend any of the reunions, given the multiple hospitalizations for surgeries he'd had to endure over the years, but Duke still did his best to keep in touch with him. John had told Duke he had undergone at least twenty-seven operations to replace the skin he'd lost on Okinawa from the phosphorous grenade he'd been hit with. He often joked with Duke that just about every bit of skin on him had been replaced, except maybe the tip of his nose.

Duke was always glad to hear the smile in his friend's voice. He couldn't imagine having to suffer from such chronic pain. Many of their phone calls ended with one or the other of them promising to get together for a visit. This time when their phone call came to a close, John brooked no argument.

He had wanted Duke to meet his family for a long time and the perfect opportunity arose in late spring.

When Duke arrived at Logan Airport in Boston, near John's home in Rhode Island, John's brother and sister were there to greet him as he exited the baggage claim area. Another brother had a large, black luxury car waiting in the parking area, and the two men wasted no time in setting Duke's luggage in the trunk and jumping back into the car to set out for their family home. An extravagant party had been planned for their parent's wedding anniversary, and Duke was honored to have been invited.

When they arrived in the circular driveway, Duke looked out his window and saw the supporting white columns that lined the front of the stately home. There were numerous windows facing the front drive, and lush landscaping surrounded the house with pink magnolia trees, lovely blue hydrangea bushes, and beautiful white lilies. It was not only an aesthetically pleasing garden, but also a sweetly-fragranced one.

As the group ascended the steps to the front door, it opened to reveal a handsome young man with blond hair and bright blue eyes. He introduced himself as John's brother, Joe, and held the door to invite Duke inside.

The entrance was vaulted, with a glistening chandelier lighting the foyer. Joe led them through some freshly painted white French doors and into a cozy family room with a fireplace. They waited only a few minutes or so before John Brady entered the room.

Duke tried to contain his shock. John's hair was stark white and stood up straight on top of his head. His skin was a bright, yet slightly pale, red.

Duke stood up immediately and threw his arms around his old friend. "John, it's so good to see you!" He hugged his friend gently, not certain of how much pressure to exert.

John returned the hug heartily with a pat on Duke's back, saying, "If it weren't for you, I wouldn't be here, my friend! It's good to see you."

Duke, John, and John's brothers and sister shared stories and answered each other's questions until they all were laughing in enjoyment.

A commotion was heard in the foyer, and Joe Brady stood and got the group's attention to receive his parents for the party. Duke was enjoying this family, appreciating their company and feeling so welcomed.

Two of John's brothers attended their father down the stairs as their father was in a wheelchair. When they reached the bottom of the staircase, Mr. Brady stood and they walked slowly with him together to the entrance of the living room.

Mr. Brady straightened his frame and looked at Duke. He took a step toward Duke, and his sons made a move to support him. He shrugged them off, determinedly. "Let me alone!" he bellowed. "I'll walk by myself!"

Duke stood straight, watching the older man move toward him. Though his steps were frail, Mr. Brady's outstretched hand rose steadily as he moved toward Duke. Duke reached out and enthusiastically shook the older man's hand.

The handshake was firm and wrought with meaning. "I want to thank you for saving my son's life!" Tears glistened in the father's eyes.

Duke nodded. "It was my pleasure, sir." Duke felt the love and appreciation, not only from the hand he shook, but from the entire family that surrounded him here. He felt like he was a part of this close-knit family. They all accepted him so readily, with complete gratitude for saving John Brady's life.

Duke spent the night reviewing the events of the day as he lay in bed staring at the ceiling. It brought a tear to his eye to consider the effort Mr. Brady had made in walking the distance of the room to shake his hand and thank him. It was a moment that Duke knew would affect him the rest of his life.

Before noon the next day, John invited Duke to have lunch at a seaside restaurant. The air was warm and the sun shone brightly as they walked the pier to the front door of the building. Duke asked John to recommend something for him.

"Well, Duke, you could have the best scallops you've ever eaten right here," he offered, smiling. "They're considered to be one of the delicacies of the sea."

Duke took him up on it and was glad he did. He savored the flavor of the fresh seawater scallops dipped in melted butter. "Delicious!" he smacked his lips together, his appetite appeased with the last bite.

He spent three more days in the Brady family's company and delighted in every moment of it, but soon it was time for him to return home. He said his good-byes to the family and promised his friend John that he'd stay in touch.

His dog, Luke, was happy to see his master when Duke arrived home from his trip. When Duke was home, the dog never left his side.

Luke jumped up on Duke and licked his face in excitement.

"I'm happy to see you, too, boy."

Luke ran to the sliding door to let Duke know he wanted to explore the outdoors. "All right, all right, Luke. I'll take you for a walk down by the lake." Duke grabbed the leash that hung by the door and attached it to Luke's collar. It felt good to be appreciated.

As the years passed, however, the dog began to move much more slowly and didn't rise as quickly to follow Duke as he once had.

Duke recognized the inevitable signs that Luke was experiencing old age, and it wasn't many months before he was forced to take the beloved old Basset hound to the veterinarian's office to have him peacefully put to sleep. Duke was deeply saddened when he felt the life leave Luke's slight, fourteen-year-old frame. Duke wrapped the dog in his favorite blanket, carried him to the truck, laid him on the bench seat next to him, and drove home.

Before stepping out of the truck, he wiped away the tear that fell from his eye. He forced himself to keep moving, carefully lifting the bundle from the seat and carrying it to the backyard. He laid Luke gently on the soft grass, and went back to the garage to retrieve a shovel and complete the task that had to be done. When he finished digging then filling the grave, Duke leaned on the shovel a few moments, remembering all the wonderful times he and Luke had shared. He'd miss that dog. Sighing deeply, he shook his head in sorrow.

Then he turned to walk back into the house, alone.

***

Duke enjoyed working at Fox Lake State Bank, and he liked keeping busy. The owners and employees were like one, big, happy family, and over the years, they'd all become good friends. They spent a lot of time in each other's company at regularly scheduled parties and picnics made to keep morale up.

Shortly after Luke died, the group got together and talked about how they should get a new puppy for Duke. Jerry O'Sullivan, vice-president of Fox Lake State Bank planned it all without Duke being aware.

Not long after the plan was hatched, Duke invited the group to his home for a party. It came as a complete surprise to Duke when he was presented with the puppy at his own front door.

His friend Jerry had arrived with the puppy in his arms, and the minute Jerry handed the puppy over to Duke, it started licking Duke's face. Duke chuckled, cuddling the pup's soft ear with his cheek. He was a handsome Bassett hound like Luke.

Seeing the familiar tri-colored pattern of white, brown and black fur tugged at Duke's heartstrings, but then the puppy barked in his face and happily began licking it again, demanding Duke's attention. He named the dog Sam and was happy to learn from Jerry that Sam was of championship lineage—the same family line as Luke. The party was a success and a good time was had by all—even Sam.

Duke and Sam became inseparable. He had missed Luke for some time, and it was nice having a dog around, again.

Duke worked another three years at the bank, retiring in 1987 at the age of 62. His friends at the bank had another big party for him to celebrate. They ate an elaborate dinner, shared stories and laughed, dancing until dawn. When Duke's head hit the pillow that night, he went right to sleep.

Duke's favorite thing about being retired was doing what he wanted, when he wanted. And that is exactly what he did.

Eventually his renter moved from the small house that he had originally lived in when he moved to Fox Lake and built his current home. Duke's son, Brady, moved into the house with his wife, Verna, and their two children, Angela and Jason. It was so nice to have them next door and to help out with some chores occasionally. And Duke really enjoyed celebrating the holidays together with them.

The years passed quickly, and in 1997, Duke received a call from Frank Aubertin's son. Chris called to invite Duke to his mother and father's surprise fiftieth wedding anniversary party. Chris encouraged Duke to attend by saying, "My dad would love to see his two favorite Marines from Peleliu at the party," referring to Duke and Stan Bitchell.

"I'll be there, Chris," Duke assured him.

***

It was a sunny summer day when Duke and Stan arrived at the clubhouse in Pennsylvania where Frank and Claire Aubertin's party was being held. All of the family was in attendance: kids, grandkids, cousins, aunts and uncles, and many long-time friends. When the time came, Chris gave Duke and Stan the signal that the couple was arriving.

With Stan, Duke opened the heavy double doors to receive the honored guests of the day. Duke and Stan each sported a specially-made red Marine cap with golden-yellow writing that read "Peleliu Survivor" on the front.

A white stretch limo pulled up to the front steps, and the driver got out to open the back door. Out stepped Frank, followed by his wife of fifty years. They both smiled as they looked up the steps at the people gathered to greet them.

Frank let out a cry when he recognized Duke and Stan standing near each of the entrances. "Well, I'll be!" he shouted in surprise. He guided his wife up the steps, then reached to shake each of his friend's hands and give them a welcoming hug.

The Aubertins, Duke, and Stan entered the building together and proceeded to the dining hall where a band was playing the "Anniversary Waltz." The guests gave the couple a standing ovation as they entered.

Once the dance was over everyone found their seats, and Frank gave a warm, humorous speech about his fifty years of marriage to Claire—the love of his life. Afterward, a delicious dinner was served. And later, there was more dancing, which of course Duke greatly enjoyed.

The three Marine comrades posed for a picture together for the Aubertin family photos. Both Duke and Stan had arranged to stay for a long weekend, and the trio got caught up with the latest news from each other's lives.

The next day the men got together over brunch and later played cards, laughing at Stan's attempts at jokes. Dinnertime was spent with all of the family in attendance, and Duke remarked to Stan how fortunate he was to have such a kind and beautiful wife. It was a fun time had by all that weekend, and Duke was glad to have spent the time reconnecting with his cronies.

***

Approximately one year later, in the afternoon hours of a spring day, Duke received another phone call from Chris Aubertin. Frank's son was calling to tell Duke that his long-time friend and comrade had passed away. Duke, stunned by the news, was silent for several moments before giving his condolences to Chris.

169

Chris thanked Duke, but went on to express his concern that his father wasn't going to receive an all Marine military burial. The American Legion had arranged for each of the Armed Forces to act as pall bearers at the funeral, but his father's wishes were that only Marine pall bearers be included.

Duke promised to look into it for him, and told Chris he would get right back to him.

Duke looked at the old picture posted on his kitchen wall, pinned to the wallpaper next to the calendar. The picture showed him standing with his comrades and fellow platoon sergeants from A Company. In the photo, Frank was wearing his red, white and blue hat with the First Marine Division patch standing out prominently against the white background on the front. Only Duke and Stan were wearing their Peleliu Survivor hats.

Duke grabbed the phone receiver with one hand and began dialing the number of the one man he knew could help with the other. General Ray Davis.

General Davis answered the phone on the first ring in a clear, firm voice. "Hello?" he said, the word used to both greet the caller and demand a response.

It had been several years since Duke had spoken with the retired general. "Hello, General Davis, this is Duke, The Indian. Do you have a moment?"

"Why, Duke! Hello, how are you?" General Davis sounded genuinely pleased to hear from him.

Duke's tone of voice deepened as he got to the point of the phone call, "I hate to give you bad news, General, but Frank Aubertin's son called me today. Frank has died."

He gave the retired general a moment to process the information and to express his sorrow. Then he continued. "His son tells me the plans for his father's funeral include a group of mixed-military pall bearers from the local American Legion. I'd like to see that Frank gets the full military honors that he deserves with all Marines. Can you help him out with this?"

"I'll take care of it, Duke," General Davis spoke with conviction.

"Thank you, sir!" Duke responded, knowing that the general would be true to his word. He placed the receiver on its cradle momentarily, then picked it up again to dial Chris Aubertin.

The young man answered the phone immediately and seemed relieved to hear Duke's voice. Duke assured him that everything would be taken care of, that he'd spoken to General Davis, and had the General's word that the details would be worked out regarding Frank's funeral.

Frank's son sounded sincerely grateful.

Duke attended his friend's funeral service in Pennsylvania a few days later. Sergeant Frank Aubertin received full military honors at his burial, with a full Marine casket team in attendance. It meant a lot to Duke to help handle this matter not only for Frank's sons, Chris and Robert, and the rest of his family, but also to see that his good friend and comrade from World War II received the proper honors due him.

As the hearse arrived at the grave site, every active-duty Marine presented arms. The team then deftly carried the flag-draped casket to the grave site, their movements slow and synchronized.

After the service was delivered by the chaplain, the team leader stepped up to the casket to initiate the straightening of the flag tightly, so it hovered above the casket. The seven riflemen of the firing party volleyed three shots under the command of "Ready! Aim! Fire!," a signal designed to declare the dead have been cared for and the remainder of the soldiers of war are ready to go back to the fight.

The command, "Present arms!" was given to the fire team, while the bugle sounded "Taps" in the formal good-bye to this Marine soldier, Duke's friend. Duke's right hand was held in still salute at the brim of his cover as he stood at attention. The command, "Order arms!" was given by the casket team leader.

Duke slowly brought his hand back to his side and remained standing at attention. The leader ensured that the flag was stretched out and level, centered over the casket, then backed away. Then he gave the order to fold the flag neatly with the help of his team, corner to corner, never allowing it to touch the ground. Once folded, the flag was handed to the chaplain.

The chaplain walked with the triangular-shaped bundle to stand in front of Claire, where he gently placed the folded flag in her arms. He then spoke these words of honor: "On behalf of the President of the United States, the United States Marine Corps, and a grateful nation, please accept this flag as a symbol of our appreciation for your loved one's honorable and faithful service." She hugged it tightly to her chest and wept quietly.

Duke heaved a heavy sigh in farewell to his good friend and Marine warrior, Sergeant Frank Aubertin, and looked at the remembrance card he held in his hand, reading it to himself. He noted the passage that was written below his friend's name. It read:

"Taps"

Lord be merciful to Your servants, our brother and sister, veterans and spouses, who have most recently departed this life. Bring them now to the happiness of eternal life in Your kingdom. We shall miss them but never forget what they have meant to us and to our Country. Give comfort to those loved ones who remain behind in the knowledge that the departed fought the good fight and lived the righteous life. Semper Fidelis.

Chapter 16

It was a Friday morning, December 24, 2004, and Duke was up early, as usual, looking forward to the Christmas celebration planned for the afternoon with his grandson, Douglas, who was bringing his fiancé. He'd heard a lot about Donna, and was anxious to meet her. Doug was his eldest grandson, and he wanted him to find happiness. Douglas was born to his daughter and her first husband, Ron Nykolaycuyk—a good father and an honorable man. Sadly, Ron had passed when Doug was still a boy of four.

That morning Duke had taken a shower and put on a short-sleeved blue and white plaid shirt, his grey trousers with red-striped suspenders attached, and his most comfortable pair of black shoes. He examined himself in the bathroom mirror, running a hand over the top of his silver-gray hair buzzed neatly just that week. Grabbing the tweezers off the counter, he plucked a few thick, grey hairs from his brows, then stood back to admire his reflection. He thought he looked darn sharp as he postured in the mirror. *Not bad for a seventy-nine year old man.*

He moved back to the kitchen and swept the floor, emptying the contents of the dust pan into a brown paper bag he kept behind the open kitchen door that led to the barbeque room. One of his two cats jumped up onto a kitchen chair. The black-brown striped-fur cat turned in circles until he was satisfied with his position and proceeded to lay down on the soft cushion.

"Rocky, you're gonna have to move once they get here," Duke told the impertinent kitty. The cat looked unimpressed as he licked his front paws individually, then settled down to take a nap.

Duke took one last look around the room and decided it looked just fine for his guests. He peered out the kitchen window and into a mirror he had strategically positioned on the outside wall of the house, so he could see who might be arriving in his driveway. When he saw the black sedan pull up, he smiled, then spun, and stepped out onto the porch to ready himself behind the wall of the sliding door to greet them.

Much to Duke's pleasure, Douglas pressed the doorbell just outside the door and the strains of "The Halls of Montezuma" filled the air loudly as he jumped in front of the door, surprising them, and slid it open to invite them in.

Doug introduced his companion, "Merry Christmas, Grandpa. This is my beautiful fiancé, Donna." He watched as she gently brushed a few strands of light blonde hair away from her blue-green eyes, then smiled at him sweetly.

He moved forward to give her an exuberant hug which she returned warmly, speaking in a soft, melodic voice, "Merry Christmas!"

"Welcome, welcome," Duke ushered them out of the cold and into the warmth of his home.

Duke remarked to his grandson, "You are a lucky man, Douglas!"

His admiration was well received, and Donna responded kindly, "Thank you!"

His great-granddaughter, Jennifer, had decided to come, too. She was getting so big. Duke took note of her shoulder-length brown hair and dark-brown eyes. She looked cute in her faded blue jeans with a wide-striped green shirt. She lived about an hour east with her mother, but Doug always drove to get her every weekend to bring her to his home to spend quality time with her.

Duke led them into the kitchen and offered for them to sit down. He picked up the cat from the chair at the end of the table and carried him to the window where he opened the screen with his free hand. Attached to the window was a small screened box with a wooden floor. Duke explained, "I built a few window boxes so the cats could sit and watch the squirrels playing outside. They love it, and it keeps them happy." He was proud of his handy work.

He noticed Doug was carrying a large platter in his hands, and directed him to set it on a kitchen shelf. "What'd you bring me, Douglas?" he asked interestedly.

"Donna baked all morning so she could bring you a delicious tray of iced cherry slices for dessert," Doug replied cheerfully.

"Well, isn't that something?" Duke shuffled over to the tray, leaned down and took a deep whiff. "Smells delicious!" he said with a smile directed at Donna, then he pivoted on his heel and proceeded to sit at the center of the kitchen table.

While Doug returned to the car to retrieve packages, Duke conversed with Donna and Jennifer in the kitchen. "Do you have any kids?"

"I have two tall, handsome sons named Brian and Adam," Donna replied with a smile.

Duke nodded his head in approval.

"How are things in school, Jennifer?" he asked.

She shrugged her shoulders and replied, "Okay, I guess."

She must be about twelve, now, Duke figured in his head.

Doug returned just then, his arms full of packages.

"Now what have you brought me?" Duke asked with a laugh.

"Oh, just a few Christmas presents," Doug responded with glee.

"You go ahead and have a seat, I'll be right back," Duke grabbed his cane from where it rested next to the cabinet and walked into his barbecue room. His leg had begun to bother him again, but he wasn't going to let it ruin a good time.

Suddenly the sounds of Native American music, replete with banging drums and melodic chanting, breached the silence of the house.

Duke appeared in the doorway of the kitchen, mimicking the forward and back again movements of an Indian performing his native dance, swaying as the music continued to stream from the speakers throughout the room. He told them it was being played from the old turntable he kept on the porch. He smiled at their surprise, reveling in his well-thought-out production to entertain on this visit.

Laughing, Doug and Donna delighted in watching him as he danced to the festive music. They clapped appreciatively as he ended his steps with a flourish. Even Jennifer had fun watching her great-grandpa, a big smile spread across her face. The Spirit of Christmas was alive and well at Grandpa Duke's house.

They took turns opening their Christmas gifts, enjoying each other's company. Duke shared his memories of Christmases past when Doug was still a child, with Donna.

"When Douglas was a young boy living in Chicago, he could hardly wait to see me pull up in my 1976 Cordoba. As soon as I rang the doorbell, Douglas was always there to open the door. Every year, I arrived carrying two large, bright red poinsettia plants I got from the bank, one tucked under each arm. 'Merry Christmas!' I'd announce.

"As soon as I found a place to set down the plants, I'd open my arms to Douglas and give him a big, warm hug," he beamed as he told his story.

"Douglas also looked forward to visiting me here in Fox Lake," he went on. "From the time he was a child, the minute he was in the door, he would make a quick trip to the small bedroom off of the living room. The room was filled with pictures from South Dakota and military books I've collected over the years. Douglas liked to look at the military books, especially while he attended Howe Military Academy where he graduated in '87. He was a curious young man. On one of the bookshelves, I kept a small box, similar in size and shape to a jewelry box," he continued.

"One particular Christmas when he was younger, Douglas lifted the lid of the small, gray hinged box, amazed to see the Purple Heart Medal I had been awarded. I watched from the doorway as he'd noticed I'd written the numbers 1944 in black ink on the inside top of the box. He was eager to ask me about my experiences in the Pacific during World War II, because he had been studying the history of the war in his fifth grade class. He was wondering what it had been like," the corners of his mouth raised as he recalled his grandson's interest.

"'Grandpa, can you tell me what you did in World War II?' he asked me with excitement. He was hoping to hear something he could share in class, I guess." Duke surmised.

"But I wasn't ready to talk about it yet," he continued, his expression growing grim. "Oh, it was awful! Just awful! The war was a horrible thing." His tone reflected his great sadness in remembering as he spoke to his grandson, Donna and his great-granddaughter.

"There were bodies all over the beach, buddies of mine," he went on.

"I didn't know if I was going to get out of the swamp alive that first night on Peleliu. On the third day, a big gun rolled out of the cave and killed my machine gunner and two ammo carriers. It blew me into a coral wall, blew holes in both my legs, and I was bleeding all over. I didn't think I'd ever get off of that island alive."

Doug and Donna exchanged concerned glances—it was apparent they didn't know what to do or say. Grandpa Duke could see their confusion and discomfort and he was shaken, as well. He decided to change the subject.

For the remainder of their visit, Duke spoke of his relatives in South Dakota and how he'd love it if the two of them could join him there for the next reunion.

Doug and Donna responded warmly in unison, "Of course, we'd love to come!"

***

In June of 2006, Grandpa Duke invited Doug and Donna to join him in Wagner, South Dakota to visit his mother, Grandma Harriet. Doug and Donna had been married on April 29th, 2005 of the previous year, and this was their first visit together to see his mother in South Dakota. The last time Douglas had visited he had been only ten years old, and his little brother, Christopher, had been only three.

Back then, Duke's mother still lived on a farm just outside of town. After Mel died, she moved into an apartment complex in the center of town, but visited family members in Chicago whenever she could.

Duke had driven to Wagner a few days before his grandson and wife would arrive and set himself up at a hotel in town. He met his cousin Arliss for dinner that night.

A few days later his grandson and wife arrived in Wagner. After stowing their bags at the same local hotel, Doug and Donna drove with Grandpa Duke to visit with Great Grandma Harriet in town. Duke was glad they had come to join him.

When they first arrived at Harriet's apartment, she was happy to receive their company. After Duke made the introductions, they all chatted easily.

Doug exclaimed to his great-grandmother, "Wow, Grandma, you look terrific! What is your secret?"

Without hesitation she answered, "I exercise every day, read the Bible, and I always have a bowl of hot oatmeal in the morning and a glass of warm milk before I go to bed at night." She smiled warmly at her great-grandson and his wife.

At ninety-six years of age, Duke's mother was the oldest living member of the Yankton Sioux Tribe. Her slight frame barely made an impression in the cushioned seat of her chair. Her hair was a soft gray, with flecks of black strands still evident, mostly at the forehead and at the nape of her elegant neck. She wore gold, wire-rimmed glasses that framed her watchful dark eyes and rested gently on her aquiline nose. Grandpa Duke appreciated that Donna spoke of his resemblance to his mother.

Several minutes of friendly conversation passed before Grandpa Duke drew their attention to the birds singing outside his mother's apartment window. A pair of house finches sat perched on a swing, enjoying the summer sun. Both of the tiny creatures were gray in color, but the male of the pair had vibrant red feathers decorating his breast and topping the crown of his head. A few days before, Duke had put up a pole with an attached perch just a few feet from his mother's window so she could enjoy the short, cheery warbling of the tiny birds as they basked in the warmth of the sun's rays.

Duke and his mother talked about what was happening in town, and he mentioned that they would be visiting the cousins, Arliss and Charlotte. She smiled as she listened to her son speak. Grandma Harriet was obviously happy to share in the company and pleased to spend time with her son, great-grandson and his beautiful wife.

After a delightful visit, Duke directed them to visit the old cemetery where Chief Running Bull and his wife, Barbara, had been buried. Chief Struck by the Ree and other ancestors were also buried there. The cemetery, located in a small town called Greenwood, just a few miles south of Wagner, which was the town where he had been born. Nearby, he showed them a monument that had been dedicated to the delegates that traveled to Washington D.C. to sign The Yankton Dakota Sioux Treaty of 1858. The names of both Struck by the Ree and Running Bull, as well as other delegates, were etched into the monumental stone tribute.

Though their visit was a short one, it was nice to have introduced Doug and Donna to his extended family. He couldn't wait until their next visit to this scenic part of the country, and to have them meet even more family members who had already announced their confirmation of attending the 2010 reunion.

***

Two years later, on May 17th, 2008, Grandpa Duke called Douglas and Donna at home to tell them the sad news that his mother had passed away in her sleep. He had loved his mother very much and always wanted the best for her. At ninety-eight years of age, Harriet Abdalla had lived a full life, but her spirit would always be with him.

He would miss her very much, but was comforted by the fact that she had passed peacefully.

***

Later that same year in December, Donna and Doug made their annual Christmas visit to Fox Lake. They brought Jennifer with them, as well. When they arrived at Grandpa Duke's, they walked through the barbecue room and entered the kitchen.

After they exchanged Christmas presents with each other, Duke announced to them that he had a special present for his great-granddaughter. Her sixteenth birthday was on December 21st, which is the first day of winter, and Grandpa Duke had this gift prepared especially for her. He hoped she'd like it. He held up a red jacket for his great-granddaughter to see. The Sioux Indian name given to her by her great-great-grandmother was embroidered in a clean, white stitching in a sort of semi-circle on the back of the Marine red wind-breaker. "Waniyetu Anpetu Wanji Win," meaning first day of winter in the Dakota Sioux language, adorned the canvas of the shiny red material.

When Grandpa Duke handed Jennifer the jacket, he smiled in anticipation of her response to the gift.

"Thank you," she said as she gave him a hug.

"You're welcome!" he stated emphatically with a big smile.

Duke was eager to see her wear it and asked her to put it on. The bright red of the jacket complimented Jennifer's dark-brown, shoulder-length hair, dark-brown eyes and olive complexion. He looked at her wearing it and thought the jacket was a perfect fit. He was pleased.

Jennifer removed her new jacket and handed it off to her father, who also gave her a loving hug, before stepping into the barbecue room, to set it on a tabletop for her.

Donna's attention was drawn to the memorabilia that decorated the walls and countertops of Grandpa Duke's kitchen. Many framed pictures and drawings lined the walls, much more so than on their last visit. He watched as she noted a framed application from Omaha, Nebraska, with Duke's signature in the lower right-hand corner, hanging on the wall next to the porch. It was evidence of his enlistment in the Marines at age eighteen. The famous picture of a Marine soldier running through Death Valley on Okinawa was hanging nearby above the window.

There were two charcoal sketches of Duke hanging on the same wall made by a war correspondent, Roland James, at different times during the hostilities. "This one was drawn shortly after I first arrived on Pavuvu," he pointed to the first sketch. "And this other one was drawn after I had arrived back at Pavuvu, while I recovered from the action on Peleliu," he indicated with his finger. There was also a framed article from a magazine describing the horrors of the battle on Peleliu.

Duke believed his great-granddaughter was humbled when she noticed several medals he had received for having served in World War II, including a duplicate Purple Heart Medal, a Distinguished Service Award and a Good Conduct Medal, as well as two Presidential Unit Citations for his service in World War II, a Pacific Campaign Medal, and a WWII Victory Medal, all encased in a glass-front wooden box. Duke explained to Jennifer that he had made the memory box himself and hung it on the kitchen wall to showcase his medals.

In the center top of the box amidst the medals was his First Marine

Division patch, known as The Blue Diamond. The patch was unique in its design. A red number one was in the center of the diamond with the word "Guadalcanal" in white stitching extending down its center, surrounded by the Southern Cross Constellation on a sea of blue. Five stars encompassed the number one.

Glancing to the left of it, Grandpa Duke pointed out to Douglas the copy of an old photo showing Duke, from the book, *The Old Breed*, also tacked to the wall. There was an arrow pointing to him, as he rested in the mud having been absolutely exhausted after three days of continuous battle against the Japanese in the pouring rains during the monsoon season on Okinawa. He waited as his grandson continued to peruse the walls of his kitchen. A map of Peleliu, drawn in Grandpa Duke's own hand, indicated the path he had taken once landing on the island. He had also printed notes concerning the various events that had taken place, to remind himself that he had endured these battles and the injuries that might have killed him.

He was grateful to be alive. The most important times of his life were pictured on his walls for them to see. Doug was silent as he viewed the memorabilia that his grandfather had collected. Pictures of both General Chesty Puller and General Ray Davis were posted on the wall near the clock.

Grandpa Duke's entire war history was hung on the walls of his kitchen. Each significant or meaningful event was framed. Donna seemed to sense the importance of the new display, though Duke hadn't yet revealed the importance of it yet.

Breaking the silence, Grandpa Duke announced that he had a special purpose in lining his walls with his war history. He matter-of-factly informed Douglas, Donna and Jennifer that when the time came, he was to be buried at Arlington National Cemetery in Washington, D.C. with full military honors.

As Doug and Donna exchanged looks, Duke went on to tell them that his military records were being reviewed to determine if he would be awarded the Congressional Medal of Honor. He also revealed that he was awarded the Distinguished Service Medal at a recent celebration of the Marine Corps birthday on November 10th at the local American Legion, where, in honor of his service, he blew out the candles on the massive birthday cake and had the honor of cutting the first piece with an officer's Marine saber.

He pointed to the wall where a recent magazine article was hanging. On the north wall of the kitchen, a magazine page from the Marines' *Leatherneck Magazine* had been carefully cut out and framed in glass hanging just above eye level as he stood and read it to them all: "The article, written June 2008, read:

Mail Call: Marine veteran Gunnery Sgt. Mike Ruffner, to locate members of A/1/1 during the battle for Okinawa and Cpl Loren "Duke" ABDALLA; Lieutenants W. P. WHITE, J. DUFFY, P. E. BURKE; Marines H. T. CLARKE from Georgia, Ace ADAMS and Corky BERNARD, both from Michigan, Stan BITCHELL from Massachusetts, and Barney ROURKE from New York." he finished proudly.

Duke informed them that he had recently received a phone call from Gunnery Sergeant Ruffner letting him know he needed two witness letters and a recommendation from a commanding officer in order for his service records to account for his heroic actions on May 5, 1945.

"I'm not sure there's anyone left alive from my company that could be a witness," Grandpa Duke said.

In his usual storytelling mode, he went on to share with them that one day after he'd eaten his lunch, his telephone rang. When he picked up the phone and said hello, the caller on the other end of the line asked him in a low and challenging voice, "Do you want to step outside?"

Immediately on the defense, Grandpa Duke said he reacted with a raised voice, "Yeah, I'll step outside with ya', who's this?"

Laughing good-heartedly, the caller identified himself as none other than his companion from Tientsin, China—Barney Rourke. The Mohawk Indian, who heralded from New York, had seen the article in *Leatherneck Magazine* and called to see how his old friend was faring.

Duke went on to tell them that he and Barney had talked friendly-like for nearly an hour, exchanging up-to-date information before they hung up. "Barney was with the Fifth NE Aircraft Unit before he joined us in Okinawa after the war was over," Grandpa Duke clarified for Douglas explaining that he was unable to act as a witness.

As he shared the story with Donna, Doug and his daughter, Duke proudly showed them his array of Ka-Bar knives that hung from or rested on, the square wooden shelves that lay beneath a small phone table, within arms' reach from where he was seated.

Deftly, he pulled one of the deadly knives out from its leather sheath. He demonstrated how each Marine would test his blade for sharpness. With the knife firmly held in one hand, he swiped it across his opposing arm, as he pretended to shave off the hairs in a smooth, clean motion. He then informed them that this was how it could be determined, during the war, whether a man was left- or right-handed.

The remembrance in his eyes showed clearly. The effects of World War II, of the singleness of his purpose during the war, was reflected there. The war had made a lasting, inexorable impact on his life. "My service is being reviewed for The Congressional Medal of Honor, Douglas! What do you think of that?" Duke asked him, a wide grin on his face.

Doug asked carefully, "Is there anything I can do to help you?"

"We'll see, we'll see."

***

One week later, in the beginning of 2009, Grandpa Duke called Douglas and asked him pointedly, "You got anything going on this year?"

"Well, no, Grandpa. Is there anything that you'd like for me to do?" Doug responded sincerely.

"I'm going to send you something in the mail. See what you can do with it." Duke hoped his grandson would be able to help him.

He had put together a portfolio of information defining his service as a Marine in World War II, accurately outlining his participation in the Battles of Peleliu and Okinawa, but specifically dealing with a battle on a long, hog-back ridge on the island of Okinawa, May 5th, 1945. There was also a handwritten letter from his grandfather explaining the specifics of his third squad performing the duties that led to the ultimate capture of the ridge. Along with this information, there were several pictures, including some of himself as a child with his grandma, Princess Minnie and his pet goat Billy, and of his great grandfather, Chief Running Bull. A copy of a notarized letter from his good friend, Marine Al Costella, who was an eye witness to Duke's heroic actions on May 5th, 1945 as squad leader for mortar platoon, A Company, was also included. Several other copies of information in Duke's handwriting that provided information of his involvement in crucial battle moments were an addition to the package.

A few days later Douglas called to discuss the information they'd received. "Up until this moment, Grandpa, I hadn't realized you had ever been on Okinawa. I thought you were sent home after being wounded on Peleliu," he said.

"Aw no, Douglas, I had a lot more fight in me after that!" Grandpa Duke exclaimed.

As they continued to read the documentation, Doug and Donna learned how the inquiries into Grandpa's military history had come about, beginning back in 2004.

***

Duke had wanted to check his property lines in Fox Lake to verify the boundaries. A friend recommended that he contact a gentleman named Richard Daniels, an attorney who had an office in Waukegan, Illinois. Grandpa Duke drove out to speak with him, and as he was sitting in his office, he noticed on the wall behind the man's desk a frame containing oversized captain's bars. There were other Marine Corps memorabilia on the walls as well. Duke asked Mr. Daniels if he had served in the Marines.

"Yes, Mr. Abdalla," the man said, "I was a captain in the Marines, but I am retired now. Did you serve?" he inquired conversationally.

Duke beamed at the man and stated, "I not only served, I fought on Peleliu and Okinawa in the Pacific." For the first time in many years, he opened up and told the retired captain about the battles he'd faced on both Peleliu and Okinawa. Somehow, the sense of brotherhood he felt with this fellow Marine allowed him to share the stories he had kept mostly to himself for all these years, and it felt good to talk about it.

Once Duke started, it was as if a floodgate had been opened. All of the memories, vibrant and real, poured from his lips as he recounted the course of his involvement in the war. Captain Daniels continued to listen and seemed excited to be the keeper of such history. The retired captain told Duke he was amazed that other than the Purple Heart Duke had been awarded for his wounds, he had not been awarded any other recognition for his incredible and harrowing actions in the face of his own peril.

In Duke's stead, Captain Daniels contacted the Commandant of the Illinois Marine Corps League, retired Gunnery Sergeant Michael Ruffner. Once Captain Daniels had shared Duke's story with Gunnery Sergeant Ruffner, he was moved to begin some research of his own. Ruffner began by retrieving Grandpa Duke's military records to confirm his eligibility for the Congressional Medal of Honor. Captain Daniels let Duke know that the research effort was in good hands.

For four years, Sergeant Ruffner informed Duke that he was collecting information. The call-out in the 2008 *Leatherneck Magazine* had prompted a letter to be written by one of Duke's good friends from the war. Marine Al Costella, then living in California, had written to Sergeant Ruffner, describing the extreme heroism and "gung ho" spirit that Duke embodied in battle. The letter read:

August 20, 2008

To Whom It May Concern:

I am writing this letter on behalf of a fellow Marine, who has put his life on the line many times to get a job done. He was a Gung Ho Marine in every respect. I saw what he did on Peleliu. Most of the Marines were stuck on the beach and could not advance because of snipers. Duke wiped out Japanese snipers in palm trees that were killing a lot of our guys. We didn't know where the shots were coming from, but he knew, and saved many lives. You would think he should have gotten a medal for that alone. Another time, while he was setting up his guns, he took a direct hit from one of the big Japanese guns, killing his machine gunner and two ammo carriers. He was blown aside and severely wounded. I don't know how he survived. I was there helping Duke and the other men, I made sure I got them back to the beach and hospital ship. The man I am talking about is none other than Loren Duke Abdalla. I call him Duke, and some call him The Indian.

Sometimes I think there might have been a little prejudice, and he could have been passed up for that reason. Let's go on to Okinawa, another bloody battle. On April 1, 1945 (April Fool's Day), we landed on Okinawa. The Army and

*the First Marine Division, and the Sixth Marine Division.
Our division, the First, was to cut across the middle of
Okinawa, which we did in three and one half days. The
Twenty-Seventh Army Division was to hit the southern part,
which they did, and was met with strong opposition. They
were pushed back—lots of wounded soldiers. The hold-up
was a long, hog-back ridge. The ridge housed a big gun that
was on tracks, inside the cave, and every time our sixteen
inch guns from our battleships would fire at them, they would
roll the gun back deep into the cave. This gun covered the
entrance to a draw. In order to proceed through the draw,
this gun had to be taken out. This job fell to the First Marine
Division. So we came south, to relieve the Twenty-Seventh
Army Division. The First Marine Division knew what the
problem was right away.*

*The job fell [to] the First Battalion, First Regiment, First
Marine Division. On May 2nd, C Company attacked the
ridge, they were pushed back. On May 3rd, B Company
tried, and was pushed back. On May 4th, the job fell to our
company (A Company). We changed our tactics. We went in
after dark, it was pitch black and pouring rain.*

*We knew what our objective was. The first platoon was to
move up the ravine to the base end of the ridge. The third
platoon was to go up the other ravine for the frontal attack.
The Japanese were well aware of what we were going to do.
They shelled us all night. We found cover in tombs, keeping
out of the pouring rain. On May 5th, at dawn, the third
platoon made their frontal attack. The first platoon made
their attack from the base of the ridge. Duke Abdalla took
his third squad up over the top. His job was to secure the
top of the ridge. Stan Bitchell, who was platoon sergeant
(Bitchell and Duke were both corporals, but Bitchell got the
job of platoon sergeant, because he was in V-12 Officer's
Training School). Bitchell took the rest of the platoon
around the base of the ridge, knocking out the spider traps,
which housed the nambus, same as our BAR's—except, they
had a front tri-pod and fired faster.*

*Bitchell worked his way forward to the mouth of the cave,
that housed the big gun. In the meantime, Duke and his third
squad (under heavy fire), took out all the machine guns and
the Japanese infantry. Duke Abdalla was standing at the
very top of the cave when he flushed the last Jap off the top*

of the ridge, the Jap jumped off to reach the safety of the cave, but he was too late, Alfonzo Calliqurei was standing with a sawed off shotgun and caught the Jap in mid-air. Buck (our demolition man) set up two pack charges, he threw one and Stan threw the other into the mouth of the cave with the big gun in it, and that was the end. Now that allowed the First Marine Division to proceed up the draw. Stan Bitchell received the Navy Cross, two other men, Joe Bureau and Alan Bleau, got Silver Stars. ???????? Duke Abdalla, who lost his whole squad, killed or wounded, was never mentioned. Just think about it, he could have been gone, with the rest of his squad. He is the guy that stood at the top of the cave that housed the big gun. If it were not for Duke Abdalla's actions, A Company would have been pushed back like B and C Company's.

It has been over sixty years, and you can forget a lot of things, but the experiences of the death of your buddies remains with you the rest of your life.

I know they will have plenty of sleepless nights. I do know this, that if anyone should have received a medal, it should have been Duke Abdalla. I know he made a difference in a war over sixty years ago.

My Name: Corporal Alexander Costella
First Marine Division
First Marine Regiment
'A' Company
Semper FI
So Help Me GOD

The letter was signed and notarized.

There was also an attempt to contact Stan Bitchell in Peabody, Massachusetts, to add an additional letter of witness about what Duke did on May 5, 1945, describing the details of the day Stan earned his Navy Cross.

But Duke learned too late, that his friend, Corporal Stanley Bitchell, had passed away on April 6, 2006. He also learned that Stan had been buried with full military honors, having achieved recognition substantiated by the awards of The Navy Cross and three Purple Hearts, as well as other accolades. Duke was saddened to hear of his friend and fellow Marine warrior's passing. He had been an honorable man.

After reviewing the piles of information on his kitchen table—papers that he'd sent copies of to his grandson Doug, Duke received a phone call one day not long after from him.

"I always knew you were tough, Grandpa, but this is crazy! You really are an American hero!"

Grandpa Duke enjoyed a laugh out loud at Doug's expense.

Douglas let him know that he was going to put his phone on speaker so his wife could join the conversation, and then spoke more seriously. "Donna is considering all of the news of your heroic acts in World War II and is thinking about writing a book about your life."

Donna asked, "What do you think about that, Grandpa?"

Grandpa Duke was thrilled at the possibility! "I think that's a great idea!" he yelled into the phone, making sure they both could hear him.

***

On March 8, 2009, Douglas and Donna drove to see Grandpa Duke in Fox Lake. They were excited to hear his story. When they had climbed the steps to the deck, Doug rang the "Marines' Hymn" doorbell and waited for Grandpa Duke to open the door.

"Come in, come in!" Grandpa Duke was all smiles as he invited them to sit at the kitchen table. He insisted that they sit down and enjoy the lunch they'd brought to share with him. After eating the sandwiches and homemade chocolate chip cookies, Donna cleared the table. Grandpa Duke was eager to begin.

"Do you know what day this is?" Grandpa Duke asked them both.

"This is Grandma Harriet's birthday. She would have been ninety-nine years old today," Douglas said, in a moment of fond remembrance.

It seemed right, somehow, that the stories about to be told would begin on this day.

Donna indicated that she was prepared to begin the interview and asked if he was ready.

"Sure, where do you want to start?" Duke asked Donna directly, as the digital video camera "rolled." Then humorously he posed for the camera and asked, "Am I on?"

They all laughed heartily.

Then Donna began the interview. "What are your earliest memories of growing up in South Dakota?" Donna asked. She seemed to encourage him with a smile.

"Ahh...that was a long time ago, let me see..."

For the most part, Grandpa Duke enjoyed telling stories from his childhood in South Dakota. He'd had to endure hardships during The Great Depression, but he felt those experiences had made him stronger and more resilient as a warrior.

Occasionally Donna prompted him to expound on a particular story. She drew the stories from him with ease. Sometimes it seemed to Duke that in sharing these episodes from his life, he was relieved of some of the burden he'd carried. And Donna was so easy to talk to.

Douglas and Donna returned to Grandpa Duke's house for additional interviews on a few more occasions, until Donna told him that she was satisfied she had enough information to begin writing his story.

Douglas told him that he was astounded to hear about his past; it was more than he had ever heard about his grandfather's life history. So many details were revealed in such a relatively short span of time, not only about Grandpa Duke's youth and about his service as a Marine in World War II, but about his personal life as well. Douglas said his head was spinning. He had no idea that his grandfather was a war hero. *It was nice to hear his grandson talk about him that way.*

During these interviews, Grandpa Duke had shared with Donna that the Sioux Indians looked at the buffalo, wolf, eagle, and other animals as brothers—as relatives. He told her that Indians were looked at as natural-born fighters, and they were gladly accepted into the armed forces because they could be relied upon to fight to the death and to remain loyal to the cause of their country. He hoped she could include this information in his story.

Donna shared with Grandpa Duke some information she'd discovered in her research. It was news that he hadn't heard before. Of the Native American population, one-third of all able-bodied Indian men from eighteen to fifty years of age saw service during World War II. According to the War Department, there were only two Congressional Medals of Honor, fifty-one Silver Stars, thirty-four Distinguished Flying Crosses, forty-seven Bronze Stars and seventy-one Air Medals awarded to Native Americans during World War II.

Grandpa Duke considered the awards that were given, even to men in his own platoon, and wondered why he might have been overlooked for the Medal of Honor. After all, Corporal Stanley Bitchell, Lieutenant Robert DeLong and P.F.C. Buck Davis had each received a Navy Cross, and Joseph Bureau and Clarence Bleau each received a citation for a Silver Star for gallantry in action at the base of the same ridge where he and his third squad cleared their way. It grated on him that he hadn't been awarded, and he could only attribute it to his being Indian.

* * *

On April 13th, 2009 Duke received a call from Douglas, and turned the volume down on the Chicago Cubs game he was watching on his television so he could hear what he had to say.

"Grandpa, I just got a call from Chuck Lomanto from Alderman Richard Mell's office in Chicago saying they want to honor you at Chicago City Hall with a resolution. I'm so glad my friend, Rick Suarez, and I visited the alderman to see if he knew who we could talk to about your story. Alderman Mell spoke to his colleagues from the City Council in Chicago and on April 22nd, 2009, the alderman wants us to report to Room 200, to attend the

Chicago City Council meeting. It looks like you might be going to meet Mayor Richard M. Daley! The City of Big Shoulders is going to carry you to Washington D.C.," he finished, waiting for his grandfather's response.

"Well, I'll be. That's great!" He wasn't sure what a resolution was, but Douglas explained it was a document meant to honor him that would state clearly the City Council's purpose to recognize him for his outstanding service in World War II.

Having been given such big news, Duke couldn't wait to contact Gunnery Sergeant Ruffner, who had been working hard on his case, to share with him his excitement about the resolution being made in his honor.

When Sergeant Ruffner heard about all that had been happening since their last conversation, he was pleased for his Marine friend.

"Duke, it sounds like your grandson is on the right track. I'm going to send you all of the military records and information I've found up to this point, and you make sure that your grandson gets it. Keep me informed as to what happens, will you, Duke?" Sergeant Ruffner asked.

"I will Gunny, thanks again!" Duke replied.

When the morning of the resolution arrived, Duke was anxious to get going. He woke up at four o'clock that morning, he was so excited. When his grandson pulled up in the gravel drive, Grandpa Duke, at the age of eighty-three, was already walking down the steps from the deck before Jennifer could climb the stairs to retrieve him.

He knew he looked dapper in his black suit, stark white dress shirt and striped Purple Heart tie. He wore his Purple Heart lapel pin on the left side of his suit jacket, and it flashed as it reflected the sunlight. He was all smiles as he approached the car. Today he wore his eye patch over his left eye under his glasses, as the old injury born on Okinawa was causing him some discomfort. He never could properly see out of that eye since the day he'd cleaned the mud out of it at The Three Sisters.

The trip downtown to the city was made more pleasant by their conversation. Duke wasn't sure what might happen here, but he couldn't wait to find out. After Douglas parked the car, he, Donna and Jennifer walked with him to the entrance of the Chicago City Hall building on LaSalle Street.

As they entered the building, Duke's attention was instantly drawn to the elaborate marble stairways with brass hand railings. *This looks fancy,* Duke thought to himself.

He climbed the short staircase, leaning on his cane a bit as he leaned forward to read the bronze tablets displayed on the walls honoring previous city halls since Chicago's incorporation on March 4th, 1837. The marble tiles beneath his feet were waxed to a brilliant shine, he noticed as they made their way to the elevators—three on each side of the central hall.

After a short ride, the doors of the elevators opened to reveal the second floor lobby, where they were all directed to an office located just off to the left of the main lounge area, room number 200, Duke read on the door.

They hadn't waited long before a man approached them and introduced himself as Legislative Aide, Jaime Andrade. He shook Grandpa Duke's hand, thanking him profusely for his service in World War II. Duke grinned widely in appreciation.

Next, the man guided them down a hallway to the backroom annex located just behind the City Council Chambers. There was a long, wooden table, varnished to a high sheen, located in the center of the large, high-ceilinged room. Dozens of council members were both standing and seated there to discuss the issues that would be addressed that day in the meeting.

On one wall was an impressive portrait of President George Washington, and on the opposite wall hung another massive painting, tranquilly depicting Native Indians arriving in a canoe along the banks of the Chicago River.

Alderman Richard Mell entered the room and walked directly to Duke. He reached for his hand, shook it vigorously, and smiling broadly said, "There's my hero!"

The corners of Duke's mouth raised in response as he returned the handshake firmly.

"Help yourselves to some doughnuts and coffee while we're waiting for the meeting to begin." Alderman Mell invited them to sit down as he spoke, extending his hand to a row of seats directly in front of where they were standing. A large array of pastries was arranged in a display on the table.

Too pumped up to eat, Duke looked around at the flurry of activity in the room. Several aldermen were present, standing and talking on their cell phones. Many conversations were taking place at the table, Duke noticed. They all sat watching the melee only a few minutes before they were approached and introduced to the Assistant Sergeant at Arms, Gary Medina. He directed them through the annex door and into the City Council Chambers to their seats, and the officials began their duties of the day.

Alderman Mell approached them before the meeting started, making sure Duke was comfortable. Then he handed each a folder that had a copy of the resolution inside.

Opening his folder, Duke looked down to see that the resolution was written on light gold parchment paper and noted at the top it was being presented by Alderman Richard F. Mell. It described the hardships that he had endured having grown up during The Great Depression. It went on to state that at the age of eighteen, he enlisted in the United States Marine Corps and engaged heroically in battles for the islands of Peleliu and Okinawa, in the Pacific. It further suggested that Duke may have been overlooked for higher honors than he was awarded during the war, having placed his own life in great danger, and having lost all of the members of his squad to either wounds or death in securing the Japanese fortress at the entrance of Death Valley. The resolution was signed by Mayor Richard M. Daley and City Clerk Miguel Del Valle. The paper was stamped with the impressive gold official Seal of the City of Chicago.

Duke couldn't help but smile. He'd never forget the sacrifice of the men in his squad and now they too, would be remembered.

Several resolutions were considered as they waited together to hear the reading of the resolution written for Grandpa Duke. In one such resolution, Chicago firefighters were recognized for their heroic actions in rescuing two victims from a raging fire, finding them hanging from the windows of their home, clinging to the ledge in the bitter winter temperatures. The firefighters were duly honored and applause was given with a standing ovation to further award their efforts as they stood to receive recognition. Next, several Chicago policemen were recognized for placing themselves in peril while in the den of a street gang where they recovered nearly five pounds of cocaine and over fifty-five thousand dollars in cash. The assailants were armed with guns, but the officers were able to disarm them, having to shoot one gang member in the process. The skillful and courageous actions of the officers resulted in the removal of the dangerous gang members from the community. These police officers were well appreciated with a standing ovation from all who were present.

Then, City Clerk Miguel Del Valle stood to speak at the podium. He read from the same resolution papers that Duke held in his hands. "A resolution adopted by The City Council of the City of Chicago, Illinois. Whereas, Loren Duke Abdalla is a member and one of the finest examples of what journalist, Tom Brokaw, has called 'The Greatest Generation…'"

Duke strained his ears above the noise of people muttering and moving in their seats in the chambers, wanting to hear every word of acknowledgment that was uttered on his behalf.

Mr. Del Valle continued to read from the resolution, summarizing the story of Duke's life from his birth near Wagner, South Dakota as the great-grandson of a chief of the Native American Tribe of The Yankton Sioux, through Duke's childhood during the worst of economic times when he learned at a very early age that he had to work hard to achieve his goals and not to give up when times were challenging. Mr. Del Valle revealed that when Duke turned eighteen, he enlisted in the United States Marine Corps at Omaha, Nebraska, in October of 1943.

As Mr. Del Valle continued, he spoke of the battlefields on both Peleliu and Okinawa, and suggested that Loren Duke Abdalla may have been overlooked for higher honors than the Purple Heart and Good Conduct medals he had received from World War II. He ended with this resolve, and stated in part,

BE IT RESOLVED, We, the Mayor and the members of the Chicago City Council, do hereby salute Loren Duke Abdalla on his praiseworthy contribution to this nation and our city, and strongly urge the President and Congress of The United States to review his service record with a view toward accolades well considered and long overdue.

The audience held their applause, waiting to hear the alderman speak.

Alderman Richard F. Mell stood. He was responsible for presenting this resolution for Duke. He listened intently. Alderman Mell referred to the recipients of the previous resolutions written for Chicago firefighters and policemen and the courage they showed in the course of their jobs, giving them due honor for their bravery. "Those stories pale in comparison to the more perilous circumstances under which Loren Duke Abdalla showed his courage and resolve in performing brave and heroic acts as a Marine on Peleliu and Okinawa," the alderman emphasized to the room. Duke sat a bit straighter in his seat.

The alderman spoke of how Duke's grandson, Douglas Nykolaycuyk, presented him with letters outlining the events that took place during World War II.

"Even after Duke was severely injured on Peleliu, and sent to a hospital in Guadalcanal to recover, he was sent back into battle against the Japanese forces on Okinawa. It was there that he took his squad up the side of a ridge to secure the way for two other squads and a demolition team to blow up the big gun at the mouth of a ridge that had killed so many American soldiers. Duke took out the last two machine gun nests on the ridge himself, after losing all of his squad to either debilitating wounds or death, and stood on top of that ridge alone as it shook from the blast of the pack charges exploding beneath his feet."

Alderman Mell's words resounded in the room. He noted that only a handful of men had survived this fierce battle, and that none in Duke's squad were there to document Duke's heroic actions. He suggested that this may have resulted in Duke's being overlooked for the recognition of courage due him. Duke nodded his head as the words were spoken. He stated that Duke was committed to his country and was prepared to sacrifice his own life in defense of it. Finally, Alderman Mell stated that Duke was truly an unsung hero who deserved to be awarded properly.

Duke watched as Alderman Ray Suarez, a Marine Corps Vietnam War Veteran, himself, stood to speak as Alderman Mell took his seat. He initially stated that he was proud to be a part of this resolution. "I don't know Duke," he began as he faced him and spoke, "but he is my friend, as a Marine."

Alderman Suarez went on as he addressed the council. "What I can tell you, is that what 'The Greatest Generation' of this country is based upon are examples of people like Duke who never thought anything about his own safety, but who went out there and made sure he did his job and helped the men that he was with in the Marine Corps. At the same time, he is a great role model for Chicagoans and the People of the United States. It is because of people like Duke that we're here today. Because they took the time and made the commitment to protect our freedoms and make sure that this country shines throughout the world."

Alderman Suarez then turned to address Grandpa Duke personally, "So, Duke, I want to congratulate you. I wish you the best of luck. God bless you. I am very proud to stand here and be associated with this resolution on your behalf, and I would hope that the United States Government would correct their mistake by making sure that they give you the proper recognition you deserve."

Duke smiled and nodded in response.

Alderman Ariel E. Reboyras stood immediately to address Duke and the council members. "I, too would like to be associated with this resolution. I don't know Mr. Abdalla. But I do know, and have read, what he has done for this country. I'd like to share with you that just yesterday morning, my twenty-one year old nephew, who is also a Marine, left for Iraq. We pray for him every day, as we will pray for Mr. Abdalla."

Alderman Reboyras turned to Duke and continued, "Because what you did needs to be recognized, and I hope that Congress does the same, just as we recognize you today."

Finally, Alderman James A. Balcer, a Vietnam Marine Corps Veteran who was awarded a Bronze Star for his heroics during conflict, and who was wearing the signature Marine tie, stood to speak on Grandpa Duke's behalf. "I too rise, as a Marine Corps Veteran, and commend Alderman Mell for bringing this story to our attention."

He faced Duke directly before continuing. "Mr. Abdalla, I salute you and commend you. It has been sixty-six years and counting since the Battle of Peleliu."

Again Duke nodded his acknowledgment.

For the benefit of the audience, Alderman Balcer provided some background information.

"I don't know if you all are aware, but the island of Peleliu is on the equator and is plagued by extreme heat and extreme humidity. It is a jungle with coral mountain ridges. It is teaming with malaria, dysentery, jungle rot, snakes and mosquitoes. This island was fortified with a determined enemy, an enemy who would fight and die to the last man. I commend the American Marine who fought them and defeated them. They defeated a determined enemy on a small island. A famous Marine was on that island, and Duke, I don't know if you know him, but Chesty Puller was on Peleliu."

Duke nodded his head slowly, meaningfully. He knew him. He gripped his leg tightly in remembrance of his good friend.

Again, Alderman Balcer faced Duke and addressed him, "Duke, when the chips were down, you were there. In the Marine Corps, I don't know how to explain it, but there is no other organization in the world quite like it. Once a Marine, always a Marine. I hope the government reads this and takes your case under consideration, and you are given the medals you deserve. As a former Marine, as a Marine, I always say, Semper Fidelis, and God bless America!"

It was then that Alderman Mell stood again to address the president of council. "Mr. President, I would like to have Mr. Loren Duke Abdalla stand and be recognized." Facing Duke, he asked, "Will the Marine warrior please stand and be recognized?"

Duke stood tall and at attention. He received a standing ovation from all who were present. The roar of the ovation lasted several moments. Duke nodded in appreciation, his throat tight from emotion, proud to be honored in the presence of so many grateful Americans.

The aldermen present voted unanimously to pass the resolution. When the service was over, several council members and members of the audience approached Grandpa Duke to shake his hand and thank him for his service to our country. Duke was all smiles.

Stanley Hollenbeck, Director of the Chicago City Council, Legislative Reference Bureau, was responsible for summarizing the words for the resolution. He joined Duke and his family in the hallway just off the council chambers following the meeting, and told them that a copy of the resolution would be sent to The President and Congress for their review and consideration.

Stan (as he told Duke to call him) shook his hand, thanking him for his service to the United States. Then he shook Doug's hand in support of all that he had done for his grandfather. Grandpa Duke could see that his grandson was close to tears with overwhelming emotions of seeing him be appreciated for his service in the war. As much as he approved of what Douglas had done on his behalf, he remained stoic—never shedding a tear. He did, however, lean forward and shake his grandson's hand appreciatively.

Once they'd all traveled back to the main floor of the building, several policemen and firemen approached Grandpa Duke to shake his hand and thank him for his service in the war.

He smiled, then nodded his head in acknowledgment.

Douglas told him that he would go and retrieve the car and meet them all in front of the building.

While Grandpa Duke exited the building together with Donna and his great-grandaughter, he was approached by many more grateful countrymen, some who witnessed the reading of the resolution at the City Council meeting, and some who recognized the Purple Heart bar and tie that Grandpa proudly wore. They were enthusiastic about thanking and honoring him, and he was touched by receiving their regards.

Once they were all in the car, Douglas announced he had made arrangements for them to have pizza at his favorite Italian Restaurant. "Chris and Sam Petrancosta are friends of the family and owners of LaVilla, where we have always had great food! Chris has graciously invited us to come have lunch at the restaurant a bit before it opens so that she can show her appreciation of your service, Grandpa."

"Well that's just great!" Grandpa replied.

Chris was at the door of the restaurant to meet the group with hugs and smiles! She directed everyone to a table in the main dining room as Grandpa Duke looked around and noticed that they had the whole place to themselves. They all sat down and a waitress appeared with menus. Before they could open up our menus to browse, Chris began bringing plates full of appetizers out for everyone to enjoy—on the house—as an honor to Grandpa Duke.

He watched as Chris and a waitress placed the plates of food around the table and announced what each dish was. There was delicious pizza bread, stuffed eggplant with marinara sauce, an Italian antipasto plate with raw vegetables, lunch meat slices, cheeses, olives and pepperoni. The aroma of freshly baked bread wafted past his nose as the final plate was set on the table along with a bowl of fresh butter for our enjoyment. Not long after that, the pizzas arrived at the table, smelling heavenly.

The food was delicious, and the rest of the afternoon was spent sharing stories and good company. Duke really enjoyed the food and Chris had been a gracious host to all.

***

On the way home, Doug dropped off Jennifer at her house. Grandpa Duke gave her a hearty hug before saying good-bye.

Doug took a detour through the town of Cary on their way to Fox Lake. His good friend, Tom Seger, lived there, and he assured Grandpa Duke that it was on the way to his home. What Duke didn't know was that Douglas was taking this detour for a specific reason. Tom was not only a good friend, but a master craftsman when it came to restoring wooden boats—specifically, Grandpa Duke's wooden boat. Duke had given the boat to Doug and Donna two years earlier, rather than seeing it scrapped. At considerable cost and with Doug's helping Tom with the labor, the ailing boat had been completely restored to its original splendor and then some—including the painted images of the top hat and cane on the sides of the bow— and was parked in the driveway of Tom Seger's home.

Duke was very impressed when he saw the boat in the driveway. He listened as Doug explained that he had spent the last two years working hard with Tom to replace the white oak panels of the floor and sides of the boat. The seats and the entire deck of the boat were replaced with a darker, African mahogany. After painstakingly applying eight layers of varnish over the wood, the 1963 Cruisers, Inc. boat shone like brand-new. The project was completed with the rigging of the motor and electrical work being done by master technician William Fitzgerald.

Donna snapped a few photos of Grandpa Duke and Doug standing by the boat, smiling. He could tell his grandson was filled with emotion as Doug turned to speak to him.

"I am so proud and grateful to be your grandson. I feel lucky to be here after all that you have been through. Thank you for doing what you did, not only to survive for our family, but for what you did for our country. I love you, Grandpa," Doug finished by reaching forward.

Duke hugged his grandson warmly, appreciative of all his hard work and determination! This was a good day.

***

It was a sunny Saturday morning in June, just a week before Grandpa Duke's eighty-fourth birthday. He knew that Doug and Donna were going to be visiting him both for his birthday and for Father's Day and was looking forward to seeing them.

After breakfast, he was putting his dishes in the kitchen sink and turned to see Doug and Donna's black sedan pull into his driveway. They must've picked up Jennifer, as she was sitting in the back seat—what a nice surprise.

When they arrived at his door, he invited them all into his kitchen. He watched his grandson as he noticed that another frame had been added to Grandpa Duke's wall.

When Doug asked him about it, Duke said, "Let's all go into the living room and sit down, and I'll tell you all about it."

They followed him into the living room and they all took a chair and waited anxiously for him to share his news.

"Well," Duke started, "I drove my Chevy pickup truck down to the post office this morning, and I saw a letter with the return address of The White House in the corner. I hurried home so I could open it and read it with my lighted magnifying glass. It was a card from President Barack Obama himself, wishing me a Happy Birthday," he finished proudly.

"Wow! Looks like things are starting to happen for you, Grandpa!" Doug said, looking at the birthday card in amazed delight.

"Congratulations, Grandpa," Donna shared in his enjoyment, smiling.

"Wow!" Jennifer exclaimed, impressed by the embossment on the card that her great-grandfather showed her behind the glass in the frame.

Grandpa Duke opened the gifts Doug had carried into the living room for him. The first was wrapped in royal blue paper that was adorned with red, white and blue stars. When he opened it he saw a large picture frame. Setting the bottom of the frame on his lap, he scrutinized its contents. The American flag was used as a backdrop to adorn and highlight a photo of Grandpa Duke standing tall in the Chicago City Council Chambers as he received a standing ovation from the crowd. Also included in the frame were the original resolution documents prepared on parchment.

"I love it!" Duke looked at Douglas and Donna, then repeated himself. "I absolutely love it!"

Next, he opened the smaller of the two gifts. It was a picture of the USS *Bountiful*, the hospital ship that had carried Duke to Guadalcanal after he had been so severely injured. Donna had found the picture online when she was researching the history of the World War II in the Pacific.

The caption read: "USS *Bountiful* with Marine casualties from Peleliu on board, arriving at Point Cruz, Guadalcanal, 29 September 1944. Red Cross workers wait on the dock."

Donna brought to Grandpa Duke's attention that he would have been on the hospital ship at the time the photo had been taken.

Duke was impressed. "Well, I'll be. That's incredible! I was busted up pretty bad right then. Wow! These are great gifts, thank you."

He got up out of his chair and walked over to the brick wall next to the fireplace and said, "Right here is where we'll put the picture with the resolution." Then he told them, "I'll put the picture of the USS *Bountiful* on the wall in the kitchen—I'll show you where to hang it."

The gifts were a success! Duke found a spot for each of them on his walls.

After the pictures had been hung, Grandpa Duke had a surprise for them for lunch. He asked them to go into the barbecue room to be seated instead of sitting at the kitchen table as they usually did. When they walked into the room, they saw he had specially made up the table there with a flowered tablecloth, plates, silverware, and glasses. He had a cooler set up with various soft drinks and loaded with ice.

Unbeknownst to them, Grandpa Duke had some big, thick steaks to cook on the grill for dinner. He asked if Donna could help him bake the tater tots, and she happily moved to the kitchen to help. While he cooked the steaks, she kept an eye on the potatoes and offered to cook the green beans, as well. When the two had finished preparing everything, they all sat down to enjoy a wonderful dinner together.

After finishing the delicious meal, Donna asked him, Doug and Jennifer to stay seated together at the table while she made a quick trip to the kitchen. She came back from the kitchen carrying a homemade yellow birthday cake with a dark chocolate fudge frosting. The cake read, 'Happy Birthday Grandpa!' and numeral candles 8 and 4 were set in the center of it marking his eighty-fourth birthday.

Doug, Donna and Jennifer sang "Happy Birthday" to him as Donna set the glowing cake down in the middle of the table. It only took one blow for Grandpa Duke to extinguish the burning candles after making his wish.

After cake, he chose to regale them, in typical story-telling mode, of a recent episode.

"Last week, Brady called me from next door and says, 'Dad, there's something in the Franklin stove. I can hear something in there.'

"I told him, 'All right, I'll be right down.' I hunted up some special welding gloves that I'd gotten recently. They were made of a thick blue suede material. I threw on my coat and made the trip down the stairs to his house."

Duke looked at each of the three of them to make sure they were paying attention, then continued. "Once I'd entered the house, Brady and I walked over to the stove. I told him to help me remove the chimney from the top of the stove. When we took the chimney off, whatever it was that had been in there, scurried down into the chamber of the Franklin stove."

His story was replete with motions as he mimicked the actions of removing the chimney before he went on. "We put the chimney back on, but closed the damper so the animal couldn't go back up into it. Now, a Franklin stove has two doors on the front that open up like a closet," Grandpa Duke continued, making sure that they got the picture by demonstrating the motion of opening the two doors from centered handles.

"I put my gloves on and laid down in front of the stove and said to Brady— 'I'm gonna open these doors! I opened up the doors, but nothing came out." He looked at them pointedly. "So, I closed the doors, but left one of them open just enough to fit my arm in, so that I could reach up in the top, back of the stove to feel up on the smoke shelf."

The excitement in his voice rose as he went on. "I said, 'Brady, I feel something soft—it's a squirrel!' And when I pulled my arm out, that squirrel flew out of the stove. We had the window open, but when the squirrel flew out, he hit the wall! Then he jumped to go back into the stove, but I was still lying in front of those doors with my gloves on. So, I closed my hands around him as he flew and caught him in mid-air, just that fast!" He snapped his fingers to show them, then went on.

"Brady patted me on the back and said, 'Dad, that was great!' My reflexes were so fast, after I caught the little guy, I flipped him onto the window ledge, then the squirrel jumped out through the window!"

They all had a good laugh. He knew they were impressed by the fact that at the age of eighty-four, Grandpa Duke's reflexes were as quick as ever.

***

About a week later, Doug and Donna were visiting Grandpa Duke when he shared again with them an explanation of his physical state of being when he was on the USS *Bountiful* hospital ship. Sharing his history of service in the war with them had brought back a flood of memories and these were moments he was reliving after years of being shelved. It helped him to talk about it.

"I didn't eat for days—and that in itself was extremely unusual for me. That little hospital on Guadalcanal was kinda like the hospital setting on the television series, M*A*S*H. All it was, was a series of tents with simple cots in them. And the hospital itself was a tent with a dirt floor," he indicated with a sweep of his hand toward the ground.

As Donna listened, Grandpa Duke could see she was moved not only by his description of the surroundings, but by the recognition he received from his peers. Grandpa explained his disembarkation on crutches from the troop ship down the long ramp in his weakened state to the dock on Pavuvu Island.

"There was a sea of khaki that lined the beaches that I could see as I got off that ship; it was something," he finished. The unspoken chasm of experience that separated seasoned Marines and new recruits was extremely evident. He said that what had struck him most about his recovery when he returned to Pavuvu was the special treatment he received from the newer recruits.

"Not only did they wait on me and the other wounded men on 'that little jungle island of Pavuvu,' but a ticker-tape parade and a seat at the Waldorf Astoria could never compare with the respect I got as a veteran who had been severely wounded while defending our country on Peleliu. They knew it, and they appreciated it," he finished proudly.

The proximity of his living quarters to the mess hall suggested the great honor given to the Marines who had served their country so well. The service offered to Duke by his peers was a testament to the brotherhood of the Marines. "The newer recruits fetched my meals, cleared my plates, and washed my mess kit after every meal. They had three barrels set up to dip the dishes in: the first one had soapy water in it, the second and third barrels were full of rinse water. Then they'd dry them off with a towel and hand 'em back to me when I got back to my tent," Duke grinned as he related the course of events.

He could see that his grandson understood the regard that he received from his companions on that island. Duke felt the appreciation and respect of those men in the moment, and he was honored by their actions.

Not long after this visit, Grandpa Duke got a phone call from Douglas who relayed a phone call from a gentleman named Fred Gajewski. Doug explained to him the gentleman was a Veterans Representative of over two hundred thousand veterans. He was a Vietnam Veteran with The United States Air Force himself, having served four years and also having served twenty-seven years in the Reserves. He had heard Duke's story and was inspired to help in any way he could.

Duke was duly impressed. Mr. Gajewski had explained to his grandson that he was a legislative contact to Members of Congress in Washington D.C., and that he sat on various Veterans committees. Douglas shared with him that the man was so moved by his story that he asked Doug if he could get a copy of Duke's portfolio packet so he could make additional copies to send to government representatives that he regarded as the proper channels for matters such as this.

Grandpa Duke told his grandson, "Let him know that I appreciate him for offering to help."

When Douglas contacted Mr. Gajewski to relay the message, he responded by telling Doug: "You can do me this favor. Every time you meet a Veteran who has served our great country, thank them for his or her service."

Doug agreed to do so, then shared the request with his grandfather on his next phone call.

Grandpa Duke hoped for something to come of the association. "I believe that you are on the right track to get this done, Douglas. Great job!"

Over the next day or two, Douglas made another set of many phone calls to update Grandpa Duke. "I was thinking about what congressional representative I might be able to share your story with. United States Senator Roland Burris served the State of Illinois thirty years ago as State Comptroller, he also served as Attorney General, and had a spotless service record."

Doug went on to say, "I think that his being an African-American, he might have more insight into the discriminatory aspect of your case. In fact,

Grandpa, he was the first African-American to ever be elected to a major state-wide position in Illinois. Senator Burris served on the Committee on Homeland Security and Governmental Affairs, and the Committee on Veterans' Affairs. He is the perfect candidate to consider your story and forward the information through influential channels."

With Grandpa Duke's blessing, Doug prepared another portfolio package and sent it off to the senator's office. A few weeks later, Mr. My'Ron McGee, who handled Veterans' Affairs for Senator Burris, responded to Doug with a letter. In it, he informed him to tell his grandfather that they would work hard for him and fight for him to receive due honor.

Using the contact number that was included with the letter, Douglas called Mr. McGee and spoke to him, personally. He learned that he also served as a Marine and was a Veteran. Douglas was happy to hear about that and immediately thanked him for his service. Mr. McGee explained that Senator Burris requested a review of Duke's service be made with the Commandant of the Marine Corps and the Department of Defense for The Congressional Medal of Honor.

After the conversation, Douglas was so excited he called his grandfather to tell him, "Senator Roland Burris is leading the charge in fighting for you to be recognized!" He explained what committees the senator represented, and the conversations he'd had with Mr. McGee.

"Yeah, I believe that you found the right man," Grandpa Duke said. "You're really working hard on this, aren't you, Douglas?"

"I am not going to stop until you are honored, federally!" Doug replied.

***

In July of 2010, Douglas and Donna made a trip with Grandpa Duke to Wagner, South Dakota, for a family reunion.

When the day of the party came, Grandpa Duke was in storytelling mode, but not until Doug had made the proper introduction. Duke had Doug inform the family that he was currently being reviewed for the Congressional Medal of Honor. He also had Douglas share that he had recently been honored at Chicago City Hall with a resolution to that effect. Doug handed out copies of the resolution to the family members, and Grandpa Duke was very proud to have his extended family read about his recent honors.

For the next several hours, Grandpa Duke enjoyed sharing stories of his youth with his cousins and their sons and daughters and grandchildren— all descendants of Chief Running Bull. Grandpa Duke pulled Donna aside to share the order of the elders in the family with her. "There are three family names," he began. "The Abdalla's are Duke and Jesse, with Richard Abdella—for some reason the spelling was different, we never quite figured that out.

"In the Pigsley family are Carol, Donald, Lois, Irma, Harlan and Lyle," he counted off on his fingertips as he spoke. "And the Pekas family includes

Arliss, Charlotte, and Francine. I'm the eldest of all the elders in the family," he finished by pointing a thumb to his chest and smiling.

His sweet cousin Arliss offered to host the gathering at her home in Pickstown, not far west of Wagner. Arliss's home had a large back yard that boasted a humungous, beautiful birch tree and many colorful birds, so it was a perfect setting for a large gathering of family members. Both she and her darling sister, Charlotte, made several baked goods and side dishes for the family feast. Much of the luncheon was catered, and all of the food provided and prepared by all the family members was delicious!

Tim Abdella, Richard's son, not only attended the reunion, but provided hand-made gifts in the traditional Sioux fashion. There were knives made of elk antler and mule-deer bone, and lovely necklaces for the ladies made with a slice of elk antler carved into a beautiful charm. The charm was placed in the center of the beads and hung from a long, tightly wound horse hair chain.

Duke helped Donna by placing her necklace over her head as she held her long blonde hair up, then dropped it to lie gently over her shoulders after the necklace was in place. The horse-hair chain was tightly wound and held four beads, white, black, red and yellow like the colors of the medicine wheel. In the center of the beads hung a hand-carved turtle made from elk antler. Tim was considered to be the family historian and smilingly offered, "The turtle is a symbol of good health and long life."

He went on to say that recently through his research, he had found information dating back to the late 1700's that Barbara Running Bull's father's name was Black and White Tail. Grandpa Duke really enjoyed hearing about his ancestral relations.

The next day, Grandpa Duke, Douglas and Donna spent some time playing in the casino at the hotel. They were joined by Aunt Carol and her son Charlie Eagleman in the gaming room. None of them were really gamblers, but they had so much fun together enjoying each other's company and sharing family stories, that playing the slot machines at the casino became an afterthought.

That evening, the group decided to have dinner in the dining room at the hotel, and Grandpa Duke noticed a gentleman sitting near the front of the restaurant, not far from where they were waiting to be seated. He asked Douglas to approach the man and ask him if he remembered a man named Duke Abdalla.

Doug readily responded to his grandfather's request, walked up to the man, and asked him within hearing of Duke, "Excuse me, sir. Do you remember a man named Duke Abdalla?"

"Well sure, I do!" the man replied right away. "He's a friend of mine. I am Tub Harrington." He extended his hand to Douglas and smiled.

"Well, that's my grandfather, and my name is Doug," he explained while he shook the man's hand. "Grandpa Duke is sitting right over there." He pointed to where Duke was sitting at the entrance. "And I'd also like to tell you that my grandfather is currently being reviewed for the Medal of Honor."

198

It was at that moment Grandpa Duke rose from his seat to come to the table. He turned to his grandson and said quietly, "Tub's brother Dusty served with the Ninety-Sixth Army Division on Okinawa, where he was killed. He was a good man."

"Thank you, Duke," Tub said, shaking his hand. Given that Duke had trouble with his vision, he asked Douglas if he could write down Tub's phone number for him, so they could stay in contact. They talked for a few more minutes before the server asked if they were ready to be seated. Tub told Duke he deserved recognition, and Duke smiled and thanked him. They made their good-byes and Grandpa Duke and the rest followed the waitress to the dining table.

***

A few weeks after they had returned home to Illinois, Duke phoned Douglas to let him know it had been nice seeing Tub again—and Doug let him know that he'd enjoyed meeting him and all of the family at the reunion.

Tub called and informed Doug that he'd told his daughter, Deb Harrington Cap, about Duke's story. She worked at Dakota Wesleyan University and was interested in writing a column for the Wagner *Post* about Grandpa Duke. Tub wanted to make sure he had the correct contact information for Duke so Deb could call and interview him for the article. Doug confirmed the phone numbers and address in Fox Lake and relayed his excitement to Grandpa Duke through a phone call to tell him that Tub's daughter was going to write an article about him in his hometown newspaper.

When the article was written, the title read, **Former Wagner Resident Possible Congressional Medal of Honor Awardee**.

Deb sent the article via e-mail to Doug, who immediately forwarded it to his grandfather. Duke couldn't have been more pleased, especially to have the article written in his own home town.

With the news that an article had been written in Wagner, Grandpa suggested that Doug contact the Lake County *Journal*, which was the local newspaper for Grandpa Duke's home in Fox Lake. Doug told his grandpa that he had spoken to a man named Colin Selbo, who was interested in writing an article concerning Duke's case.

Doug and Donna were present on the day of the interview at Grandpa's home. They all sat at the kitchen table (after Grandpa had removed the kitty to the window box) and shared pertinent information about the events that led to the review. Grandpa Duke shared specifics from the battles that he participated in, and Mr. Selbo told Grandpa that he would let him know when the article would be published.

Family Fights for WWII Vet to Receive Medal of Honor was the title of the column that was published. Again, the journalist forwarded the article to Doug via e-mail, and Doug sent it on to Grandpa Duke, who was pleased to see that another article had been written on his behalf.

"What do you think, Grandpa?" Douglas asked him when he called to see if he had received the article.

Grandpa responded happily, "You have done more for me than I can ever thank you for. I really appreciate it, Douglas."

***

On December 7ᵗʰ, 2010, Pearl Harbor Remembrance Day, Doug asked his wife to help him compose a letter to President Barack Obama on Grandpa Duke's behalf. It had been two years since he had begun the quest for his grandfather, and this day had particular significance to him. He wondered how much longer it would take for his grandfather to be honored federally, and told him so once he'd called to inform him of his actions.

"Donna and I prepared another portfolio package, Grandpa, and Donna wrote a letter to send along with it. This was the first time we've ever written to the President, telling him that your case was currently with the Department of Defense. We've asked for the President's help as Commander in Chief to see you honored for your service in World War II," he told him.

"We also sent a copy of the letter to the *Indian Country News*. It's an independent national Native American newspaper," he said.

The newspaper was eager to include the news in their publication. After an introductory paragraph, a copy of the original letter that Donna had composed from the information she had about Grandpa Duke's service, was included in their published article in February 2011. Doug had printed a copy of the article and sent it to him to read.

Grandpa Duke called immediately to let him know that he'd received it.

Doug told him with excitement in his voice, "Your story has made it all the way to the top! There really isn't anything else I can do at this point, Grandpa. It is all up to them. I believe it's an honor just to be reviewed for The Congressional Medal of Honor. Congratulations, Grandpa!"

"Thank you, Douglas!" Grandpa Duke answered sincerely. "Well, I guess we'll just wait and see what they say."

***

James F. Amos, Commandant of the Marine Corps, with a Formal Standing Board, convened for a review of Loren Duke Abdalla's service in World War II. After a thorough review, it was determined that regulations required, in order to be considered for the award of a personal decoration, including the Congressional Medal of Honor, an award recommendation must be submitted by an officer of the chain of command in accordance with Title 10 U.S.C. § 1130. A commanding officer's recommendation had never been submitted on Duke's behalf. The Commandant did say, "Although his sacrifice on behalf of our Country is noteworthy, and deserving of unending thanks."

Grandpa Duke called Douglas about two weeks later, having received a letter from the Department of the Navy that read:

DEPARTMENT OF THE NAVY
Office of the Secretary
1000 Navy Pentagon
Washington D.C. 20350-1000
March 30, 2011

Dear Mr. Abdalla:

Thank you for your letter to President Barack Obama requesting consideration for the Medal of Honor. While it would understandably mean a great deal for the President to assist you, responsibility for Marine Corps awards and promotions is delegated to the Secretary of the Navy and Commandant of the Marine Corps.

I found the story of your actions and those of your fellow Marines to be truly inspiring and recognize how tremendously difficult it must have been to recount the events of May 1945 in your letter to the President. Your desire to have your actions acknowledged is understandable.

On your behalf, a member of my staff researched your case. Our records indicate that Headquarters, United States Marine Corps (HQMC) reviewed a petition for the Medal of Honor, which was initiated by your grandson, Mr. Douglas P. Nykolaycuyk. Their response informed him that in order to be considered, an administratively complete award recommendation package must be submitted through a Member of Congress. HQMC carefully and objectively considered your record and all other evidence submitted on your behalf.

Please know that the value of your actions is not defined by awards received, but by the contributions you made to our Nation's defense during the Battles of Peleliu and Okinawa. You and your fellow Marines experienced untold hardship and demonstrated extraordinary courage. Your family, community, and Nation are forever indebted. Thank you for your service, and again, thank you for writing the President.

Sincerely,
A.G. LIGGETT

LCDR USN
Director, White House Liaison Office

Throughout the next year, Duke received a huge wave of recognition and appreciation. Over the course of several visits, Doug and Donna watched him hang his new treasures on his Walls of Recognition in the kitchen and by the fireplace in his home. It seemed everyone knew he was a war hero.

The list of recognition on his behalf was long:

Prior to July 1st, 2011, State Representative Deborah Mell heard about and forwarded Duke's story to Illinois Governor Pat Quinn who presented a proclamation on that day to Loren Duke Abdalla, recognizing and thanking him for his heroic service in World War II.

Grandpa Duke was also honored with the Illinois State flag that flew over the State Capitol in Springfield. This was presented to him by Secretary of State Jesse White with a certificate and an additional letter of recognition.

Douglas contacted Congressman Joe Walsh, Duke's congressional representative. On November 11th, 2011, Veteran's Day, Congressman Walsh met with Grandpa Duke, Doug, Donna, Duke's son Brady and his grandson Jason at his office. The congressman was extremely warm and cordial, as was his staff. After hearing Duke tell his story, the congressman was moved to ask Doug what recognition he had received.

After telling about the events and recognition his grandfather had received, Doug explained the letter from the Commandant of the Marine Corps, stating that based on the law, Title 10 U.S.C. § 1130, his grandfather would be unable to be recognized with a military award. Everyone involved who had researched Duke's case tried contacting any officers that his grandfather had served under, but no one had been successful.

Congressman Walsh looked Duke straight in the eye, shook his hand, and said, "I want to do more."

Later, Congressman Walsh wrote a letter to Duke, thanking him for his service to his country and the sacrifices he and his family made to preserve and protect these freedoms. He told Duke how his grandson had informed him of Duke's heroism as part of the First Marine Division during the Battle of Peleliu, for which he was awarded the Purple Heart; and in May of 1945, how he fought in the Battle of Okinawa "as the last man standing" on a ridge near Dakeshi. He commended him for his bravery and courage during several of the toughest battles in World War II.

As the month progressed, Congressman Joe Walsh contacted the National Archives and Records Administration in order to find any information as a matter of record regarding Duke's acts of valor in the Battle of Okinawa on May 5, 1945, during World War II. Timothy K. Nenninger, Chief, Archives II Reference Section (RD-DC), answered him with a letter, which he forwarded to Douglas, which was shared with Grandpa at his home, that stated in part:

We are enclosing courtesy copies of excerpts from the Special Action Report, Okinawa Operation filed by the First Marine Regiment. Included are the cover page, table of contents, order of battle, and the narration of Phase III of the invasion covering the period April 30 to May 31, 1945. In the May 5 entry, there is a description on how Companies A and F withheld a Japanese attack. This report represents the lowest command level report in our custody. It is rare to have company or even battalion level reports because those reports are used to write the regimental reports, and once that is complete the lower command level reports are disposed of.

The Special Action Report cover showed a picture of the island of Okinawa, surrounded by the Pacific, with OKINAWA OPERATION stamped over it. Directly below it read, First Marine Regiment, First Marine Division, UNCLASSIFIED. The next page showed a detailed map and was included in the report. The map showed the areas that had been secured, results of the operation, period 30 April to 15 May. The pages following gave a detailed description of heavy combat that the First Regiment participated in each day. Doug read the pages aloud, and found it heart-wrenching to hear of the multiple casualties in black and white. The death toll was high.

"You can't imagine fighting until you're simply exhausted, then having to see all the dead bodies of your fellow Marines lying all over the ground," Grandpa Duke somberly shared.

The information in the report was interesting, but as for any records stating the specific heroic actions of Duke—there were none.

On Grandpa Duke's behalf, Douglas and Donna thanked Congressman Walsh for attempting to locate the precise information needed to forward Grandpa Duke's case. Based on the letter from Mr. Nenninger, and his pointing out that this information represented the lowest command level report in their custody, it seemed a military award was not possible, as there were no commanding officers available to recommend one.

Doug considered that his grandfather had received recognition at both the city and state levels and thought to write two commissioners from Cook County, Illinois, Commissioners John Fritchey and Edwin Reyes. In the first week of February 2012, he received news from both offices that Cook County wanted to stand with the City of Chicago and honor his grandfather with a resolution, which they presented to him at City Hall.

Having received the exciting news, Doug contacted Chairman David Stolman from Lake County, where Duke currently lived, who responded by offering to honor Duke with a resolution of their own.

On March 19th, Lake County Chairman David Stolman and President of the Veterans' Assistance Commission Norm Arnswald both honored Loren Duke Abdalla with a resolution at an unveiling of the new Lake County Vet

Drop-In Center. Doug and Donna attended, as did Brady, and his son Jason. There were also veterans, as well as a significant number of the Military Order of The Purple Heart Organization, attending. The podium had been placed outside near the new sign for the Veterans' Center which was to be unveiled.

The chairman presented the framed resolution, stamped with the gold Seal of Lake County, to Duke and shook his hand. The chairman and the president unveiled the new sign, announced the center was open, and invited everyone inside. As the long line of veterans and others attending made their way into the building to continue the celebration with cake and ice cream, Doug held the door open for the Congressional Medal of Honor recipient Allen James Lynch.

As Doug shook the man's hand and thanked him for his service to the United States, his eyes fell to the impressive medal suspended by the blue ribbon hanging from his neck. It was the first time Doug had seen the Congressional Medal of Honor. He could well imagine seeing the medal worn by his grandfather.

Captain Rick Daniels, who had been the first to hear Duke's story back in 2004, was there, and he invited everyone to join him for a celebratory lunch following the ceremony.

On the ride to bring Grandpa Duke home to Fox Lake, Doug received a phone call from Governor Dennis Daugaard's office announcing that in honor of Duke's service in WWII, he was pronouncing June 18th, 2012 as 'Loren Duke Abdalla Day' in the state of South Dakota.

Governor Daugaard also had written a proclamation which was signed both by himself and Secretary of State Jason M. Gant. In addition to the proclamation, Governor Daugaard sent Duke an official State of South Dakota flag, along with a certificate stating that the flag had been flown in Duke's honor over the State Capitol in Pierre.

United States Senator Tim Johnson of South Dakota wrote a letter thanking Duke on behalf of himself and the entire nation. He shared in his note that he was the father of a military man himself and had an especially high regard for the men and women of the armed forces.

Duke was very happy to have had the two states where he had lived all his life provide him with such honors.

Having had such success in receiving written and presented honors for his grandfather, Douglas told him he'd decided to contact all of the United States. He did so by contacting all the offices of governor for each state, from Alabama to Wyoming. A total of fifteen states responded with recognition for Grandpa Duke, along with the original honors, in this order:

The State of Illinois—
  Alderman Richard F. Mell with a Resolution from the City of
  Chicago
  Congressman Joe Walsh, with a Congressional Commendation

Governor Pat Quinn, with a proclamation
Secretary of State Jesse White, with a letter of recognition
Chairman David Stolman, with a resolution from Lake County
Commissioners John Fritchey and Edwin Reyes, with a resolution
from Cook County
Congressman Brad Schneider, with a Congressional Record
Statement
State Senator Jim Oberweis, with a State Senate Resolution
State Representative Barbara Wheeler, with a State House
Resolution

The State of South Dakota—
Governor Dennis Daugaard, with a proclamation honoring him
with Loren Duke Abdalla Day on June 18, 2012
U.S. Senator Tim Johnson, with a Congressional Record Statement
Yankton Sioux Tribe Resolution, Chairman Robert Flying Hawk
and Secretary Glenford Sully
U.S. Senator John Thune, with a Congressional Record Statement

The State of Montana—
Governor Brian Schweitzer, with a letter of recognition.

The State of Alabama—
Governor Robert Bentley, with a governor's commendation.

The State of Florida—
Governor Rick Scott, with a letter of recognition.

The State of Georgia—
Governor Nathan Deal, with a governor's commendation.

The State of Maryland—
Governor Martin O'Malley, with a governor's citation.

The State of Washington—
Governor Chris Gregoire, with a letter of recognition.

The State of Oregon—
Governor John Kitzhaber, with a letter of recognition.

The State of Tennessee—
Governor Bill Haslam and Commissioner Many-Bears Grinder,
with a letter of recognition.

The State of New Mexico—

Governor Susana Martinez and Cabinet Secretary Timothy L. Hale, with a letter of recognition.

The State of Rhode Island—
Governor Lincoln D. Chafee, with a governor's citation.

The State of Wyoming—
Governor Matt Mead, with a letter of recognition, as well as a Wyoming Military Coin.

The State of North Carolina—
Governor Bev Perdue, with a letter of recognition.

The State of Indiana—
State Senator Allen E. Paul sponsored a resolution with the State Senate.

The Speaker of the House John Boehner, presented a memorial of the House of Representatives of the State of Illinois, relative to House Resolution No. 1086 urging the Congress and the President to review the case of Loren Duke Abdalla's actions during World War II; to the Committee on Armed Services. Each document was written with words of thanks and accompanied with each state's own seal, and signed by the relevant officials. With each recognition, , Grandpa Duke was excited to hear of the latest accolades.

Ms. Jean Miller, Director of Development for the Howe Military Academy also honored Duke with a letter of recognition. Grandpa knew that Douglas had graduated from Howe in 1987. Another of the school's alumni, Class of 1963, was the Indiana State Senator, Allen Paul. Jean forwarded the information to the senator on behalf of Grandpa Duke, and Senator Paul responded with the honor of a resolution.

***

Duke received a phone call from Vera Costella in early September, letting him know that her husband of forty-six years, Al Costella, had passed away on August 31, 2012. She told him that Al was eighty-nine years old and had been buried with full military honors by Detachment 942 out of Lafayette, California. Duke remembered when he had spoken with Al the last Fourth of July. His friend had told him he had walked the entire distance of the parade in Lafeyette with the Marine Corps League. The parade included a fly-by of World War II era planes and a release of balloons following the parade.

Vera recalled her husband often talking to Duke on the phone and ending with, "Okay, buddy. I'll talk to you soon." It was his routine end to every phone conversation. Duke expressed his sorrow at the passing of his good friend and offered his condolences to Vera Costella and her family.

The news of his passing hit Duke hard. He was alone now. He didn't know of any other living members of The Marines' First Battalion, the men he'd fought with in World War II.

***

One of the more personal honors Duke received came from a group called The Warrior's Watch Riders. His first wife had two children from subsequent marriages—Phillip Grandinetti and stepson Michael Saubert.

Uncle Phil relayed to Doug and Donna at a family gathering outside of Grandpa Duke's hearing that he and Uncle Mike Saubert had recently participated in a motorcycle tribute ride for a returning veteran, with a Chicago Police escort. Mike, who also belonged to The Warriors' Watch Riders, was a retired Army Captain, having served in The Iraq War, flying Blackhawk helicopters. Phil described it as *rolling thunder* with lights and horns and American flags waving. The honored veteran appreciated the welcome home immensely. Brady, a Vietnam veteran himself with the United States Air Force, liked the idea of the tribute ride. He looked at his brother Phil and said, "Let's do one for Dad!"

"Good idea," Phil replied. "I'll talk to Mike, and see what we can do to coordinate it."

Over the next several weeks a conspiracy was in the works. Douglas was in contact with Mike Saubert, who was coordinating The Warriors' Watch Riders welcome home for Grandpa Duke. He was also corresponding with Phil Grandinetti, who was a co-coordinator in the process. The date had been set, and Mike suggested to Doug that they take Grandpa Duke out to a restaurant in his hometown, with the idea of surprising him when they exited the restaurant and the riders escorted him home.

It was Doug's job to convince Grandpa Duke to go to lunch with him on the specified day and to persuade him to wear clothing depicting his association with The United States Marines. Doug also contacted Captain Rick Daniels to invite him to lunch with them, making certain to tell him that The Warriors' Watch Riders welcome was to be a surprise. When Grandpa found out his good friend Captain Daniels would be joining them for lunch, it became much simpler for Doug to talk him into wearing his Chesty's A-1-1 red Marine jacket and Peleliu survivors' cap for the pictures they would be taking with the captain.

October 20th, 2012, Doug, Donna, Jennifer and a dear family friend of nearly twenty-five years, George Truhlar, all piled in the car. George was a veteran, having proudly served in the United States Navy during the Vietnam War. He was happy to join and honor Grandpa Duke.

They drove to Fox Lake to pick up Grandpa Duke to take him out to lunch. As promised, Duke was wearing his red jacket and cap when we arrived at his home. Grandpa rode in the car to the restaurant, and he saw Captain Daniels there to meet us, riding up on his bright royal blue motorcycle.

207

The conversation flowed smoothly over lunch, although Grandpa Duke couldn't figure out why Douglas, Donna and Jennifer were all exchanging glances and looking out into the parking lot so often.

After everyone had finished eating, precisely at twelve noon, Doug's cell phone rang. Grandpa Duke watched him leave the table to take the call, then Doug returned shortly afterward to hurry Grandpa out the door with Donna, Captain Daniels and Jenny following behind. Doug told Grandpa to stand in the grassy area outside the restaurant so they could take pictures with Captain Daniels.

As they were all standing outside in the sunshine, Duke's truck, with his son Brady driving and his wife Verna in the passenger seat, pulled up next to the grassy strip. Grandpa was standing poised for pictures and was surprised to see his son approaching with his wife to give him a hug and a handshake. Right behind Brady and Verna was a motorcade of motorcycles, some with lights flashing and all of them honking their horns.

Duke turned in surprise to see what all the noise was about and Gunnery Sergeant Michael Ruffner approached him it seemed out of nowhere with his hand outstretched, thanking him for his service and saying, "It looks like you've got an escort here, Duke!"

"What a surprise!" Duke responded, shaking Sergeant Ruffner's hand with enthusiasm.

As Grandpa Duke stood shaking hands with the sergeant, Doug's Uncle Mike Siciliano and Aunt Susie showed up to thank Duke as well, Susie giving Duke a big hug as soon as she saw him. Next, it was Mike Saubert. Then Phil Grandinetti approached Duke to shake his hand and thank him for his service. A long row of veterans lined up behind him to express their thanks to Duke for his service in World War II. With a big smile on his face, Grandpa shook every hand, overcome with emotion.

After the large group of supporters had gathered close, Phil started off the welcome home celebration by informing everyone that they were all being rather quiet...which initiated loud whooping, clapping and shouting on behalf of Grandpa Duke. Mike proceeded to give everyone an introduction by paying tribute to Grandpa Duke for his service. Phil continued the tribute by reading a condensed version of Duke's heritage and history, including the stories of battle in Peleliu and on Okinawa. The concise biography included the story of the boxing bout Duke had with his drill sergeant when he was at Camp Elliot. The entire group laughed and clapped upon hearing that Duke had flattened the sergeant in the match. Phil also read about how when the fighting on Okinawa had stopped and World War II was finally over, A Company celebrated with a fifty-five gallon drum of jungle juice, which provoked more laughter and cheers from the group. Then, after relaying how Duke had spent an additional eight months with his regiment securing and residing in Tientsin, China, Phil told of Duke's return home to the States.

Phil read from his notes, "Duke's ship finally hit the docks in San Diego, and there was no one there to welcome Duke home." Then he added cheerfully, "Well, sixty-six years later, now is the time. Welcome home, Duke and God Bless the United States of America!"

A bevy of cheers and clapping erupted from everyone who had gathered to give Grandpa Duke his welcome home. Mike then presented him with The Warriors' Watch Riders beads, explaining their significance. "So what we'd like to do is present something which is near and dear to The Warriors' Watch Riders hearts, our honor beads. Beginning with the blue, which represents our Blue Star Families, those families who have a son or daughter in harm's way who are deployed overseas fighting a battle. The black is for those who have served, our veterans and POWs and MIAs. The gold are really special beads, because they represent our Gold Star Families, and we honor them, those whose families have lost someone, a family member in battle, and they live with that today. And we support them, we pray for them, and we honor them, with the Warriors' Watch Riders this day. And finally, the red, white and blue beads are for the flag and the United States of America under which we all serve. We'd like to present these beads to you with our thanks for your service."

Mike turned to face Duke and also presented him with The Warriors Watch Riders Coin, which has their motto engraved on it, "We have your backs here at home."

After more cheering and clapping, Mike explained to Duke that due to the efforts of his son, Brady, the town had been put on notice. Grandpa Duke was speechless. Fox Lake's finest, The Fox Lake Police Department, had sent an officer to conduct a police escort for the ride home. An official Marine Corps Jeep was in the procession with attending Marines. Also, Ms. Michelle Mathia was there representing Congressman Joe Walsh's Office and showing their support. All of The Warriors' Watch Riders, a group of men and women dedicated to honoring veterans, along with other supporting friends and family, would be escorting Duke home.

Police vehicles led the procession out of the parking lot, followed by Grandpa's Chevy pickup truck, the Marine Jeep, and all of the cars and motorcycles that had gathered for this special event, horns honking, lights flashing, American flag tribute. For three miles on Route 12 in the city of Fox Lake, intersections were blocked off—all the way through the small town, and around the turn, then up the hill to Grandpa Duke's house.

After everyone arrived at Grandpa Duke's home, a few more visitors shook his hand to honor him. Doug's friend, Thomas Dosch, and his son, Brandon, walked up the long gravel driveway carrying a United States flag. After gathering in the direction of Mike for a group photo, Doug pointed out the flags waving off the deck of his grandfather's house. "First, is The American flag, which was flown over our Capitol in Washington D.C. and presented to Grandpa Duke by Congressman Joe Walsh, along with a Congressional Commendation.

Next to it is the Purple Heart flag, which he earned in the Battle of Peleliu.

Then, the Illinois State flag, which was presented to him by Secretary of State Jesse White, having been flown over our State Capitol in Springfield. Next, the flag of South Dakota, which which was flown over the State Capitol in Pierre, and presented to him by Governor Dennis Daugaard. Then, the United States Marine Corps flag and The Marine Raider's flag.

Finally, The Yankton Sioux Tribe flag, presented to him by Vietnam Veteran Ron Sully Sr. and Sergeant Dennis Rucker, stating there is Honor among the Ihanktonwan Dakota relatives!"

Everyone clapped and cheered, and Duke stepped back to join the crowd in hearing a fellow Marine call for everyone's attention. The young man began by explaining the tradition of the Marine Corps to have the youngest Marine honor the eldest Marine by sharing the history of the battles he fought in. Having done the research of the Battles of Peleliu and Okinawa, the young man went into some detail of the fierceness of the battles, the extremity of the heat and conditions, and the nearly impenetrable strongholds of the Japanese Imperial Army. Due honor was given to General Chesty Puller, as he was and is known throughout the Marine Corps as an outstanding general. Every Marine knows the nightly tribute— "Good night, Chesty Puller, wherever you are!"

At a break in the presentation, Mike Saubert stepped up to announce that The Warriors' Watch Riders were also honoring the speaker that day. He was introduced as Marine Corps Sergeant Ryan Bentele, who had served seven years with The United States Marines Corps and been injured in The Iraq War. Having returned to the States in 2005 without a welcome home, he was receiving a welcome home from The Warriors' Watch Riders.

After shouts and cheers of welcome for Sergeant Bentele, he humbly continued by stating that the World War II veterans deserved high honor, having survived such a fierce enemy in the Pacific. He presented Duke with a Marine Corps Coin, one that he had carried with him through his years in service, including during The Iraq War. On the back of the coin was a picture of the Marines raising the American flag on Iwo Jima, during one of the most photographed Marine Corps battles.

Sergeant Bentele further explained the rank structure, and the importance of recognizing that as a corporal, a non-commissioned officer (NCO), an eighteen/nineteen-year-old corporal becoming a non-commissioned officer had some serious responsibility, having anywhere from about fifteen to thirty-five men under his wing, if he were lucky.

"Anything he says to do, to shoot, you do. So it is a great honor to meet this man." He shook Duke's hand then continued, facing him, "I want to present you with your insignia for corporal. And next, I'd like to give you another pin, the American flag, with the United States Marine Corps emblem on the bottom. Lastly, I want to give you, according to the new vs. old Marine tradition, I'd like to give you the new cover with the digital camouflage pattern that the Marine Corps came up with. I did carry this cover in combat with me, but I never used it, because I always wore my helmet."

Everyone cheered and clapped for the great honor shared between young and old Marine brothers.

Mike then introduced Duke to Mrs. Kim Bentele, sharing that she and Sergeant Bentele had driven all the way from Michigan to attend this welcome home ceremony.

More of the afternoon was spent admiring some of the motorcycles in attendance that day. Duke commented on the fact that Mike Saubert actually wore his Blackhawk helicopter helmet as a motorcycle helmet.

Mike informed Duke that it was indeed bulletproof.

Duke took a closer look at his bike and saw that it was embellished with the sun shining over the desert, represented by the metallic gold color that was the background on the side of the gas tank, with two Blackhawk helicopters shadowing one another as they traversed the terrain. Flashing strobe lights highlighted the front and back of the bike, with a rear carrier emblazoned with the Army Star on a background of dark gold. In fine detail, on the top of the gas tank in front of his seat, Mike had a tribute to his father written prominently: "In Memory of Wild Bill Saubert" with the Marine Emblem painted beneath it.

Next Duke moved to where Phil's motorcycle was parked. It was painted royal blue, with charcoal flames spreading out on either side of the gas tank and on the rear fender. The extensive chrome was polished to a high shine. He moved on to see Sergeant Ryan Bentele's motorcycle which had been custom-painted the color of Marine Dress Blues—Duke liked that. The golden Marine emblem held a prominent spot on either front side of the gas tank and its meaning was heartfelt: The Eagle, Globe and Anchor. The eagle representing the proud nation the Marines defend, standing at the ready with our coastlines in sight and the entire world within reach of its outstretched wings. The globe represented the Marines worldwide presence. The anchor points both to the Marine Corps naval heritage and its ability to access any coastline in the world. Together, the eagle, globe and anchor symbolize the Marines commitment to defend our nation—in the air, on land, and at sea. On each side, directly underneath the tank was Sergeant Bentele's emblem—red, with three gold stripes and crossed rifles underneath. On the rear fender, were the numbers 0311, Infantry, and the exclamation "Ooh-Rah!", and on the bottom of the fender were the words "Dress Blues"—painted in blue, of course!

On the top of the gas tank he saw the universal tribute to those who had been killed in battle. The Fallen Soldier Battle Cross is a symbolic replacement of a cross on the battlefield for a soldier who has been killed, boots as the base, rifle standing on its nose, with the soldier's helmet placed carefully on the head of the rifle. Finally, Grandpa Duke looked at the front fender of the bike which boasted the Marine motto, originally adopted in 1883, "Semper Fidelis" Latin for "Always Faithful." It was quite impressive, and Duke understood his devotion to the Marines.

Both Phil and Mike had dedicated themselves to searching out and welcoming home those military warriors who had never received a celebratory "Welcome Home" and Duke was pleased that they had honored him with his welcome home.

After the riders left, Grandpa Duke visited a while longer with Doug, Donna, Captain Daniels and Jennifer on his outside deck overlooking the lake. He shared with them some of the comments that had been written by fifty-one Warriors' Watch Riders in support of his service. Phil had given Grandpa a printout of the comments from their website. The final entry was written by Mike, and Grandpa asked Doug to read it aloud:

Corporal Abdalla,

It is an extreme honor to know someone who has done so much in the service of his Country! Your story is one that will go down in history and be honored by generations to come. I am proud to know a true representative of our greatest generation, who has gone through so much and showed us all how important it is to endure and persevere together— and what that means for our future generations as well. Your values are impeccable, your actions are exemplary, and your life is an example for all.

Semper Fi Sir!
Maddog81 (Wild Bill Saubert's son)

It had been a good day indeed.

***

Grandpa Duke knew that his grandson Douglas had sought to engage any and all individuals throughout the country who may be able to help in his quest to have his service in World War II honored. Douglas had told him that he'd been in touch with historian/author USMC Colonel Jon Hoffman, retired, who authored the book *Chesty, The Story of Lieutenant General Lewis B. Puller, USMC.* Doug explained to the historian the results of all the inquiries that had been made over the past four years and Colonel Hoffman was very helpful in providing as much information as he could to assist him. After all of the information was collected and reviewed by the colonel, he wrote Doug a return letter that he shared with Duke:

Hi Douglas,

As you have discovered, the process of awarding a military decoration for valor is very stringent in the Marine Corps, but even more so long after the fact when most witnesses of action are gone. The nature of the award system, of course, is never entirely fair. Two men may perform similar feats of valor, but those who witness it in one case are killed or wounded in action and are never able to participate in initiating a recommendation for award, while the other person is recommended and ends up receiving it. Or the supporting statements and documentation in one case may be stronger than in the other, simply because immediate superiors are better at processing such administrative actions. It's like the six men who raised the second flag on Iwo Jima-they became household names at the time and the survivors were widely feted by their Country, while the vast majority of those who fought were equally heroic and suffered just as much, but never received any particular accolades. Those of us who have studied WWII know that in battles like Guadalcanal, Peleliu, Iwo Jima, and Okinawa, almost every man who participated was a hero just for continuing to fight day after day in such incredibly heavy combat.

Your grandfather did not receive an award for valor for his action of 5 May, but it says a great deal about how his chain of command valued him that he was promoted to acting platoon sergeant. As you probably know, Chesty Puller himself thought that NCO's were more important than officers. Rising high in the NCO ranks was neither automatic nor something conferred lightly by the Marines, so it is a great honor for your grandfather to have made it to that rank in the few brief years he was in the Corps during the war.

It appears to me that you have exhausted all sources of possible information that would help in your quest, and you have already been through the review process by the Marine Corps, so I don't have any other ideas I can provide that would help.

I wish you could have a better outcome for your grandfather, but at least you have been successful in obtaining wide recognition for him, which I'm sure he appreciates.
He walked among giants with Marines like Chesty Puller and Ray Davis, and all those who served on the front lines in WWII were giants in their own right!

Semper Fi,
Jon

After hearing the colonel's words read by his grandson, Grandpa Duke realized that he truly had exhausted all avenues in his quest for federal recognition. Doug responded with a letter on his behalf to thank Colonel Hoffman, saying he was grateful for his interest and efforts, as well as his kind and eloquent response.

***

In November, 2012, Congressman Joe Walsh lost his bid for a newly defined 8th Congressional District. He would no longer be representing Duke in Congress. Doug received a letter from the congressman:

November 20, 2012

Dear Mr. Nykolaycuyk,

Thank you for contacting my office with regards to your Grandfather Loren Duke Abdalla. His service to this Country is exemplary and is truly symbolic of those of The Greatest Generation with never ending patriotism and love of Country.

I wish you the best as you continue to honor the history of your Grandfather's military service. It was a privilege to meet Mr. L "Duke" Abdalla, and his family. It has been an honor to serve you in The House of Representatives.

Sincerely,
Joe Walsh
Member of Congress

March 18, 2013, Congressman Bradley Schneider stood on the floor of The House of Representatives, honoring Loren Duke Abdalla with a Congressional Record Statement:

HONORING LOREN DUKE ABDALLA FOR
OUTSTANDING SERVICE
TO HIS COUNTRY DURING WORLD WAR II—
HONORABLE BRADLEY S. SCHNEIDER

Mr. SCHNEIDER. Mr. Speaker, I rise today to honor the service of Loren Duke Abdalla. Duke is the great-grandson of Chief Running Bull of The

Yankton Sioux. He enlisted in the Marine Corps in 1943, and for his courageous service, Duke earned a Purple Heart and a rank of Corporal.

In September of 1944, at the Battle of Peleliu, Duke's machine gun team was shelled. Duke lost his machine gunner and two ammo carriers, while himself taking shrapnel that left him with holes in both legs. Rather than being sent home, Duke recovered and then quickly was promoted to leader of Third Squad, First Platoon, A Company.

Beginning April of 1945, Duke and A Company began an assault on Okinawa. In early May, Duke demonstrated true bravery in a series of heroic maneuvers and actions. Over the course of the day, Duke carried a wounded fellow Marine to safety and successfully neutralized six machine gun nests, clearing the way for U.S. Forces to advance. Duke lost his entire squad after clearing four of the nests, but he continued on and cleared the final two by himself.

Duke and his fellow Marines fought valiantly and withstood fierce counterattacks from enemy forces. Their commitment and selfless dedication to their Country was emblematic of the effort put forth by "The Greatest Generation" during the world's time of greatest need.

I thank Loren Duke Abdalla for his service to this Nation. We all owe a great debt of gratitude to Duke and to all those brave men and women who sacrifice so much for the good of this Country.

***

April 24th, 2013, Senator Tim Johnson of South Dakota stood on the floor of The Senate, to give tribute to Loren Duke Abdalla for his service as a Marine in World War II:

TRIBUTE TO LOREN DUKE ABDALLA

Mr. Johnson of South Dakota. Mr. President, today I wish to recognize the military service of Loren Duke Abdalla, the great grandson of Yankton Sioux Tribe Chief Running Bull. Loren Duke Abdalla, a native South Dakotan, fought valiantly as part of The United States Marine Corps in World War II.

Loren Duke Abdalla, or 'Duke' as he was known by his fellow Marines, began his service to this Nation when he enlisted in The Marine Corps in 1943 at the age of eighteen. He completed his basic training at Camp Elliot in San Diego, California, where he was trained as a rifleman and machine gunner.

On September 15, 1944, Duke displayed his bravery at the Battle of Peleliu in the Pacific. In the struggle, three of his comrades were struck down next to

215

him, but Duke still carried on, despite injuries, through the six-day battle. At the end, Duke survived as one of only twenty-nine Marines left standing in his Battalion. Shrapnel left holes in both of his legs, yet instead of returning home, he recovered in only a few months on the Island of Guadalcanal and returned to Pavuvu Island. He received a Purple Heart and was promoted to Corporal, and became squad leader of the Third Squad, First Platoon, A Company.

Duke returned to combat and quickly became a hero once again in the Battle of Okinawa. On May 5, 1945, he rescued Second Squadron Leader Corporal John Brady, throwing him over his shoulder and carrying him to safety under heavy fire. Duke immediately returned to the battle where he began neutralizing machine gun nests leading up a ridge along with his twelve-person squadron. When he reached the fourth nest, he realized he was alone. With his comrades killed or wounded, he forged on to take out the last two nests by himself and reached the top of the ridge. In taking the ridge, he allowed The First Marine Division to advance. Although many of his comrades were honored for their bravery on that day, Duke was not recognized for his action.

Duke ended his service with an honorable discharge on February 28, 1947, ending four years of selfless sacrifice for our Nation that will not soon be forgotten. At the battles of Okinawa and Peleliu, some of the bloodiest battles in The Pacific Theater, Loren Duke Abdalla proved time and again his courage, perseverance and ability to sacrifice, preventing many potential casualties. I ask my colleagues to join me in recognizing Corporal Loren Duke Abdalla for his exemplary service and dedication to our Nation.

***

In May of 2014, resolutions were written by Duke's State Representative Barbara Wheeler and State Senator Jim Oberweis. They were adopted and passed with the Illinois General Assembly. They requested that Loren Duke Abdalla's service records be reviewed for his actions during World War II by the President, the Illinois Congressional Delegation, the Speaker of the U.S. House of Representatives, the Minority Leader of the U.S. House of Representatives, the U.S. Senate Majority Leader, and the U.S. Senate Minority Leader, in hopes of his being honored with a Congressional Medal of Honor as it was believed that Duke was passed over for an award because of discrimination against his Native American Heritage.

State Representative Barbara Wheeler announced a press conference regarding Duke's story and The Northwest Herald responded with an article, **Push Ongoing to get Marine veteran the Medal of Honor**, which was written by Kevin Craver and published on July 4, 2014, in Duke's honor.

"You're front page news, Grandpa," Douglas proclaimed to Duke when he called to talk about the article. "I got several copies for the family to have."

Excitement was high until Doug contacted him after receiving news from the Department of Defense and somberly related to him, "Unfortunately Grandpa, too much time has passed since your actions in World War II, and we are unable to locate any more living witnesses for the Department of Defense to consider their testimony. One more witness letter is needed, along with a recommendation by an officer who you served with. It appears that only the President as Commander in Chief can honor you with a military award."

"So," Doug continued, "we are knockin' on the door of The White House and I heard today that Senator John Thune of South Dakota is honoring you with a Congressional Record Statement, and he's telling me that the fight goes on!"

"Well that's just great, Douglas," he told his grandson. "You are standing like a man!"

And Duke, The Indian knows, beyond any medals or lack thereof, that his story has been told.

Grandpa Duke then confided to his grandson, "Now I've got one final request. At the end of my trail and when I am buried at Arlington, I want the bagpipes played."

Doug said, "I like the bagpipes, and you deserve it!"

Grandpa replied, "Don't forget, I'm half Scotch!"

Doug smiled and chuckled as he hung up the phone to begin his search for a set of bagpipes, so he could learn to play them for his grandfather.

Loren Duke Abdalla at the age of eighty
wearing his Marine Corps League uniform.

Illinois Marine Corps League V.P. Gunnery Sergeant Mike Ruffner.

Restored 1963 Cruiser's Inc. - Duke and his grandson, Douglas.

Al Costella standing in Marine Corps League uniform.

Warriors Watch Riders and Guests.

Warriors Watch Riders motorcade escort Duke - Welcome Home!

House that Duke built in Illinois.

Flags flying at Duke's house on days he deems worthy.

Loren Duke Abdalla, grandson, Douglas Nykolaycuyk, and
Captain Rick Daniels at the Lake County Resolution.

Illinois State Capitol – President Lincoln Statue with Loren Duke Abdalla.

Duke, The Indian (wearing his Indian Buffalo ring).

Dear Reader,

Thank you for purchasing *Stand Like a Man, The Story of Duke "The Indian"*. I hope you enjoyed reading the story.

For updates on Duke's recognitions, you can check my website: www. DonnaKingAuthor.com. Please feel free to leave a review on the website where you purchased the book.

Thank you!
Donna King-Nykolaycuyk

A special note from Duke Abdalla

I am very appreciative of all the work that my grandson and his wife, Donna, have done on my behalf. Looking at my Walls of Recognition in my home, I'm thankful for the efforts of those who have participated in honoring my service. It has been an incredible journey.

Duke, The Indian
December 2014

About the Author

Donna King-Nykolaycuyk is a writer and a poet who also has an ardent love of baking and cooking. She is a member of the Chicago Writers Association and an avid reader. Though she has always had a passion for writing, **Stand Like A Man** is her first endeavor at writing a biographical novel. She currently resides in her home town in Illinois with her husband, Douglas, and their family.

Upon hearing the story of her husband's grandfather having been raised during the Great Depression, and then hearing how he served heroically as a Marine with Native American heritage in The Pacific Theater during World War II, she felt both challenged and compelled to write his story. She hopes she has done it justice. Please visit her website at DonnaKing-Author.com.